"Another gem from Martin Butler – required reading for anyone looking for retail success."
Sir Stuart Rose, Chairman and CEO, Marks & Spencer
(UK & international)

"This book is like getting the world's leading retailers to help you run your shop..."
Ian Cheshire, CEO of Kingfisher Worldwide
(Global)

"Learning from the great entrepreneurs of our time, if I'd read this book when I started out I think our success would have been greater and faster."
Jack Smith, founder, The Sports Authority
(USA, Japan & China)

"If you can't learn from this book perhaps you shouldn't be in retailing or you've been in it too long."
Hugh Perrett, founder, Pak 'N Save
(New Zealand)

"A book to be congratulated for the quality of its research and the light it has shone into many of the world's leading retail Corporations."
Jesus Echevarria, CCO Inditex (incl. Zara)
(Global)

"A must read for anyone who cares about customer perception, market differentiation and effective leadership."
Len Roberts former CEO, Radio Shack
(USA)

"I found this book to be superbly focused and very succinct!"
Jeremy Hobbins, Li & Fung
(Great China)

"I am particularly impressed with the collection of shared experiences from industry leaders; each with an in-depth perspective and varied approach to retail."
Casey Lim, COO, Sprint-Cass
(Singapore)

Also by Martin Butler:

People don't buy what you sell

*For a complete list of Management Books 2000 titles
visit our web-site at www.mb2000.com*

THE ART OF BEING CHOSEN

Secrets of Success from the Giants of Retail

Martin Butler

2000

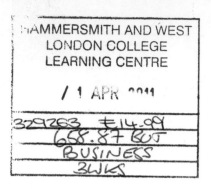
Copyright © Martin Butler 2010

First published in 2010 by Management Books 2000 Ltd
Forge House, Limes Road
Kemble, Cirencester
Gloucestershire, GL7 6AD, UK
Tel: 0044 (0) 1285 771441
Fax: 0044 (0) 1285 771055
Email: info@mb2000.com
Web: www.mb2000.com

Contact author: martin.butler05@btinternet.com or on his blog: Martin-Butler.com

British Library Cataloguing in Publication Data is available

ISBN 9781852526634

CONTENTS

ACKNOWLEDGEMENTS

Simply couldn't have written this book...

There are many who have helped me write this book.

Some have lent their names, some have opened doors and some have been kind enough to read snippets of what I've written. And I thank them all.

But there is a great buddy of mine who has done all these and a great deal more.

Until he retired, David Simons CBE was a titan of British retailing and in non-executive capacities still is. He is an accountant by birth and an extraordinarily good bridge player, also, he insists, from birth. Both involve accurate counting – shame this logic doesn't work for his golf.

But without doubt David is a remarkably questioning, remarkably strategic thinker. He has 40 years of successful retail management experience to prove it. For a bean-counter, he is particularly well tuned to the softer things in life. And with the exception of this acknowledgement, he has generously taken the time to read, digest and critique every single word in this book.

Now there are some who say that authors are their own worst critics, but those writers haven't been fortunate enough to have David. From the very first case study he has given me exacting comments on content and style. Indeed he has been sufficiently objective to critique his own suggestions unfavourably when he's seen them in print. No wonder he is a good accountant.

But the simple truth is that I couldn't have completed this monumental project without his support and encouragement. And I just wanted to publicly acknowledge his contribution. I also wanted to thank his wife Ellie for patiently letting me interrupt their breakfasts so David could read my midnight ramblings. David made a point of replying to my e-mails immediately.

You will note he was the boss of Somerfield and some might even be interested to know he fired my advertising and marketing agency when his business was at its most successful... something to do with a new-broom marketing director he assures me. But we became even closer friends following this divorce. The observant may even notice I have included his time at Somerfield as the final case study.

To me this is a fitting tribute to his passionately supportive and often robust contributions to my book. He has the last word.

Thanks David.

With thanks and shameless networking

The only way to write a book like this is with the help of people who generously give their time, liberally sprinkled with excessive portions of shameless networking.

It goes without saying I couldn't have done anything without the world's leading retailers agreeing to be interviewed. There are too many to mention but each and everyone I thank.

And equally importantly I'd like to thank the executive assistants who I prevailed upon to help me get through to all the other bosses their boss had referred me to. Of particular note are: Beverly Richmond, Jane Bryett, Lydia Dawson, Monica Brady, Nancy Kent, Margaret Cirillo, Michelle Harley, Caroline Muller, Marian Milne, Joy Trout and Elaine Russell.

I'd also like to acknowledge the phenomenal help Ian McGarrigle of the World Retail Congress gave me. It was almost embarrassing the number of times I'd ask him for help and guidance. I couldn't have presented myself to the world's retail leaders without his endorsement of my project. Particular thanks are also due to Ric Comins and Sue Shipley of the Odgers Berndtson organisation who seemed to know almost everyone in retail around the world. I'd also like to thank Glynn Davis and Alison Clements, two wonderful retail journalists for their invaluable help. Speaking of help I'd like to particularly thank Jurek Leon based in Perth, Australia for his unstinting assistance and stimulating monthly newsletter, Terrific Retail Tips. Thanks also to my literary agent, Sally Tickner, for skilfully opening firmly locked doors as well as encouraging me to blog and tweet. And thanks again to my publisher Nicholas Dale-Harris for agreeing to support this latest book. It's all the more incredible he should want to publish me again having suffered the process just four years ago.

And finally my thanks to three gentlemen who I've leaned heavily on for advice and guidance. Roger Jennings a fine retailer, an ex-client and now a wonderful friend. Russell Wailes and Mark Brandis, respectively my fellow creative and managing partners from our agency in Soho. All three made a priceless contribution to the content, shape and creativity of this book.

On a personal level I owe a huge debt of gratitude to my wife Judy for again letting me keep the light on in bed to proofread. Also for her valuable advice and gentle put-downs when I've pontificated on how women shop. Big thanks also to my number three daughter Hannah, a truly talented creative who designed my fabulous front cover.

Thank you all.

FOREWORD
by Ian McGarrigle

Having been an observer of the retail sector as journalist, publisher and now Congress Director for over 25 years, I can honestly say that I have never ceased to be fascinated by this industry. As a consumer-facing business, retailing is, by its very nature, about constant change and evolution as stores vie with each other to be better and more appealing than their competitors.

But for me, retailing's appeal is more than that. It is also about the many extraordinary characters and personalities that tend to dominate the retail sector. They are either the founders of their businesses or the larger-than-life executives who have stamped their personalities on their organisations. What unites them all is a very clear sense of what makes their formats and brands unique and how they have been able to build a sustainable retail business. So, when Martin Butler proposed the idea of writing this book around the learnings from scores of interviews with retail executives from around the world, I was very happy to offer the support of the World Retail Congress.

Many of the personalities interviewed for this book match the profile of our audience at the World Retail Congress. Their style and turns of phrase will be familiar to those who have heard them speaking. This book goes a lot further than that, though, and with great skill has drawn out some inspirational and provocative learnings that are invaluable for anyone involved in the business of selling to today's demanding consumers. Martin has travelled extensively and invested considerable time to reach and interview an incredible list of retail leaders from around the world.

Knowing how busy and often elusive these executives are, he has been able to achieve an unprecedented level of access and in all cases the interviewees have been candid and willing to share their business secrets, helped along by Martin's detailed questioning. In many ways, the content and objectives of Martin's book have a parallel with the aims of the World Retail Congress which seeks each year to assemble the very best retail leaders who can give insight to their peers. In this it serves to reinforce why we are happy to endorse this publication.

At its heart, retailing is a simple business and is, as this book is called, about learning "the art of being chosen". There could be no better way of learning that than from many of the proven masters included in this book.

Ian McGarrigle
Congress Director
World Retail Congress

For Judy, Georgie, Letty, Han & Toff –

this book is for you and I'm coming out of my study now.

INTRODUCTION

What's it all about

Today one of the largest and most successful businesses on the planet is a retailer which just 40 years ago almost went bust.

Since growing up working in my parents' shop, I've always wondered what it takes to be a success. In particular, what it takes to be a successful retailer.

So after a lifetime in and around retail, I decided now was the time to find out. Find out who's doing it and how it's done around the world. Find out what the secrets of success look like.

On a more personal level, busy retail executives journey to far-flung destinations to do the same thing. Jumping from plane to plane, wearily snooping on other retailers. Shamelessly pinching ideas, guessing what strategy lay behind awesome initiatives. But this book has done all this and a good deal more. It has also taken the guesswork out of the equation by speaking to the retail bosses to understand their thinking, and better still, readers don't even have to check-in two hours before they start.

From Wal-Mart to Woolworths, from New York to New Zealand and from Fashion to Food.

With the support of the *World Retail Congress* and others, I have been privileged to interview some of the-best-of-the-very-best retailers across every continent. From Wal-Mart to Woolworths, from New York to New Zealand and from Fashion to Food. It's been a fascinating and informative glimpse behind the scenes. I am delighted so many of the world's top retail bosses have decided to 'spill the beans' and let me publish their case studies.

Inevitably, I have approached some who preferred not share their secrets. And I've met those I couldn't stop talking. But through brazen networking and with never-ending gratitude, I have been fortunate enough to ask many of the world's most distinguished retailers, a simple question: *What is it you've done that's had a profound and positive effect on your business?*

I've enjoyed interrogating these executives, understanding what innovative thinking has helped shape and make their businesses the successes they are today. Even quizzing them on the seeds they are sowing for greater success tomorrow. I've always tried to ask the questions my readers might want answered, but it wasn't easy. I never knew what I was going to be told. Sitting down face to face, I had to think on my feet, so to speak.

Intriguingly, I don't think a book like this has been written before. And like my publisher, I'm hoping and expecting this has more to do with the logistics of interviewing almost a hundred retail leaders around the world than any underlying indifference! But those who have read the case studies tell me which they find most absorbing. And pleasingly, no two readers agree. So I'd like to think there are insights and

a profound and positive effect on your business

learnings here for *anyone* interested in retail. I think Ian Cheshire, CEO of The Kingfisher Group, sums up best what I have tried to achieve: "The idea of this book is almost like getting the world's leading retailers to help you run your business..."

I couldn't have put it better myself.

Simple not easy

So what's actually in this book?

Well, the interviews have thrown considerable light on many issues, but probably the most illuminating thought is by a former client and now great buddy of mine, Stan Kaufman, who, borrowing from Sam Walton, the founder of Wal-Mart, said: "Retail is simple, but it ain't easy!"

Most agree with this retail truth. And, from my experience, the truly great retailers agree with it too. Only they tend to see things rather differently. Often the key challenge is perceived as delivering the right merchandise at the right price. But I have found the retailers who enjoy the most success tend to concentrate their efforts on the softer issues, the issues that require careful stewardship of others' emotions.

No-one is saying being good with product isn't important to retailers – of course it is. But being good at product is like a footballer being good at kicking – it's a prerequisite. I would argue true retail success is defined by the emotional understanding and engagement leaders bring to their businesses. I sum it up as product being important... but everything else being that little bit *more* important – especially in the world today.

> *retailers who enjoy the most success tend to concentrate their efforts on the softer issues.*

Rightly therefore, this book concentrates on the 'everything else'.

Travel and tantrums

I have spent the last two years researching and being infatuated by world-class retailing – *I've loved it.*

It would be disingenuous to claim I haven't enjoyed whizzing around the globe asking polite and hopefully searching questions of the world's most revered and respected retailers. I've seen places, airports, hotels and shops that have blown me away and others that emphatically have not.

I've interviewed a shop-owner who purposely hid the exit signs to increase 'dwell time', and while *en route* from the UK to Sydney had my meeting cancelled for the following day – hoping it hadn't inconvenienced me! I've travelled day and night expressly to interview busy executives who have not understood the purpose of my book nor had the time to sneak a look at the 'typical interview questions' that always precede my arrival – but somehow we've always managed to unearth a gem of an insight. On the other hand I've met charismatic leaders who have at once given me goose-bumps with the lucidity of their vision. And I've been changed forever by the humility of executives wanting to put customers at the centre of their orbit.

Soul

Understandably, when presenting my research findings at conferences and workshops I am often asked who impressed me most. And I always answer that there are those with soaring intellects and those with the charisma of gods, but the ones who impress me the most are those with retail's vital ingredient – Soul. For these three or four precious and unnamed individuals I would pay the ultimate compliment and come out of executive retirement, out of my beloved home on a golf course in Surrey, England and, if they wanted me, back into full-time commerce. But I'm not telling who they are – it would spoil my negotiations if they knew how besotted I am, and trigger the first shots of an expensive divorce.

Strangely, for a business that prides itself on interpersonal skills, I can't tell you how many interviewees, on initial contact, protested they didn't have the time to meet with me personally and couldn't we 'do' a phone interview. After some gentle persuasion with their personal assistants I've always managed to squeeze a 30-minute face-to-face interview. Ironically, these same executives would often ask me if I'd seen their wonderful new initiative or innovation in their nearby flagship store – by answering in the positive the interview became a richer experience for all.

I've lost count of how many lonely 'spaghetti vongole' I have eaten at what (according to my body clock) seemed like breakfast time. But I do reflect positively on the umpteen time zones I have skipped, just to look into the eyes of the interviewee so I could 'listen between the lines' of what they were saying. And throughout the exercise, I have built on my understanding of how different the world is but how similar the emotions of shoppers are.

Understandable but disappointing

Most audiences are really surprised, when I present my research findings, to find that with one notable exception, sustainability is not cited as a key initiative that has driven or is planned to drive retail success. But to be fair it is often mentioned in passing under the general heading of a desire to reduce carbon footprints or a commitment to reducing plastic bags or packaging. With most interviews taking place 2008/9, timing clearly had something to do with this. The world was preoccupied with the banking crisis, with global sustainability seemingly relegated by the world's retailers from an imperative to a 'nice to have'. Also, the world's governments and various administrations were still struggling to achieve a 'tipping point' of consensus – with my interviewee at the UN in New York succinctly but dismissively talking about environmental detractors as flat-earthers. I guess, for the executives I interviewed, there was also an element of not wanting to be seen to green-wash or showboat their environmental credentials for fear of accusations of profiteering.

Retail is uniquely positioned to effect tectonic change and help save the planet

But on a personal note, I *am* disappointed. Retail is uniquely positioned to effect tectonic change and help save the planet. It has a unique relationship, if not duty of care, to its customers – it would be so easy to inform and then persuade them to value 'how & why' merchandise and retail businesses are sustainably robust. Retail is also unique in that it has a superior, unequal relationship with manufactures to insist they deliver merchandise produced accordingly.

Retail is the largest business in the world and its influence, if harnessed through appropriate association, could be enormous in terms of insisting on clean energy and sustainability in all its dealings. Retail has, after all, revolutionised working conditions throughout the third world's manufacturing and supply chains – so arguments that customers would not pay the premium nor value sustainable practices have been disproved.

And before I stop riding this particular hobby-horse – any legal concerns about anti-trust abuse or protectionism by retailers ganging up need to be set aside in the greater interest of *saving the planet*.

On a brighter if not saddle-sore note, my more recent conversations lead me to confidently expect to be 'not so disappointed' when writing any follow-up book.

Six for success

Although retail is in my blood, I chose to spend most of my professional life owning or working in advertising and marketing agencies. But I love retail. Unsurprisingly, I ended up specialising in it and from this objective point of view, I have been fortunate to work with retailers of every persuasion. Always inspired by the great leaders, undoubtedly learning much from those who failed. This book has added greatly to a deeper, more profound understanding of the secrets that separate success from failure.

There are many outstanding retailers still to be interviewed but I am giddy with my dervish-like travels around the world. Internet retailing is really coming of age (Amazon must be one of the most customer-centric retailers on the planet) and 'clicks with bricks' is at last properly finding its feet. But we all know retail is about *change,* so I have decided to pause, rationalising that I will write about all this and more after the banking system, along with its bankers, has moved back into credit. And when, as I confidently predict, the world has better embraced its environmental fragility.

What I am pleased to report, however, is that with nearly one hundred interviews done so far, not one executive has duplicated another – and equally fortunately for my theories of retail success, not one has mentioned *merchandise* per se.

But as my research numbers became more robust, I did notice clear trends.

At the risk of stating the 'blindingly obvious', I have realised that there are as many facets to retail success as there are visionary leaders. No surprise there. But what I've also noticed is that the mechanics of the success described in each case study tend, to a greater or lesser extent, to cluster into six thought-processes or understandings – there may have been more but I didn't notice them! So as an adman at ease with hyperbole, I have decided to call *my* observations 'the six secrets of success'.

Please, please remember: none of these secrets are mutually exclusive

Please, please remember: none of these secrets are mutually exclusive. Inevitably, there's huge cross-over and certainly more than an element of each in every case study. But it is interesting to note how the centre of gravity of any given case study tends to speak particularly eloquently to one of these six secrets.

For the rhythm of the read, I have been asked to choose up to ten very different case studies to illustrate the various dimensions of each secret. The first secret is why *being chosen* is the very essence of all business success – fortunately something Wal-Mart came to terms with 40 years ago.

LET ME NOW START
RIGHT AT THE END...

"Meet me by the iron gates near the hole in the land."

So in April 2010 began my last interview, it was to be the most illuminating store visit of my life.

South Africa must be one of the most beautiful places on earth. Vast open spaces. Deserts, mountains, intense greenery and long natural beaches. Diamonds, wild animals and two great oceans colliding at its southern tip.

Two great societies learning to live together under Mr Mandela's forgiving and generous ideological guidance.

South Africa has a remarkable infrastructure given its African heritage. I was told to leave the efficient N2 motorway near Cape Town at the Khayelitsha exit. Turn left and left again. This was the entrance to one of South Africa's notorious Townships. Intensely populated areas, clustered around train and bus stations, where people come to live in the dream of *it was to be the most illuminating store visit of my life* finding work in nearby cities - there's almost no work in the countryside. Trouble is, the cities have very little work either. The majority of Township dwellers are unemployed.

I knew most of this but what I didn't know was what I'd see and feel.

I'd asked Nick Badminton, the Group CEO of South Africa's Pick n Pay retailing empire, if I could interview one of his amazing new franchisees. I was particularly interested to find out more about his new retailing initiative that specifically targets the *previously disadvantaged* in South African society.

As directed I met Steve Mavuso by the iron gates and he took me to his store in the heart of the Township. On a relatively small piece of land nearly one million people live, sleep and bring up their children. The lucky ones squeeze onto transport and crowd into Cape Town to work, the others stay behind and simply exist. Weekdays the children proudly don smart school uniforms and cheerfully make their way to the wonderful schools on the edge of the Township. Like everyone, the children see education as their path out of Khayelitsha.

But with music blaring, people bartering and animals roaming, the scene was set for retailing as I've never seen it before.

Against a backdrop of cars in every stage of repair and a seemingly endless supply of worn-out tires, we drove through Steve's catchment area. Corrugated tin sheds providing the most basic form of temporary 'long term' shelter crushed uncompromisingly beside tiny, government-built brick houses promising more permanent shelter. Some even boasting a TV satellite dish. Then, as if happening across a clearing in a forest of humanity, we pull alongside Khayelitsha's very own Pick n Pay – one of Africa's most admired and respected supermarket chains. I am told to park my car and follow Steve into his shop. I ask if it's all right to just leave my car outside and a surprised "of course" is all I get. We pass through a shopping centre which, when finished, will have a Checkers store, a national discount food retailer, and Woolworths, South Africa's closest thing to the UK's Marks & Spencer, as its two anchor stores.

I ask if it's all right to just leave my car outside and a surprised "of course" is all I get

We also pass what can only be called independent traders on every corner, if there were corners. Street kitchens selling all manner of cooked animal parts, if there were streets. But if corners and streets were lacking, there was no absence of laughter and vibrancy.

But this is daylight and things may change later, when the bars are in full swing.

As we bustle our way through, Steve checks the prices of giant watermelons, dark brown cuts of meat and DVDs on open stalls.

Everyone knows Steve. And Steve seems to know everyone. He is a major personality known for his regular Township radio broadcasts, complete with 'agony aunt' phone-in solutions.

I am shown around Steve's frenetic, cramped, 9,000 sq ft supermarket. People queuing for freshly butchered meat, freshly baked bread and freshly delivered, locally grown, vegetables. People queuing for Steve's daily menu of freshly prepared hot food, each item a local delicacy and each highly successful – a welcome innovation since he and his business partner Dean bought the business 18 months ago. People courteously and contentedly standing at the long checkout queues. Everyone seems happy!

Business is booming.

Turnover has doubled since the store changed its name to Pick n Pay from Score (Score was Pick n Pay's specialist budget operation – see Nic's case study on page 171). Steve has a wonderful relationship with the various Township authorities and works hard with them for mutual benefit. Raising and giving much money to help to the needy. He makes sure that as many residents of the Township work in his store as possible, though he refuses to employ them just for the sake of it. He makes a point of training his staff in new skills if they show the aptitude. And he is clearly skilled at all this. He was the regional manager for Score stores and knew this business for many years before raising the money to take over the franchise. He grew up in Soweto, an even more notorious collection of Townships near Johannesburg and knows what's required. He knows how the system works and knows how to work the system. Along with his brothers and sisters he enjoyed a comprehensive education – all of them ending with university degrees. He was immersed and brought up intuitively understanding and enjoying the process of buying and selling. Instinctively understanding his customers and how modern retailing can be geared to answer their specific needs.

I ask why people chose to buy from him and not the cheaper traders in the Township.

As expected he tells me price is critical but people know and appreciate the quality Pick n Pay demands and guarantees. Even though money is scarce his customers know that quality food is essential. And even though money is scarce his customers know they must eat cooked foods they can trust, especially their children. And even though money is scarce his customers still want the things they see other people enjoying. His customers also know that Pick n Pay sponsors the national sports teams they passionately support. His customers have learned to respect the brand. To them Pick n Pay is not expensive; it simply represents value for money and they know this is key, not price alone.

even in this socially challenged environment, the laws of modern retailing hold true

His customers know the brand represents fairness. Steve's customers choose Pick n Pay because they trust and respect it.

So even in this socially challenged environment, the laws of modern retailing hold true. Steve always makes a point to:

- know the business he's in, emotionally engaging his target audience;
- painstakingly protect the trust his customers have for his brand;
- acknowledge the importance of his team in delivering his point of difference;
- make sure his business moves with the times;
- know exactly how to make his new ideas memorable;
- constantly strive to be different from what else is around.

I am amazed and shocked in equal measure with Khayelitsha and Steve's store. Steve isn't.

Retail may not be the oldest profession in the world, but it's certainly the largest. On this store visit I have been reminded of its importance and reminded of its responsibilities. It also made me reflect on the complex inputs it demands and reflect on how it influences the lives of every living person.

In one unimaginable store visit, my last two years of research flash before me.

On my very last store visit, could this be the most powerful evidence yet for my assertions – six secrets of success, with Steve skilfully demonstrating them all.

Skilfully practicing *the art of being chosen.*

SECRET 1

BEING CHOSEN

BEING CHOSEN

Just what I'd hoped for

It was perfect. When interviewing the world's retail leaders on success there were no duplications, only recurring themes.

One theme, however, recurred more often than others.

Sometimes protesting its relevance, often silently underpinning what had just been said, *being chosen* was insisting it be heard above all else. I have therefore made this my first secret of success. In fact, so germane is it to what I discovered about retail success, it forms the title of my book.

Metaphorically speaking

Interestingly, Secret One was often disguised in the form of one giant, metaphorical question: *How can you get people to turn left into your store, rather than right into your competitor's store?*

From Accountancy to Zoos, we all realise that very few businesses have a truly unique offering. Some may be more conveniently placed than others, but history dictates that another convenient business will soon pop up close by if demand is there.

> *How can you get people to turn left into your store, rather than right into your competitor's store?*

It's the same for retailers but more so.

I can't think of one I've met, anywhere in the world, who sold unique product. Sure, some of the very big boys have exclusive ranges. But that's more a marketing ploy than genuine uniqueness – a different facia to a washing machine with an extra spin speed option or a little black dress with a 'to die for' scoop neckline. But *fundamentally* these products are still similar to what you can get elsewhere. Indeed there's always another facia and spin speed option in another store and another 'to die for' neckline just begging to devastate someone. There's always someone who will copy a unique widget and sell it next door to you and always someone prepared to cut that extra discount. Very few people truly offer anything unique for very long.

Three clear steps

But with just three clear steps it appears the world's most successful retailers manage to attract and retain customers:

1. They understand what business they are in.
2. They ensure emotional engagement is at the heart of all relationships.
3. They make sure everyone 'gets it'.

Step one: It's a simple thought and applies to all commerce. The really successful businesses, and indeed retailers, acknowledge first and foremost that they are in the business of *being chosen*. And their route to success is defined by how effectively they orientate the mindset of the whole business to embrace this fact. If, broadly speaking, the merchandise they sell can be bought elsewhere, rigorously implementing a company-wide mindset to be chosen, (rather than one of purely buying and selling), is the process that will eventually generate the answers to persuade customers to choose their shops. Turning the desire to be chosen into reality may sound obvious, but it is in the deep appreciation of this simple fact that I believe success lies. I have found philosophically that the really successful retailers don't view themselves as being in, say, the fashion, food or furniture business; in mindset terms they are in the business of *being chosen* – fashion, food or furniture is just the expertise the business has... that's why the really successful businesses can, for example, develop non-core add-ons like financial services to deliver incremental growth! In the Wal-Mart case studies in Secrets One and Four of this book, the world's largest retailer talks about 'every day

in mindset terms they are in the business of being chosen

low pricing'. Its founder Sam Walton always dreamt of 'giving ordinary folks the same things as rich people'. Through ever-improving execution and by perpetually challenging itself, this global giant has been, and believes it will continue to be, *chosen* by bringing this fundamental thought to life. To this day the company implores its customers to *live better* by choosing to save money every single time they visit. It surely won't be long before Wal-Mart breaks US\$ half a trillion in sales each year and in 2010 already claims to interface with 200 million customers a week. A beautifully crafted bit of global thinking that insists the brand is chosen every day.

Step two: In my first book, *People don't buy what you sell, they buy what you stand for*, I argued the importance of emotion in customer choice. Simply put, you have a better chance of being chosen if you're unique and if you can't be unique in what you sell, you need to be unique in what you do. I have found that all successful businesses seek to be unique and therefore appeal, by *if you can't be unique in what you sell, you need to be unique in what you do* wrapping themselves in an 'honest' customer promise (their brand) that is compellingly different. If customers like what a business promises and delivers, 'what it stands for', it gives them a reason to remember and choose that business over and above others selling the same things. But the harsh reality is: emotional engagement is the *only* way to stand out from the crowd.

The added benefit, however, of emotional differentiation is that when you get it right, as Virgin has done, or Google or even Harley Davidson, you have an edge, an emotional edge, that others find near impossible to copy. Interestingly, Carrefour, the world's second largest retailer, talks in Secret One about a 'simple' plan for international growth. By emotionally engaging the middle classes, and specifically respecting the cultures and ambitions of emerging markets, more often than not they have gently muscled into hostile territories to enjoy phenomenal success. A massive percentage of what they sell is local but by listening and actively respecting their diverse audiences around the world, this international retailer is winning hearts and minds where others have failed. Indeed, to *be chosen*, all the retailers in this book brilliantly engage their audiences at an emotional level. Carphone Warehouse, in Secret Two, is also a beautifully crafted piece of business modelling with trust at its heart – I am a real fan of this brand and what it stands for.

Step three: Not unreasonably this demands that everyone, without exception, appreciates and understands Steps one & two. The great retailers place enormous store by getting this right, ensuring that everyone, as we say, 'gets it'. Effective communication is always essential and I have found that the really successful brands start internally before contemplating any exposure externally. Customers or interested third parties certainly can't be expected to 'get it' if the workforce doesn't! Myer Department Store group, in Secret Three, provides a fascinating example of internal communication speedily overcoming huge geographical barriers. New Look, in Secret Two, made sure that those who financed their 'change programme' were the kind of people who would 'get it' before they became partners. And once everyone internally has 'got it' there are brilliant ideas in Secret Five, by Desigual and Saks Fifth Avenue where they highlight wonderfully unique examples of high impact external brand building. Making sure that whole new swathes of other people 'get it' – known affectionately as key influencers and customers.

Customers or interested third parties certainly can't be expected to 'get it' if the workforce doesn't!

It may sound the same

The business of *being chosen* is not the same as simply acknowledging customers have a choice.

Unlike those perfunctory announcements from airline scripts when taxiing after landing, I am not talking about saying 'thank you' for choosing a particular company. Although politeness is fundamental in business, to me that's looking at life through the wrong end of telescope.

The world's most successful retailers always make sure that *everyone* in the business knows and appreciates that they, as individuals, are in the business of *being chosen* – which in turn means the business they work for is in the business of *being chosen* too. These retailers make sure everyone appreciates they are *being chosen* each and every time they serve a customer, *being chosen* each and every time they ask for something out of the ordinary from a supplier or third party. And critically, making sure that through these deliberate actions customers and others *feel* what's special about the business they work for. Macy's Inc in Secret One and Starbucks in Secret Three have case studies that are wonderful examples of this.

The business of being chosen

- Am I over simplifying? Yes.
- Are there exceptions to what I've found? Yes.
- Do any of these apply to your particular business? I doubt it.

The world's most successful retail bosses dedicate their lives to creating an internal mindset with a simple ambition of being in the business of being chosen.

Let me personally explain

I recently visited South Africa. A big celebration trip. I treated my wife and myself to first class. I was looking forward to being pampered and sitting in a nose, so to speak. As we glided through the dedicated, marble-clad mausoleum to the first-class check-in I bumped into my wife's trolley. Golf clubs and luggage went tumbling. Charged with anticipation and excitement we both dissolved into laughter. Fortunately a smart-looking airline official was walking towards us with a cup of coffee in his hand. It had one of those lids that ensured he scalded his mouth when he drank. To my surprise, as we scurried around picking up our luggage, he very deftly sidestepped our mess. He had to do this to avoid treading on my fingers on his determined way to the smoking area. I was astonished; he made no attempt to come to our assistance.

Truth be told, when we were treated like royalty and escorted to our comfy haven in one of the nostrils of the airplane, I couldn't let go of this earlier incident. Instead of luxuriating in the attentive service I was receiving in first class, it just all felt smarmy and superficial.

Contrast this with our experience when we disembarked. Of all people (and I feel guilty for stereotyping them now) I was courteously dealt with by an *immigration official* – ending with a 'happy big birthday for tomorrow' send-off. I immediately fell in love with Dora. Well, well, bureaucrats can be nice and I now love Cape Town too.

What's this got to do with a business book specialising in retail?

Well I got my luggage checked in, and I was checked into South Africa. So the core competencies were delivered. Which experience did I enjoy and more importantly, which experience do I want to go back and enjoy again? That's a no-brainer. Dora knew that part of her job *should be* to welcome me, not just process me – and the chap in London *knew* he was in customer service but was on a break and in a hurry to burn his tongue. Presumably he felt this meant he didn't have to serve customers just then.

Someone had managed to convince Dora and someone had failed to convince the coffee man that it's how I feel emotionally about the whole process that will get me to come back. Presumably someone had told Dora that foreigners have a choice where they spend their holidays and she could impact this decision. Presumably Dora realised if people liked everything to do with South Africa, it would be good for her, good for her family and good for her friends. Indeed if everyone in her country understood that tourists have a choice and did their little bit, it would be good for the country – tourists and money would flow in.

Dora knows she can't stop all the negative issues surrounding her country from happening but she can do her job as effectively as possible. Orientating her actions to acknowledge that she, on behalf of her country, is in the business of being chosen. Obviously Dora needs to be helped to understand how she can do this but if she is in the right mindset these won't just sound like instructions, they'll just make common sense. She can then make the right decisions every minute of her day. She can help her country be chosen.

Of course, Dora may be just a lovely person, naturally given to look for the good in every situation.

If this is the case, thank goodness Dora is in the front line of welcoming people to her country. Maybe the people who selected her for the job recognized this quality. But interestingly, at the airport car hire desk *and* when we eventually checked out of Cape Town to come home, I was again congratulated on my big birthday. Three officials who needed to look at my passport, three officials who knew they're in the business of being chosen.

One gigantic coincidence, maybe? Three nice officials who all happen to have been chosen to be in the right job. I doubt it but I don't care.

I felt good and I'm choosing to go back. But guess who I may not fly with?

Enough of me

Let's hear from a few of the most successful names in retail.

It's no surprise that some of the biggest retailers in the world are in this section. Being chosen is absolutely central to their continued business success and the initiatives they recount explore various facets of this.

The interviews

- **Wal-Mart,** the largest retailer in the world, is famed for its ruthless pursuit of low prices. But few really know the mechanics that led to them being able to deliver their deeply held beliefs on such a grand scale. Indeed according Jack Shewmaker, Wal-Mart very nearly sunk without trace back in the 1970s before giving customers a reason to choose them every day.

- **Carrefour** has grown to be the world's second largest retailer by *loving and respecting* the people whose lives they touch. This retailer has invested heavily in understanding the rich cultures in the countries it serves and is now being chosen in 35 countries through its 16,000 stores.

- **Inditex** is the world's largest fashion retail group. From humble beginnings in a northern Spanish town, Zara and its sister brands have become a global phenomenon. By listening hard, acting swiftly and fiercely guarding the customer experience, its loyal customers choose it above all others.

- **Best Buy,** the world's largest electrical retailer, not only talks about putting customers at the centre of everything they do, it re-defines what this means. Being chosen is the only business they consider themselves to be in and expands the point with a radically different vision for the future.

- **Macy's Inc** is huge but the company has decided the only way to get bigger in the enormous North American market is to think as small as possible. With millions of customers, this business is re-orientating itself to be chosen by one customer at a time.

- **Marks & Spencer,** one of the world's most famous retailers, was suffering at the hands of its new competition. By re-orientating the mindset of the business, its customers were given a reason to choose this much loved brand once again. Customers were given their brand back.

- **Bloomingdales** may have a legendary reputation in the USA but it took a visionary, if not brave leader to realise people would eventually stop choosing to shop if things didn't change. The successful solution was to restore the emotional values of the brand.

- **Sportsgirl** is now part of the largest privately owned fashion retail group in Australia. Its owner is as creative as she is determined, saving this brand from oblivion by encouraging her team to value the 'art' in being chosen.

- **HMV,** the respected international music retailer must be in one of the fastest changing retail businesses on the planet. With supermarkets discounting its products, and file downloading (both legal and illegal) threatening its very essence, customers are now successfully being brought closer to the things they love and are again choosing the brand.

Case **1**History

Jack Shewmaker
Former President, Wal-Mart

Interviewed April 2008

Smooth Operator

Retailers prefer not to be surprised.

Proof comes from the biggest and most successful of all the 'winning' initiatives in this book. An initiative so successful that in under 50 years it changed the world of retailing forever, inspiring generations of imitators. It's recounted by Jack Shewmaker, former President of Wal-Mart who along with the company's founder, Sam Walton, was one of the architects of EDLP – every day low pricing.

As Shewmaker recounts, "In the midst of a horrible recession during 1973, we took the bold decision to buy a number of stores in the Mississippi area to give scale, deliver profits and get us through a difficult time. This meant we grew to around 100 outlets but it didn't deliver as planned. Very soon around a quarter of our stores were bleeding to death, losing big money – we needed to do something. And quickly."

Now retired, but until recently still a

Jack Shewmaker left, with Mr 'Sam' (Walton), Saturday morning meeting c1970s

Director of Wal-Mart, Shewmaker is a charming gentleman from the American deep south. Polite, courteous and considered – facts and figures slip from his tongue with a slow surgical precision.

Stung into action following the Mississippi expansion plans, Shewmaker's initial tactic was a typical retailer's response. Mark-up 'low' profile items and use this to offset a series of 'high' profile mark-downs. As Shewmaker explains, "We identified hundreds of products but I specifically remember one of the high profile targets – a 12oz can of private label spray paint priced at 88 cents. It cost us about 52 cents so we were making a profit but like others, we were advertising it six times a year at two-cans-for-a-dollar, which was below cost! This was footfall generation and pretty normal."

But realising his closest competitor was regularly selling the similar paint at $1.29 Shewmaker argued it made sense to, "increase our regular price from 88 cents to $1.18, still advertising the sale price as before…we expected this to be more profitable, but it wasn't. Before, we sold about 70:30 regular versus sale price, but when we marked it up to $1.18 we began to sell 25:75 regular versus sale price – do the maths!"

With unacceptable mathematics happening to merchandise across the store, a brave yet inevitable decision was made to stop the long established below-cost advertising promotions. Wal-Mart launched their now legendary, *Roll Back* campaign. So staying with the spray paint as an example, the regular price was rolled backed to 87 cents and the 63 cents Sale price was offered just three times a year. As Shewmaker now admits, this tactical change had a secondary benefit too. "Like our rivals, we found with below-cost prices our supply chain couldn't credibly handle demand – typically we'd run out of deep-cut advertised items within hours and offend customers when they arrived too late."

It's difficult to manage costs out of a business with inconsistent sales

Impressively, this tactical price switch meant the company starting selling 80 per cent of the paint at the regular price and only a small amount at Sale prices. Indeed when replicated across the business, sales and gross profits grew by 118 and 87 per cent respectively – effectively becoming the commercial model for the entire business.

But in future, improved performance figures owed more to operational issues than customer attraction. The *Roll Back* price started a chain of events where, over time, savings on operational costs could be compounded and passed onto customers. The peaks and troughs associated with high/low pricing were greatly reduced and Wal-Mart found it easy to strip-out operating costs.

As Shewmaker says, the company conceded the notion of every day low *costing* (EDLC) along with every day low *pricing*: "It's difficult to manage costs out of a business with inconsistent sales. But by flattening out the sales curve whilst still maintaining momentum upward, it's easy to take cost out of the back & front end of a store and distribution centres too. We took the trading week and smoothed it out, we took the month and smoothed it out, we even took the year and smoothed it out.... the efficiencies we gained were phenomenal. By constantly taking out costs, we managed to keep the price of the spray paint at 87 cents for many years."

EDLP had been born and was coming of age.

But extremely low prices were a great way to entice customers into a store when the store wanted them in, not necessarily when the customer needed to visit. By systematically phasing out high/low pricing, how did Shewmaker and the team deal with the loss of a proven call-to-action. "Good point, we actually had a decline in our like-for-like sales at first during the sale periods but because we were committed to it for a period of time, *80 per cent of our people would've voted to abandon it, probably abandoning me too* what began to happen was that on the weeks where we had no comparable sale advertising we had a huge increase and when you averaged them out, it was a positive trend upward," explains Shewmaker.

While this all sounds relatively simple, it took a huge amount of time and effort. It involved breaking away from ingrained methods. "Back then business wisdom was focused on increasing margins and the whole concept of *taking out* cost was pretty insignificant in any industry," says Shewmaker. "To roll EDLP out across the business took us 10 years and if you'd taken a vote half way through, 80 per cent of our people would've voted to abandon it, probably abandoning me too.... it's human nature, it took the control away from people, especially those associated with sales and marketing."

And on the subject of marketing, Shewmaker wryly acknowledges those retailers who 'dabble' in EDLP. "I've seen it countless times, they concentrate on deep cuts for 100 or so items, the ones most recognisable to the customer.... trouble is, when these customers buy anything that's not one of the 100 special items they soon realise it the next time they go to a genuine EDLP store. They see them cheaper and recognise their mistake. Believe me, this insidious message is soon understood and reinforces the proposition of true EDLP to the obvious detriment of the poor imitators – great bit of marketing for the likes of us, though!"

As Shewmaker confides, "Sam Walton's roots were in delivering a better value to his customers." Strange then that the very thing to have crystallised Walton's dream, from the dark days of the early 70s, would initially involve removing the deepest price cuts – especially when his retailing ethic had always involved low costs, cheaper store fits and cheaper locations.

in effect stripping out costs based on known quantities

Obvious as it may be today, it took a while for Walton, Shewmaker and the team to understand that by taking the up's and down's, *the surprises*, out of trading they could deliver operational savings – in effect, stripping out costs based on known quantities.

Jack Shewmaker talks of how, in the early days, Sam Walton tolerated his almost maverick attitude. But the passage of time has shown what Walton really saw in him: a kindred spirit and a great lateral thinker. Sam Walton's original vision was to be chosen by *giving ordinary folk the chance to buy the same things as rich people,* and with low prices every day his team succeeded.

Wal-Mart now posts an annual turnover of nearly half a trillion dollars and has become the world's largest retailer. By being chosen on a daily basis, it has become one of the largest businesses on the planet – surprising to think putting up the price of spray paint helped.

Case History 2

Daniel Bernard
Former CEO, Carrefour

Interviewed October 2009

A simple idea

The French philosopher Voltaire once profoundly observed, "There are men who can think no deeper than a fact."

Sexist quote or not, retail executives venturing into foreign territories would do well to heed this thought especially when aspiring for their businesses to *be chosen*. Experience shows few have reflected deeply enough on what lay ahead.

But for Frenchman Daniel Bernard, former CEO and a key architect of Carrefour's global success, this was something he mastered to unquestionable effect during a distinguished international career. Before landing the top job at Carrefour he spent 12 years running Metro International. And it was here that he saw first-hand the importance of a truly engaged workforce, robust business systems and cultural respect. In 1992, armed with this experience, Bernard seized the opportunity

Daniel Bernard, with the Mayor of Beijing in China, 2002

to take Carrefour's hypermarket concept truly international – well beyond the handful of overseas stores existing in Spain, Taiwan, Brazil and Argentina. And in little over a decade he had masterminded Carrefour's transformation, creating the world's second largest retailer.

"The big idea was to go global at a time when retail was local," explains Bernard. "Initially we decided to grow rapidly in Latin America, Europe and the Far East. But having visited China, when it was still the China of old, we soon realised this was *the future* and must be included too – I remember the Mayor of Shanghai asking what we would sell. I said rice. He was astonished and said many people sell rice. But I said we will sell it cheaper. He said you'll go bankrupt. I said no, because we'll sell big volumes. He wasn't convinced – he is now, we've 150 hypermarkets there."

Bernard is a mathematician by training yet somewhat philosophical. He is also charm personified – a confection of Gallic values, deep emotional intelligence and a self-belief that never spills into arrogance. With his colleagues he decided Carrefour's future lay in the burgeoning buying power of the newly prosperous in the emerging economies

Retail must always be simple and our simple idea was to follow the middle class

of the 90s. "Retail must always be simple and our simple idea was to follow the middle class. For every country with emerging industrialisation, you could imagine an emerging middle class," reasoned Bernard, explaining that with wealth and aspiration comes a thirst for new lifestyle choices. "When people have a car they need more freedom.... they want to be free to go to different places.... one of the applications is shopping. But I concede it wouldn't work everywhere. Hong Kong, Singapore and Japan, for example, all had middle classes that were well catered for.... car use was low and homes too small to buy the volumes needed to fit our business model."

But with Bernard's *simple* vision, his team acquired partner businesses, built hypermarkets and supermarkets, setting in motion a programme to target more than 30 countries. "We'd say, how many new countries can we take on? So besides our established countries we would have newly maturing businesses and, at any one time, we would always be fitting-out three new countries. When the new countries went on-line, we started three others!" But far beyond the systems, management teams and operational expertise essential to complete such a 'hasty' vision, was Bernard's deeper thinking. With a simplicity that betrays its complexity, he knew that to be chosen it was important to adapt to the 'tastes, customs and cultural anomalies' of every new country. And all to be achieved without compromising Carrefour's fundamental model – high volume, low margin, delivering low prices & promotions to repeatedly tempt shoppers. As Bernard explains: "There's no greater accolade than succeeding internationally. It's difficult. It's a balance between adapting and respecting your concept."

So in Thailand, Carrefour developed state-of-the-art stores, but each respected the ancient tradition for feeding the spirits of the land – food was left out to appease them and bring good luck. "That's what locals do, so we did it," recounts Bernard adding, "In Malaysia, our butcher shops were fitted with two identical air-extraction systems – one for halal meat

to be chosen it was important to adapt to the 'tastes, customs and cultural anomalies'

and the other for non-halal, satisfying the needs of different religious groups. In Taiwan a fortune-teller was consulted about where the door should be, in line with local beliefs!" In a chameleon-like mindset, Carrefour spared no effort to harmonise with local communities. One of the greatest compliments paid to Bernard was when a government minister in Brazil said he thought Carrefour was a Brazilian company.

It takes time to drill down to this level of local empathy. Typically, almost 24 months was set aside for 'prepping' a new region. During that time, the international team carried out research to ensure locals liked the way Carrefour did business and equally importantly, to see if Carrefour liked and could work with the way locals liked to live and shop. As Bernard explains, "Retail is about relating to communities and I'm not just talking about the big issues. Amazingly, in China, customers shop our huge 200,000 sq ft hypermarkets every couple of days. The cities are so big our stores can be located in the centres. Locally, we came under huge pressure to charge for bicycle parking – we never, ever, charge for parking, so that *simply* didn't happen."

Rightly, in order to be chosen the workforce played a huge part in

Carrefour's international success. "When we go to a country, we go with our own people, our own systems and train the locals. The secret is then to adapt to the country, not adapt our *values* during the process. It's important our managers are totally engaged with this. They are expected to understand the issues, understand the big picture and are incentivised accordingly – this leads to unusually high loyalty. Churn is low." Bernard adds: "Our existing Taiwanese managers were used when we moved into China, greatly easing a complicated process and outsmarting the competition. It meant promoting a lot of women. You can imagine it was a big thing for them; they had a car, chauffeur and a highly prestigious position. It all worked very well."

As expected, around the world Carrefour has training facilities and universities for nationals and locals alike. And true to Bernard's 'local-respect' agenda he proudly remembers, "The wife of one of my executives posted to Shanghai set up a French school on arrival. She started with 12 pupils in an apartment. 15 years on it's a school with 3,000 students!"

Wal-Mart may be the biggest retailer in the world, but with a turnover of US$160 billion and almost 16,000 stores in 35 countries, Carrefour succeeds internationally where most fail. Indeed, the true learning from this case study is how a huge global operation and brand has embraced the need for 'local' orientation. It's not just

love and respect the people whose lives you're touching

the half million predominately indigenous workforce or the 90-95 per cent of products sourced locally (depending on the country) that cause it to be chosen. It's the endless passion and thought that the company insists on putting into 'listening' to the communities it serves.

Bernard stepped down as CEO in 2005 with a legacy best expressed by paraphrasing him: "On your journey bring something new; if you don't, it's not worth going. And on this journey, love and respect the people whose lives you're touching."

Voltaire would approve, n'est-ce pas?

Case **3**tory

Jesús Echevarria Hernández
CCO, Inditex (including Zara)

Interviewed September 2009

Obsessive listening

Many retailers *talk* about giving customers what they want – few deliver.

But Spain's fast-fashion powerhouse, Inditex, has become a global giant by doing just that.

These days it's the norm for high street fashion groups to swiftly replicate catwalk designs. But no-one is quicker at identifying and responding to consumer trends than Inditex, an organisation whose quest to be chosen frequently starts by 'picking up' on a few customers' requests for a certain cut or colour tone – which they then have designed, *the group's listening and rapid-response ethos* manufactured and transported from Spain to anywhere in the world in less than three weeks. In fact, Inditex pays such attention to live sales data and customer feedback that typically 50 per cent of the much adored Zara fashion collections evolve and adapt during each season.

In immaculate English, on behalf of the group's founders, the CCO, Jesús Echevarria Hernández proudly explains the group's *listening and rapid-response* ethos. "Maintaining frontline customer-centricity across our 4,300 stores in 73 countries is central to our group's success.... the company's founders are obsessive about this."

"From the very beginning, every day, the thing that drove this business was talking to the stores and asking – What's liked? What's good? "What are customers asking for? Today this type of qualitative feedback is a formalised procedure, reliant on a powerful *triangle* of three key roles: store managers, store directors (who effectively manage regions) and the commercial team based at head office. At each of these three levels, conversations are taking place with detailed customer feedback streaming its way to IT-linked merchandisers, marketers and 250 fashion designers at head office."

Echevarria says that store managers love this role and perform better as a consequence. They know they are an essential part of the Zara fashion-driving process. Rightly, they have a degree of autonomy when ordering and around 80 per cent of initiatives are set up internally by the individual stores.

Germane to the business and arguably unique, Inditex does not publicise its collaborative customer model. As Echevarria explains, "If customers want to share something with us they are most welcome, but we do not promote it. We want it to happen spontaneously; we want our teams to 'pick up' on things. That way we are managing expectations and the process too. *Listening hard* is a better way of describing the relationship."

Like so many great retailers, Inditex is effectively making use of the valuable market research their customers give freely. Then reacting quietly and swiftly to what they've heard, delighting their customers.

Now the world's largest fashion retailer by sales, Inditex grew from famously humble beginnings in La Coruña, North Western Spain. As a young retail sales assistant, the budding entrepreneur Amancio Ortega Gaona always believed people didn't listen enough to customers. So he and his family borrowed the equivalent of 90 euros in 1963 and, having bought a sewing machine, they started manufacturing garments including bathrobes. They were absolutely fixated on giving customers something 'better'. Studiously monitoring customer feedback, they soon developed other lines too – finding their products becoming increasingly popular.

But over time, the Ortega family realised their lovingly designed and produced goods were not always merchandised with the same degree of care and attention. So in 1975 the first Zara store opened its doors. The merchandise was presented exactly as it should be. By 1980 there were five stores within a 100km radius of La Coruña. "Their factory was producing for these five stores and delivering new garments twice per week – the same philosophy that applies to this day," says Echevarria. "Today every one of our 4,300 stores around the world receives new merchandise twice a week, quickly replenishing or responding to design inputs. Just as it was in the beginning, it's a quantitative as well as qualitative reaction to the information our stores give us from their daily conversations with the customers."

These *effective conversations* between regular shoppers and attentive store staff affect what merchandise is pulled into the stores. Echevarria concedes such conversations may not always be possible in the vast, frenetic flagships of London or Barcelona, but guarantees they take place in towns and smaller cities around the world. "All the time store advisors and managers are suggesting products to customers, noting reactions, understanding what's popular and feeding back specific requests for colours, styles and cuts. In Tokyo a store manager was asked repeatedly for shorter skirts by young *fashionistas*. This nugget of customer interaction fed back through the company. Very short skirts were produced in record time, and the trend took off in Zara stores – and competitor stores – internationally." With Echevarria explaining further, "We manufacture small runs of coats, dresses and skirts at the beginning of each season. We then modify colours and styles over the coming weeks depending on sales data, even discontinuing designs that aren't an immediate success. But in our terms, we never produce huge runs of anything – our customers don't like to be seen in the same fashions!"

it's a quantitative as well as qualitative reaction to the information our stores give us

La Coruña is still home to the company's HQ and main manufacturing plants. There are other factories worldwide producing around 50 per cent of the merchandise. But all product comes back to one of three logistics 'platforms' in Spain before being sent to stores globally. Inditex's supply chain is state-of-the-art and exquisitely complex. Simultaneously dispatching winter coats to the southern hemisphere and swimsuits to the northern hemisphere. Yet Inditex's ability to control costs while supplying stores globally is legendary – considered by many to be one of the greatest achievements in modern retailing.

Listed on the Madrid Stock Exchange, Inditex launched a second brand, Pull & Bear in 1991, and since then six more brands have been added to the portfolio – Massimo Dutti, Zara Home, Uterqüe, Bershka, Stradivarius, and Oysho – with nearly US$ 13 billion turnover, the company's magic is now working for women, men, kids and the home too.

they change 4,300 store interiors every five or six months!

But interestingly, one of the world's most respected retailers is a manufacturer.

It all started with the founder's vision of simply wanting to *be chosen* by giving customers what they really wanted. Making sure it worked on every level:

- Operationally, they've created a near-unique manufacturing and speedy supply chain model where 'opening orders' are relatively small – giving them the choice to either replenish or refine. Not only does this delight the customers; it means that costs are lower and end-of-season (if there is such a thing in the ever-changing world of Inditex) mark-downs kept to a minimum.

- Emotionally, the Ortega genius was the desire to truly engage with customers. As a manufacturer with unassailable retailing instincts, they knew that simply delivering what the customer wanted was not enough. They knew they had to open their own shops to control the shopping experience too – maybe one reason why, to this day, they change 4,300 store interiors every five or six months!

What's the learning from this case study?

The need to engage and listen. The need to set out to endlessly surprise and delight. Because that's what customers love and the reason they choose where they shop.

Case History

Robert Willett
CEO, Best Buy International

Interviewed May 2009

Shopping heaven

"Simply 'selling boxes' is the past, selling 'solutions' is the future," declares Bob Willett, CEO of Best Buy International.

Best Buy, the world's largest electronics retailer, has an audacious plan to extend greater 'customer-centricity' to revolutionise how it will stand-out on the global stage. To be chosen, it will remain a ruthlessly efficient retailer of competitively-priced TVs, music, white goods and laptops, but within a few years is targeting that up to 20 per cent of its massive global revenues will come from providing additional services to its customers – helping them make the best of the technology they've invested in.

A bright, articulate Welshman who started as a management trainee at Marks & Spencer, Willett is now a member of a select club of highly rated global retailers. "Consumers around the world are struggling to network their homes, get their electrical products to speak to each other or fathom the functionality of laptops and digital cameras – offering help and advice as well as *Simply 'selling boxes' is the past* contracts through our celebrated service club, *Geek Squad*, will give Best Buy a unique and highly lucrative edge," says Willet adding. "The interesting part about all this is, the emotional and commercial relationship with our customers is massively elongated and aligned once they sign up. You're not just taking their money and saying goodbye; you're engaging with them over the next 18 months or so – get it right and you have customer lifetime value too."

Bob Willett, enjoying Geek Squad transport

Best Buy has ambitions to be the 'trusted friend' of customers who need gadgets to work properly once they get them home. Willett is very clear that this will only happen if all 180,000 Best Buy employees feel they have a very real role to play. He sees this massive retail workforce as 'the secret sauce' and considers them as 'internal customers' whose day-to-day involvement in the business, and commitment to its brand values, is what ultimately drives success. Colourful expressions, full of meaning.

When Willett began working with Best Buy as a management consultant, before joining full time in 2003, he recognised that the company had fully mastered the art of customer segmentation. "We were becoming highly proficient at matching product in stores to different audience needs around the business." But along with Brad Anderson, Group CEO, they both felt there was a need for something more. As Willett explains, "Customer segmentation is a fact-based approach to service excellence but it only goes so far. It doesn't stick as well as it might. What can make it stick, however, is the internal culture you wrap around it. This, to me, is customer-centricity and is effectively the glue that makes employee and customer relationships on the shop floor (and beyond) really stick, and work better every single day.... it's our new battleground!"

Best Buy runs 3,500 stores across the United States, Canada, China, Europe and Mexico and is expanding carefully, having come late to the international theatre. Over the last six years a painstaking process of re-engineering to deliver customer-centricity has been under way. Store operations, supply chain and service procedures have been updated to the agenda of *total* customer satisfaction. A whole new culture has been introduced whereby commission on sales has been replaced with an accountable and obsessive customer service ethic – meeting every customer's precise personal need.

To facilitate this, sales staff known as 'Blue-shirts' are now more empowered, leading to higher engagement. "Rather than expecting everyone to carry out standard operating procedure, Blue-shirts have flexibility and are able to bring their own character to bear – delivering innovative ideas that cannot be created centrally," says Willett. "So for us, customer-centricity is about taking the fact-based approach that segmentation gives you, applying cultural elements to *Customer segmentation is a fact-based approach to service excellence but it only goes so far* it, and enabling our people to adapt standard operating procedures to every customer experience. And make a career of it."

Willett gives a basic example: "If there's a 'bundle' promotion in store, with a free printer when you buy a PC, but the customer doesn't need a printer, the Blue-shirt can create a better-suited bundle for that person. We're simply trying to get closer to the customer.... we're not close enough yet but already the competition is suffering. Research shows that Best Buy's identity as the retailer that will give you 'value for money' *and* 'help you with any problems that arise' is penetrating consumer consciousness."

Already five per cent of Best Buy's massive turnover comes from the 'Geek Squad' service contracts, sold at point of purchase, but Willett is confident 'services' and 'add-ons' will soon make up a significantly greater total of the business. "We don't make very much money on the hardware when we sell a PC, but it's the attachments of the software, the application, then the insurance and Geek Squad contract that becomes important." By partnering with Carphone Warehouse, (the UK and Europe's leading independent mobile phone store group) and other brands that sit well with Best Buy's customer-centric, *provider-of-services* approach, areas of weakness are targeted. "Our Carphone Warehouse partnership now helps us sell mobile phones in 800 Best Buy stores across the US, enabling our market share in phones to double."

The challenge going forward will be keeping the vision focused around the world. Willett is realistic about how big the training and education task is when rolling out this revolutionary culture change in locations as diverse as Turkey and China. "We need to be really in tune with the local customer," he says. "The product might be identical and the Best Buy values non-negotiable, but the ways people want to shop and be treated are going to be different around the world – I am estimating around 15 per cent flex will be needed to deliver our vision. We're not going to make the same mistakes as others when developing overseas!"

moving increasingly to the retail model used by mobile phones

Best Buy is certainly fixated with getting customers to choose them, by giving customers what they want.

Willett reckons they are 60 per cent of the way to bringing their giant global workforce and sophisticated operations fully up to speed. But even during their transition period and the economic upheavals of 2008/9 they were out-performing the market. Their competitors are in negative territory. Customer-centricity augurs well for Best Buy.

But get Willet talking the theory of customer-centricity and you hear him muse that with the massive deflationary pressures on electronics it's not a big step to imagine the likes of Best Buy moving increasingly to the retail model used by mobile phones. Hardware given away in exchange for service agreements in order to get customers to choose his brand.

Just imagine for one moment – free televisions, free washing machines, free computers and free mobile phones not only talking to you, but to each other. Technology that's our servant, not our master. Technology costing nothing to purchase except a service agreement that ensures that it works, that you know how to work it, and you know someone who'll fix it immediately when it doesn't!

This may or may not be the future of shopping, or your idea of shopping heaven – but it's certainly one hell of an idea.

Case History

Terry Lundgren
Chairman, President and CEO, Macy's Inc

Interviewed, March 2010

Relevance is key

Macy's Incorporated, the parent company of Macy's and Bloomingdale's, is the largest department store group and largest mall-based operator in the gigantic North American retail market.

But as Chairman, President and CEO, part of Terry Lundgren's vision is to be chosen by thinking as small as possible.

The Macy's brand accounts for around 90 per cent of the parent company's US$ 23.5 billion turnover and just over 800 of its 850 stores. As Lundgren explains, this iconic mid-market department store chain is embracing monumental change attitudinally and operationally. "Over the years, Macy's has grown organically and through regional acquisition – we've more than doubled our size, become truly national and consolidated our operations to leverage scale. Right now, we have just one *determined not to lose 'local relevance'* central operation handling merchandise, planning and marketing functions. It's more efficient, quicker and ensures key talent is in one place: New York City. The rationalisation made perfect business sense but I was determined not to lose 'local relevance'. So we created a programme called: *My Macy's.*"

Having worked in retailing through college and university, Lundgren became a career retailer. After just 13 years and at age 35, he was the youngest ever CEO of Bullocks Wilshire, the renowned California-based upscale department store group. Clearly a natural retailer, he is a polished and charming individual. Openly relaxed, he's a bright and phenomenally successful leader. Enjoying a varied retail career, he departed Niemen Marcus in 1994 as Chairman and CEO to join Federated Department Stores, eventually taking the helm in 2003 and changing its name to Macy's Inc in 2007.

My Macy's is a massive logistical challenge. It's taken almost three years to execute. Besides closing down the individual headquarters of more than 75 businesses acquired over the years, Lundgren and his team have recently closed their own regional business units too. But to deliver Lundgren's 'locally relevant' mantra, a unique clutch of customer-centric intelligence units have been formed. An enthusiastic Lundgren explains, "what we've created is 69 districts – because that's how many we needed! Each strategically located and staffed by a small team of 18 or so executives.... mostly former regional and national buyers and planners. But we were very fortunate, this process was funded from our rolling consolidation programme – we ended up with highly experienced, locally based, merchandise executives focused purely on the customer base of just 10 to 12 stores – we've never had that before. This structure doesn't exist in retailing to my knowledge. Certainly not in the United States. So imagine, while we have one central buyer in NYC for, say, men's dress-shirts, there are 69 district merchandisers and 69 district planners who specialise in men's apparel. Each *qualified* to help and advise, each visiting their stores every week, in communities where they live, in markets they understand. Each feeding back highly localised intelligence in real-time, through dedicated channels and technology."

For the early days of the *My Macy's* project, Lundgren talks in glowing terms of like-for-like tests delivering a substantial, three percentage point positive differential for the new districts when benchmarked. "However you cut it, stores served by the 'district units' performed best. And there's no doubt *My Macy's* is changing our merchandising model too. Instead of a push mechanism for merchandising as in the past, pushing down from central, it's now a pull system. While there's a basic inventory that will satisfy the needs of customers in every market, there's now a substantial change in the 'size detail' of how merchandise deliveries are packed for individual stores. We're seeing major differences in the colour and the weights of fabric, substantial shifts between classic and contemporary.... and while we had a general idea before, it was usually our big stores taken care of first and the little stores barely getting their voices heard. Now I'd say it's the smaller stores that are the biggest beneficiary so far in this programme."

But talk of 'push' and 'pull' can disguise the emotional benefits of *My Macy's*.

Imagine the very real engagement enjoyed by the company's 100,000+ sales associates when interacting with their district executives. Lundgren quotes an example from a recent store visit: "The famous rapper, Diddy, has a unique suit range, Sean John. It proved a massive hit when a district merchandiser brought it to the Pittsburgh area. Although his colleagues in Palm Beach or Boston would never entertain the idea, he knew this type of suit style would sell in *his* stores. They did – his sales associates in the stores thought

But talk of 'push' and 'pull' can disguise the emotional benefits

they'd died and gone to heaven. At last their voice was being heard and responded to.... they're very, very excited about it. Imagine, too, the extra commitment when selling *their* requested merchandise from *their* district executive. Only the other day, another sales associate said to me: Man, I asked for it, somebody finally listened and gave it to me and now I'd better sell this stuff."

My Macy's is acknowledged as a great engagement opportunity having brought about a major shift of emotional ownership for the associates. To formalise this, a 'log-book' protocol has been developed where associates can formally request merchandise and variances. "There's a 48-hour deadline to respond to requests and an imperative to say yes. Central executives are questioned harder when rejecting a local request than when accepting them – I'd like to think we say 'yes' first, and 'no' only as a last resort. Interestingly, even though 95 per cent of the buying decisions are currently centrally based, to be honest the central buyers and planners are still finding it a whole new game. They're used to being in control, but we're getting there – the benefits are obvious."

And the benefits of being 'locally relevant' are obvious to customers too, but there have been some surprises. Lundgren again recounts his recent visit to Pittsburgh where a local, much-loved 80-

year-old company, Betsy Ann Chocolates, was going out of business. "The local Macy's team rallied round and ensured that a concession

*good intentions can
be easily lost in
implementation*

opened in its store. It was front page news in that city because it mattered to local people, which made it good news for us too. Betsy Ann Chocolates sold phenomenally well but we can't sell them elsewhere – they wouldn't be relevant. But that doesn't matter. If it's important in that particular market, it's important to us."

And that's what *My Macy's* is all about.

There's nothing new in an aspiration to edit merchandise like this. But when you're one of the largest retailers on earth, specialising in the ruthlessly unforgiving world of fashion and home apparel, good intentions can be easily lost in implementation. Getting customers to choose you isn't just a numbers game; it's about empathy.

And Lundgren understands this. That's why he has ingeniously crafted a customer-centric business model that demands 'local relevance' no matter how large his store estate.

Eloquently, *My Macy's* engages both workforce and customers by encouraging brand ownership. It's a perfect piece of joined-up retailing – and proof you can never be too local.

Caseistory

Sir Stuart Rose
Chairman and Chief Executive,
Marks & Spencer

Interviewed October 2009

Giving back

Received wisdom dictates brands don't die; it's their management that kills them.

In the late 1990s, for the first time in over 100 years, UK customers fell spectacularly out of love with one of the most famous retail brands in the world. Why?

Competitors, new *go-getting* fashion retailers as well as ambitious supermarkets, had left Marks & Spencer in their wake. Tempting once famously loyal shoppers to walk past the M&S brand for unprecedented choice and lower prices. Equally worrying, for those who did venture into M&S, conversion rates fell dangerously low. *Customers were simply expected to remain loyal* Research paradoxically revealed that even as market leader, M&S was often fifth choice for clothes shopping. Management had taken their eye off the ball and the consequences looked dire.

The brand simply wasn't being chosen; it was dying.

In 2004, with a near-unique expertise in fashion and food retailing, Stuart Rose was parachuted in. He was appointed Chief Executive and tasked with returning M&S back to its glory days. The challenge he faced was as wide-ranging as it was detailed. He soon realised he needed to address product, systems, stores, morale and the shopping experience – he had to resuscitate the M&S brand.

From the start and to this day the marketing thought, *Your M&S*

championed Rose's programme of change. "The institution that most British shoppers felt deep affection for, but believed they had lost, was about to be *given back* to them," enthuses Rose.

Rose is urbane. A gifted retailer with a ready smile. He's intelligent, frighteningly succinct and charmingly self assured. "The business had become introspective. Previous management failed to look outside their windows every day and see what the competition was doing. Deflation in the clothing sector from the mid 90s was blithely ignored by the top brass at M&S, as were the aspirations of pushy supermarkets offering premium foods. Customers were simply expected to remain loyal. The company had become complacent, become arrogant."

"The business had also been run with short-term financial *wins* in mind. It was squeezing profits up. Not only by squeezing prices higher, but also by squeezing costs down, sometimes the wrong costs – keeping capital expenditure and depreciation too tightly controlled," explains Rose. "Everything was being squeezed in an unsustainable way, driving profits very hard for the short term.... the trouble was, customers stopped buying; business fell off a cliff."

This lack of investment in infrastructure – logistics and systems – means Rose has been playing catch-up ever since he arrived. "We will have just about caught up in 2011, having by then spent £3.5 billion," calculates Rose.

Politics at head office in the years before Rose came aboard had been a damaging distraction too. "At the time, the company was heavily involved in an internal battle about succession, so the eye was off the ball." Equally detrimental was the fact that many board directors did not have specialist food or high street fashion experience – all issues Rose addressed immediately.

Rose knew that reviving M&S could not be done single-handedly. He brought with him two close colleagues – his successful lieutenants from previous 'turn-around' ventures: Steve Sharp, for brand building and customer engagement and Charles Wilson, to oversee operations and stores – leaving Rose to concentrate on leadership and *product*. As Rose explains, "The secret of our success was close and constant communication. Putting management-speak to one side, we simply talked to each other. We tried to set an example." Interestingly, as soon as Rose arrived he interviewed 70 of the top and middle managers. Individuals he says who knew *exactly* where the problems lay but weren't talking to anyone about it. "From the start it was obvious M&S needed to start talking. It needed direction, it needed clarity, and above all, everyone needed a simple message," claims Rose. "They needed their self-belief back, they wanted somebody to give them confidence and assure them it was going to be a struggle, but together we'd get there."

Right at the very beginning of his involvement, marketing guru Steve Sharp articulated Rose's simple message with the clarity of simple words, *Your M&S*. Much admired and now highly awarded, "It was designed to give the business a direction. It was designed to tell customers look, we're back on the radar screens," says Rose. "It flagged up the re-launch of M&S, reminding customers

The secret of our success was close and constant communication

this was *their* M&S - the iconic retailer they had loved during their childhood, through their parents' childhoods, and through their grandparents' childhoods, and it was worth a second look."

An extremely effective yet straightforward thought, the colloquial *Your M&S*, was adopted enthusiastically by Rose. Not just for customer-facing marketing campaigns, but internally too. It 'spoke' to staff about how a sense of purpose was being returned to the organisation. About how M&S was putting customers back at the centre of everything it did. Rose also needed a central thought for the big defence speeches he was making in the City six weeks into his tenure at M&S. And again, *Your M&S* summed up what needed to be said to a sceptical audience of institutions and business analysts.

M&S still has much to achieve. But then again, it always will. Retail is about change and that's what the previous management failed to recognise - incredibly, credit cards were only accepted in the new millennium! But it must continue to change, constantly outsmarting competitors and constantly striving to delight its customers.

The key thing Rose and his team have done is mastermind an immediate halt to M&S' deteriorating status. Progressively they are now grabbing back their place in the hearts, minds and pockets of millions of shoppers. Re-engaging with them emotionally and persuading them to choose M&S once again through an increasing reputation for quality, value and innovation. "I'm delighted changes in product, systems, store design and marketing have now bedded-in. For 2009 we've seen footfall and conversion up almost six and seven per cent respectively," says Rose, "which makes a real difference when you're dealing with a US$ 20 billion turnover and 20 million people each year."

Even during the extraordinary banking crisis, not to mention a period of unprecedented retail and societal change, Rose has managed to steer this monolith into safer waters. And as if repairing years of apparent neglect were not enough, his *the essential skill of* team have had to contend with the *never taking customers* 'future of the planet' too – *Plan A* *for granted* *(because there's no Plan B),* is M&S's much lauded and far-reaching environmental project. It's injecting much needed energy into the brands reinvigoration programme, assuring customers that M&S, once again, is doing the right thing by them, giving an added reason to choose the brand.

Now honoured by the Queen for services to retail, the key learnings Sir Stuart Rose has brought to the M&S business are the essential skills of never taking customers for granted, the need for a simple vision that demands customer relevance and the fundamental art of talking to each other.

Accordingly, the business now truly understands it doesn't own the M&S brand – it's owned by others.

They'll forget that again at their peril.

7 Case History

Naomi Milgrom
Owner of Sportsgirl

Interviewed June 2008

Life's rich tapestry

"Art is not a mirror with which to reflect the world, but a hammer with which to shape it." So claimed the early 20th century Russian poet, Vladimir Mayakovsky.

What, you may ask, has this got to do with shops?

Well, one meeting... correction, one *minute* with the charismatic, feisty Australian from Melbourne, Naomi Milgrom, will explain all. Born into a retailing dynasty she is as passionately committed to art as she is an intuitive retailer. Two worlds colliding and informing her very being.

One of the impossibly difficult jobs in retail is to fix a broken fashion brand and get it to be chosen again – especially one aimed at young women. But for Milgrom, owner of the now hugely successful Australia-based Sussan, Suzanne Grae & Sportsgirl Group, this was the challenge she faced when in 1999 she bought the troubled Sportsgirl business out of administration.

One of the impossibly difficult jobs in retail is to fix a broken fashion brand

"The brand had sunk into the depths. There were problems in every area. No capital was being spent, there were no systems, no product, and the business was being so price-driven that it was competing on every level with the discounters! Instead of being the proud fashion-led brand it had been in the 80s, Sportsgirl was losing US$20 million a year, offering absolutely nothing other than cheap prices," explains Milgrom.

Of all the failures out there, why did Milgrom choose Sportsgirl to prove the Australian retail establishment wrong? "I have no interest in brands which aren't emotional because if they're not emotional you can't get true buy-in from customers. I'll never buy a menswear business because most men aren't emotional about their clothing; they can do without."

The unspoken truth being that like great art, female fashion brands only succeed if they emote – hence the appeal to Milgrom.

Having convinced the banks to support her vision, Milgrom bought the troubled brand. Using an appropriate artistic metaphor, she explains: "We set about unpicking the tapestry of the failed business – identifying the constituent parts and ensuring each of these were ruthlessly interrogated and targeted to become better than its best-in-class competitors."

her tapestry analogy was so clever – it focused everyone in on the detail yet never lost sight of the bigger picture.

At the beginning of her recovery process, Milgrom's economic model only worked for 60 or 70 employees, so the remaining 140 had to go. Milgrom was very clear: "Obviously the senior managers of the business were wrong – rigid systems and no feel – they went first!"

Left with a team who felt highly valued and part of the process, Milgrom set about creating a progressive and inclusive environment that remains to this day. Openly valuing and encouraging creativity, the teams not only confidently mastered the art of lateral thinking; they learned to ruthlessly and single-mindedly quantify 'known issues'. This is where her tapestry analogy was so clever – it focused everyone in on the detail yet never lost sight of the bigger picture, the importance of each individual element in the overall 'creativity' of the piece. "We also established databases of competitors' successes and Sportsgirl's failures and overlaid this with a matrix of customers' emotions. For a fashion brand this was all very technical but all very necessary," explains Milgrom.

Crucially Milgrom's team identified 11 specific competitors. It was important to have a finite number as it stopped the challenge being amorphous. "We said, this one has taken the jeans business away from us, this one has taken the shirt business, this one the accessory business and so on. We then set a target of taking 50 per cent of *their* market share within a given period of time," explains Milgrom adding. "So for the competitor that had taken our denim business away we drilled right down on every part of their business, especially understanding the emotional elements. We found out what their customers loved about them, what they hated, and what really frustrated them?"

"We had this phenomenal intelligence that individually analysed our key rivals' businesses. But we didn't only 'unpick' our competitors; we unpicked Sportsgirl, too," says Milgrom. "And most of the answers had been staring the business in the face. We had a bunch of 20-year-old girls working in our shops and, for example, coming to work in denim. The problem was, Sportsgirl hadn't been selling the sort of denim they wanted to wear; they'd been wearing fashions from elsewhere – it was crazy, evidence in front of everyone's eyes, every day."

Sportsgirl offices with chic vertical garden at reception

So no great intellectual theories in the early days, just raw retail common sense laced with the right amount of emotion. A strategy that rigorously challenged the business to ensure it won back what had been lost. And as the success returned, Milgrom allowed her passion for the arts to increasingly inform the business and help develop its unique brand character.

Undeniably, Milgrom believes in creativity. Unlike normal corporate 'showing-off', her offices have become a homage to modern art. But critically, the exhibits are revered as essential business tools by Milgrom and her equally passionate workforce. Loved and appreciated, this art cleverly sets the creative agenda, influencing and inspiring those it touches as well as the brand it supports. "As soon as the group could afford it, we put a lot of money back into the 'equity of our environment'; the art pieces we bought are a fundamental part of our inspiration, part of what makes us tick," explains Milgrom.

"People who visit our offices see what I think an environment needs to look like for people to be creative, for people to 'love' to come to work. I never forget that a lot of people don't *have* to do this anymore; they have a choice and we want to be the preferred choice for the best of them.... I often have artists come and talk to the teams. I want everyone to be truly inspired and give them reasons why they want to work for me."

Visual merchandising is imported from the best practitioners around the world with nothing slipping past Milgrom's creative quality controls. She can get very emotional about these things. But then, Milgrom is an emotional type and proud of it – the art she likes has always spoken to her emotionally and through her retail brand; she likes to speak to her teams and customers the same way. And

we put a lot of money back into the 'equity of our environment'

it's clearly working. Within eighteen months of buying the business she turned a five-year string of losses into an immediate profit. Milgrom now has 110 Sportsgirl stores throughout Australia and recently spun off a standalone accessory business called SG. Her passionate workforce has grown to 1400 and now offers customers creative new fashion ranges every single week of the year.

Milgrom did not reflect what the world thought when she bought the Sportsgirl business. But to be chosen, she and her team knew exactly what they were going to 'stand for' and used an enviable mix of ruthless common sense and creativity to hammer & shape a phenomenally successful fashion retail brand.

Vladimir Mayakovsky may have had a point.

Case History

Mike Gould
Chairman and CEO, Bloomingdale's

Interviewed June 2008

An unthinkable thought

Some things in life are learned, others you're just born with.

The ability to truly *think the unthinkable* is often regarded in the latter category. It is one of the most precious gifts any business leader can possess and always marks out the great retailers.

In the 1980s Mike Gould used his innate talent for thinking the unthinkable to great effect during his stewardship of the Los Angeles-based fragrance house, Giorgio Beverly Hills. To get this brand to be chosen, he broke just about every accepted practice of the international perfume houses by creating new ways of marketing product, and fashioning a *we needed to decide what we wanted to be when we grew up* 'new world order' for fragrance. Now, more than 20 years on, he is still surprising colleagues and competitors alike as Chairman and CEO of the much loved American department store group, Bloomingdale's.

Studious by nature, a retailer by choice, Gould joined Bloomingdale's in the early 90s when, as he says, "it was making its numbers.... each year sales and profits were growing. But around 2000, I realised we needed to decide what we wanted to be when we *grew up!*"

What could he mean?

This 125-year-old business was an iconic institution. Why change a profitable formula? As Gould explains: "We were focusing on the wrong things, focusing on promotions and the like; we were not focusing enough on the customer. I honestly thought we were going to hit a wall."

Gould was determined to find out how Bloomingdale's was distinguishing itself in the market place. He commissioned a comprehensive survey. Hundreds of questions were asked of 21,000 customers, across all the company's stores. Gould was struck by two key findings. "Firstly, the customers said they didn't want us to play in the department store arena…. you had Neiman Marcus at the top and others at the bottom; they felt we were stuck in the middle, trying to be many things to many people. They wanted us to play in the more upscale 'specialty store' arena. Secondly, and this was something of an epiphany for us, our customers were effectively saying we weren't differentiating ourselves enough just by trying to be the best in contemporary merchandise. Adding to which they said we could not win with our current service levels. By that they not only meant the quality of the sales associates but the environment of the stores, the ease of shopping, etc. They didn't expect service as good as the exemplary Nordstrom department store but did expect service to be on a par with Saks and Neiman Marcus."

brave enough to change what was working

These findings spawned a new brand strategy for the business to be chosen for all the *right* reasons. Gould was brave enough to change what was working. As he puts it: "We needed to create the only nationwide 'full line' department/speciality store with an upscale focus and contemporary bent." Acknowledging this was much easier said than done. He broke the task into five parts:

- As Gould explains, number one centred on merchandise: "When we started, 44 per cent of the business was defined as limited, upscale merchandise. The five-year plan was to move this to 55 per cent. It now stands at 72 per cent. The knock-on effect is that we've moved our average unit sale at a compounded rate of about 9 per cent – so we have almost doubled the average unit price going out the door over the course of the last seven years."

- With a significant shift of emphasis to increase emotional engagement with loyal customers, the second element involved marketing. "Promotional days and general advertising were dramatically reduced and our spend more focused towards regular direct mail-outs. We were determined to build stronger, deeper relationships with customers."

- The strength of a well defined strategy is that it naturally informs a business, it encourages management to make the right decisions. "Number three was a no-brainer. We knew our shops were cluttered and not easy to shop. We eliminated 85 per cent of our signage almost overnight. We decided we would not merchandise in the aisles anymore. We created environments in the stores where people enjoyed sitting. All pretty basic, but a significant shift in mindset as it reduced selling space. We also took over precious space to create bigger changing rooms – as one of my store managers said, standing on line waiting to try something on is not giving great customer service! He was right; turnover has doubled in those departments! We spent millions of dollars refurbishing our rest rooms, customer service areas and the like – all crucial."

- Currently accounting for 25 per cent of the business, the New York City flagship store was to represent the fourth part of the strategy. "For all the tourists and iconic status we never forget 59th Street is a neighbourhood store, with local needs, but we do celebrate it as a headquarters store too. We invest heavily here and experiment a lot. One of our guys came up with an edgy fashion concept of mixing designer and bridge (fashion that is classified just below designer level) together. We have Ralph Lauren Black Label and Burberry sitting across the aisle from DKNY; it's worked well for us, because that's exactly *who* we are. I define our DNA as approachable upscale, and here on 59th Street we're always testing and fine-tuning our 'understanding' of this."

- And for number five, Gould talks about his people strategy. "This is the most critical, the single most important thing for our business. Fundamentally there is nothing I sell in this building that you can't get within six or seven blocks, and that's the same the world over – this means your people become your key differentiating opportunity. Crucially our programmes seek to give our people the skills and opportunities to excel. We have developed an enormous number of 'educational' syllabuses. *We don't train our people, that's what you do with animals.* We specifically nurture passion for what they do and compassion for others. And with all this education our people progress financially too; that's good for them and a good reason not to leave – which is good for us."

Now more profitable than ever, Bloomingdale's has always been considerably more famous than its size would suggest. When Gould took control there were 25 stores. There

We don't train our people, that's what you do with animals

are still less than 40 across America. But this iconic store group has always managed to own a special place in the heart of the American shopper. When Gould arrived, Bloomingdale's had been around for a very long time and was *doing* its thing and *doing* its numbers. But over time Gould realised things needed to change – customers needed to be persuaded to choose the brand in a more sustainable way. Bloomingdale's *raison d'être* had become focused on making money rather than delivering outstanding customer satisfaction. Decisions were being made that were harming the brand and its future – Gould thought this unthinkable.

In the fast moving world of retail the learning here is simple: periodically a business needs to dig deep, very deep and think the unthinkable.

If that's too difficult – *do* the unthinkable.

Get someone in who knows what they are doing and was born to the task!

Case story

Simon Fox
CEO, HMV Group

Interviewed March 2010

Getting closer

"By thinking of ourselves as music retailers we were confined to being about stores and product, serried racks of packaged goods. Now we think of ourselves as an entertainment brand."

So says Simon Fox, the young, visionary CEO of the UK's HMV group.

Since arriving at HMV in 2006, Fox explains he has led a full strategic review, aggressively re-focusing the business to become more relevant to the ever-changing world of entertainment. "People have an emotional connection with what we sell in a way they don't with other things – we're now celebrating this, going out of our way to be chosen by getting customers closer to what they love."

Following a degree in economics and various management positions, Fox used a well-timed redundancy package to start his own business. From humble beginnings in his bedroom he created and eventually sold the UK's first out-of-town stationary superstore group, having built an empire of 60 stores in just nine years. He is extremely *People have an emotional connection with what we sell in a way they don't with other things* personable and clearly very bright. Besides natural talent, Fox has an authority and logic that effortlessly earns respect.

With 280 stores in the UK & Ireland and a further 150 stores in Canada, Hong Kong and Singapore the HMV chain has been a traditional music specialist for much of its 90-year history. But through necessity the business and brand has had to re-invent itself. Despite benefiting from competitors who disappeared without trace following the supermarkets' decision to move into their product areas it is the sales-crushing arrival of digital downloads and file-sharing that potentially represents the sector's biggest challenge. But as Fox acknowledges: "Still less than ten per cent of our business is online, with very

Simon Fox, centre, with 'Take That' band

little money in this for us. We knew we had a respected brand, to survive we simply needed to adapt with the times."

But to be chosen, how far can the HMV brand credibly stretch?

"We have an enormous amount of highly detailed customer research that guides us. Opening the horizons of a business like this needs a mechanism that allows teams to make the right decisions quickly," explains Fox. "We've developed a metaphorical 'funnel'. It's a business model that, as best you can, separates winning ideas from losers. It's a progressively rigorous thought-process that requires any new idea, service or product to successfully tick boxes in order to progress to the next stage. The overriding filter for everything is: 'personal *media-based* entertainment'. Filters from research then refine further. It works very well allowing the right amount of intuition too. The 'funnel' is fast and keeps us on track – we know where our magnetic north is, so to speak."

Indeed it's a logical process that graphically explains how a business that knows it must reinvent itself stays focused.

"So we now sell a lot of MP3 players, but won't sell televisions. Both are media entertainment but TVs are family-based, not personal. We weren't selling MP3 players, headphones and speakers a few years ago; now they make up nine per cent of sales. We have nearly a quarter of a billion US dollars in sales from products that weren't in our stores just three years ago. Concert tickets also meet our criteria – so ticket offices are going into all stores. Mobile phone offerings with strong entertainment packages are now in 60 of our stores. And a clothing franchise with licensed TV and film show merchandise called 'The Studio' is rolling out."

In recognition of the importance of *live music* to their customers, HMV has diversified into this market too. Following the recent purchase of MAMA Group, it now owns 13 live music venues including London's iconic Hammersmith Apollo, aptly renamed the HMV Apollo. It also owns five summer festivals and has a fledgling management business with artists like Franz Ferdinand and Kaiser Chiefs.

We've developed a metaphorical 'funnel'

With live gigs and personal appearances continuing, the stores are becoming increasingly experiential. "They're becoming more immersive," explains Fox. "We are currently testing Gamerbase 'pay-to-play' gaming centres, boasting banks of PCs where customers can rent stations by the hour. People come in small groups or large parties. We run competitions and special events, making gaming more sociable, more competitive. In partnership with Curzon AE we're also opening specialist small cinemas in selected stores for the *cognoscenti* – complete with a glass of wine (no popcorn). It's all about being more relevant to our broad customer base."

Get closer, HMV's marketing strapline, perfectly communicates the company's promise, beautifully tempting customers to chose the brand.

"Our full vision is no-one gets you closer to the music, film and games you love," says Fox. "And *Pure*, our new loyalty programme, has proved an excellent way to endorse this. We charge £3 for customers to join. The assertion being that only committed fans of music and film should and would apply. We wanted them to genuinely value belonging – in under a year, over one million customers have signed up. The rewards aren't primarily about discounts; they're about experiences *money can't buy*." By being commercially connected to artists, labels and venues, securing a dazzling array of experiences appears relatively easy. When members accumulate points with purchases they browse the rewards online. They could find highly prestigious and rare BAFTA tickets, opportunities to be 'extras' in films, seats at music venues, all-areas passes, premieres – reward opportunities both big and small are endless… local gigs, signed paraphernalia, tickets to the 'Brits'. Even one million points recently earned a delighted customer a signed Metallica guitar.

Fox claims *Pure* really is getting his customers closer to what they love and they love it. "We're targeting half of all sales to come through the *Pure* programme within 12 months – the data mining opportunities are phenomenal.

Fox doesn't know what the business will look like in a year or two's time – but that's OK

Customers' spending patterns, shopping habits and preferred shopping channels are easily understood, effortlessly translating to highly personalised and 'welcomed' marketing campaigns. Imagine, we'll know someone went to the 'Florence and the Machines' concert at the Apollo because they bought a ticket through us. We'll then offer a relevant download or bundle that download with the ticket; we're just understanding what works and what doesn't. The potency of this vehicle is real – cross selling will be enormous."

With the digital revolution claiming huge retail scalps, the metamorphosis of HMV has been timely to say the least. With over US$ 3 billion group turnover in 2009, annual profits are up 50 per cent to US$ 115 million since Fox arrived. But successfully being chosen needs a committed workforce and here *get closer* is working its magic too. A record-breaking 92 per cent engagement was recently verified amongst HMV's 12,000 staff, with churn well below 20 per cent.

Fox calls it magnetic north. Marketers call it brand.

And the business is growing by trusting it.

Get closer skilfully tempts customers to choose HMV to be part of their lives. And customers are loving and cherishing the whole idea. The good news is, it's inherently future-proof. So like his committed teams, Fox doesn't know what the business will look like in a year or two's time. But that's OK. In a digital age that's speeding up, he trusts his customers will drive the business in the direction they want – in truth not even *they* know where that'll be, either.

But be in no doubt. Fox, the 'funnel' and his team will *get everyone close.*

SECRET ONE – SUMMARY

Being Chosen: Tips for success

- Always remember there's nothing you sell that can't be bought elsewhere.

- In effect, this means you're in the business of 'being chosen'.

- To be the truly preferred choice you need to *wrap* whatever you sell in some form of uniqueness.

- The best form of uniqueness is to 'stand for' something that emotionally engages and inspires your workforce and customers.

- What you 'stand for' is called your Brand and most successful businesses acknowledge this as the genesis of their success.

- When a brand is born from heartfelt values, competitors find it more difficult to copy and a workforce tends to self select.

- Well articulated brands help businesses swiftly recognise what 'good' decisions look like.

- Listening is free and a necessary ingredient if you want to be chosen.

- Brand, don't *be* branded. If you don't go out of your way to grab the agenda of what people think you 'stand for', they will make something up for themselves – and that's a stupid thing to allow.

So if you only remember one thing from this section, remember:

You're in the business of being chosen.

SECRET 2

TRUST

TRUST

Nothing bigger

In life it seems nothing works properly without trust.

Certainly my research shows that after the fundamental re-orientation of being chosen, the successful retailers place an unparalleled premium on being trusted. Looking to be trusted in all they do, looking to be trusted in all they stand for. Trust therefore demands to be my second secret to retail success.

Indeed I would argue there's nothing bigger in a retailer's armoury than being trusted.

But the first rule of trust is you can't ask for it, you have to earn it – everyone knows this but take a moment to look around and see how many times *the first rule of trust* trust is requested. Trust such-and-such for *is you can't ask for it* the best price around or such-and-such is your trusted supplier of.... How many times do you hear, trust me when I tell you.... ? If anything ever validated the maxim, *actions speak louder than words,* it's my second secret of success.

Just how important?

How powerful and exactly what role does trust play in our lives? Well I'm no great philosopher but without too much reflection you must agree:

- Spiritually speaking, Faith is all about trusting what you've been told.
- Governments find life notoriously difficult because experience dictates most politicians can't be trusted.

- Commerce thrives on reputations. Successful companies insist on putting trust at the heart of their brands, bundling customer promises around this to differentiate themselves.
- Relationships. People simply don't like people they can't trust.
- ....there are more but you get my point.

Where's this taking us?

Without getting too deep, the really successfully retailers are those who reflect the society we live in, often helping shape it. Retailers know that to be chosen and trusted they must care what people think, care about their role in communities and obviously care that customers choose to revisit them. The progressive retailers even lead the way on ethical issues: fair trade, sustainability, etc. For retailers none of this is worth doing if people don't trust their motives or trust that they will deliver what they promise. Honouring your word is, of course, morally sound and people will love you for it. But in this modern age there's a compelling business reason too. The simple truth is, if a retailer lets people down - betrays their trust - web-based communications will rip the heart out of its reputation at the speed of light with blogs and networking sites.

Battling for trust

Unsurprisingly, research confirms that people prefer to work for businesses they trust. The workforce is first to know when a business is not keeping its word, ripping people off, so to speak. In these businesses it's the workforce that is encouraged to do untrustworthy things. From experience many of these *successful companies don't just do the 'easy' bits of trust* businesses refer to their customers as 'punters'. I hate it. Apart from the accepted use of the word in betting circles, I believe it positions the customer experience and expectation as one big gamble. It's disrespectful and sets the wrong tone. The customer experience should have nothing to do with chance.

And obviously trust is about relationships with other stakeholders too. I am not talking about trust being simply written on the company's corporate wish list, neatly filed under the heading of company Values. Here I am acknowledging how the most successful companies create an ethos of trust. Genuinely challenging themselves to deliver trust at every stage of their operation. And I am always struck how successful companies don't just do the 'easy' bits of trust. They bravely face the tough decisions to ensure trust is totally embedded in everything they do.

Asda, the UK arm of Wal-Mart, is raising its profile by claiming to drive trust and transparency in literally all it does. They are trialling a programme of web-cams throughout their business and supplier base – cameras in boardrooms, in Bangladeshi garment factories and even viewing milking parlours twenty–four/seven. Extreme as all this sounds, it does send a big signal in the fight for trust. Asda are not asking for trust, but confidently *earning* it.

Almost paradoxically, trust is so important to retailers it has become a major competitive battleground. Supermarkets have elevated running out of fresh bananas on Saturday afternoons from an 'out-of-stock' position to a breakdown of trust – acknowledging the negativity it generates when customers aren't able to get the ingredients they need, when they want. An interesting mindset but as an observer of retail I understand where they're coming from!

Tempting but wrong

As a marketing man it has always struck me that advertising & marketing promotions seem to be a trust *blind-spot* for many retailers. It seems to be a tempting place for even the most conscientious of companies to fall short on their ambitions to be trusted. I suspect it's a consequence of wide-ranging laws aimed at rogue traders that push honest retailers to bend some incredibly prescriptive rules. How often have retailers hidden merchandise in remote parts of the shop floor, for a given number of days, just to 'establish' unfeasibly high prices ready to be reduced in blitz of publicity.

But interestingly, research shows that customers understand what's going on with this fake discounting. Customers being almost complicit, refusing to buy certain categories of merchandise unless heavily marked-down – furniture being a tarnished example. It's as if normally rational customers need to lean on huge discounts to give themselves permission to make the larger purchases. We all know specialist retailers that are on 'Sale' 50 weeks a year – where's the trust component in this? It must surely be a warning that the customer trust-contract has been broken – a fitting epitaph in the making. Certainly a sector the faceless merchants of internet discounting are circling, licking their lips.

But over the years *every day low pricing,* EDLP, has taken this trust conundrum head-on. In reality, retailers find weaning themselves and customers off high-low pricing is very difficult – it is, after all, a mechanism that puts the retailer in control of stimulating sales and gives the customer a reason to buy. Some retailers I've spoken to look longingly at EDLP but reckon it takes half a generation and a good deal of pain to successfully achieve.

We're seeing a similar breakdown of trust around the world at Christmas-time too. Customers hesitant to buy in the run-up to the festive season for fear prices will be reduced before the big day. Who hasn't been tempted to give an IOU as a Christmas gift to guarantee a saving in the January sales? And note I said 'tempted'! How often do you hear observers of retail saying Christmas is getting later every year? No wonder. It's because there has been a breakdown in trust. It's become a case of who will blink first – somewhat ironic at this special time of year.

Christmas trading needs to be re-invented with some form of 'goodwill' on prices

I believe Christmas trading needs to be re-invented with some form of 'goodwill' on prices. How about a price guarantee? Retailers and shoppers would certainly be happy with that – please make sure you read the first case study in this secret from Carphone Warehouse. They have a wonderful policy on promotional prices.

The web we weave

In my line of work I buy books and airline tickets, a lot.

I like to think I know my way around a keyboard and website. So when last year I was reduced alternately to tears of rage and admiration,

I knew these two emotional experiences would find their way into this book. And it's no secret which part of the book and why.

Let me tell you about two experiences within a month of each other bringing one into stark relief against the other. Two poignant reminders that third parties are no excuse for a business not to manage trust. A perfect demonstration, in the first instance, of how some businesses *never miss an opportunity, to miss an opportunity*. And a reminder, in the second instance, of how some businesses see every opportunity as a chance to demonstrate that trust is at the heart of everything they do.

Last year I was speaking at the World Retail Congress and booked my own flight. The airline I chose, I now know, had a 'code share' which meant *they* took my money but *I* flew another airline. When I asked for a snack in flight I was told there would be a charge. I argued I'd booked with a full service carrier, with a flight number to prove it, who boasted free in-flight service.... but I lost. I was encouraged to ring customer service and was put through to the web designer's *some businesses never miss an opportunity, to miss an opportunity* department (?). Here I was told if I had scrolled down to the terms and conditions of the booking protocol I would see one of the paragraphs stated 'services may vary' – a neat little catch-all and a guaranteed loop-hole for trust to disappear. I asked if I had to read all the small print every time I booked a flight and was told the font size was the same.

Contrast this with Amazon. I went on line to buy a rare book. Before I pressed the 'buy button' Amazon flashed a warning to me that my order would be re-directed to a specialist bookshop in the tiny Welsh village of Ross-on-Wye. When I did hit the buy button I was asked to let Amazon know how things subsequently went. The book arrived on time, everything went perfectly and I marked the experience ten out of ten. More importantly I didn't *feel* I needed to scroll down to see what services may vary as a consequence of my Welsh diversion.

I have to confess both these brands are impressive operations but now I'm on a trust journey with each of them. One has taken me forward and the other backwards – different service sectors, one an opportunity missed, another taken.

The trust dimension

As I've said it's no great blinding insight announcing that trust is a secret to success. I can't believe anyone reading this section hasn't nodded approvingly throughout.

But retailers are three-dimensional brands with thousands of touch points where maintaining trust is a challenging reality. So let me now introduce you to some fine exponents of the craft.

The interviews

- **Carphone Warehouse** is one of the most trusted brands in the UK and Europe. Its founder explains how a dynamic young business must constantly review its operations to make sure the special bond with customers is not broken.

- **Liz Claibourne** has always placed huge emphasis on its social responsibilities. Following a phone call from the White House and with the help of the President's wife, this trusted fashion brand was amongst the first to re-define working practices in Asia.

- **Comet** is one of the UK's oldest and largest electrical retailers. Its road to success is being re-routed through a programme of 'four behaviours' aimed at building the customer trust contract. It's a low margin, high service operation where profits are hard won, easily lost.

- **The John Lewis Partnership** has become one of the world's most admired retail models. Trust and integrity guides every action of this UK business with everyone working there being a partner and every customer publicly acknowledging its unique shopping experience.

- **Trinity Group,** part of Li & Fung is the very essence of entrepreneurialism. Understanding precisely the role trust plays in building the individual business empires it acquires and grows throughout Asia is core to its success.

- **Tesco** is undoubtedly one of the most revered retail brands in the world. A company with global ambitions, it puts customers at the very centre of its thoughts with trust being a non-negotiable value pervading everything it stands for.

- **Lane Crawford** is a sparkling success story in the heart of Asia, delivering what many believe to be one of the finest luxury shopping experiences. It's an intimate speciality fashion brand where customers trust it to deliver exactly what they want.

- **New Look** is one of the leaders in the ruthless world of European value fashion retailing. After a long period of success it was time to re-invent itself, and a trusted relationship in the provision of finance proved to be as important as the vision itself.

10
Case History

Charles Dunstone
Founder, Carphone Warehouse

Interviewed May 2009

Esprit de corps

If the big *question* for retailers is how to be chosen, executives with vision will always put trust at the heart of *their* answer.

Carphone Warehouse was on a mission to offer shoppers impartial advice about mobile phones from day one – since 1989 it has prospered on the back of its 'customer-centric' brand values. While competitors' commission structures encouraged sales staff to push specific handsets or particular network contracts, Carphone Warehouse stores have always felt refreshingly trustworthy to customers. Simple, honest advice is guaranteed, because salespeople haven't been incentivised to sell higher-priced products or tariffs – they receive a flat commission no matter what price the phone or which type of tariff. The company even keeps an eye on prices of phones after a purchase is made, *automatically refunding the difference to customers if there's a price cut in the following 30 days* – a remarkable retailing initiative, made all the more powerful by the fact that it's not widely publicised.

Now with more than 2,300 stores across 10 European countries, Carphone Warehouse's founder and CEO Charles Dunstone feels it's time to step up the trust factor even further. He is introducing a scheme to abandon commission altogether and instead, reward 'stores' for providing exemplary customer service. From mid 2009, following successful trials in its London stores and broad staff acceptance, the scheme is being rolled out across the estate. It's an initiative that's perfectly in tune with the Carphone Warehouse brand essence, and Dunstone is visibly enthused at the prospect of evolving the way workforce view their relationship with customers, super-charging customer satisfaction levels, and re-asserting the brand as a customer champion.

"A really big change that is happening now is that we're taking commission out of the stores all together," says the affable, intelligent and straight-talking Dunstone. "It's simply done now on customer service. Everyone has a salary with a bonus based on their customer service scores." The preferred means of measuring customer approval, or disapproval, is the Net Promoter Score (NPS), a system developed by US customer loyalty guru Fred Reichheld and now fast becoming a popular alternative to traditional customer satisfaction research. *super-charging customer satisfaction levels* "We're lucky. We sell a device that we can use to communicate with, which obviously would not the case if we sold cameras for example. We can get one stage further to asking about customer service – implementing NPS – simply because our product lets us!"

Dunstone says that after a sale, "customers receive a text which asks them to rate, on a scale of one to ten, how strongly they would recommend Carphone Warehouse to friends and family." The results from this 'ultimate question' are centrally processed and made visible to store teams. "Employee bonuses are then allocated depending on how well 'their' store has performed according to the NPS." Peer pressure to deliver excellent service for the good of the whole team pushes individuals to give their best, and the desired results are already coming through, explains Dunstone. "The average NPS score that we are getting goes up month by month the longer we run our business this way – doubling in participating stores to date. And importantly, our internal employee happiness survey, which we run pretty consistently, has also continued to climb. So people feel more professional and better rewarded. Overall employee satisfaction is the highest it's ever been with over 80% of staff either happy or very happy. So everybody has changed dramatically. What's great is that we are rewarding them for doing the right things."

Does this translate to greater sales? Of course, many factors are at play, says Dunstone, but he is delighted the company is growing market share in a shrinking, recession-wracked market, and the company has out-performed the mobile and telecoms market in the six months since the changes were introduced.

It's not missed by anyone that a major move away from commission-based selling could have sent shockwaves through the workforce, with diehard salespeople feeling deprived of personal commission. But Dunstone is sanguine about this. He acknowledges that a few high-performing salespeople have 'walked', but feels they were probably not fully in tune with the Carphone brand ethos anyway. "I think to be frank there are some people who've left because of this – but probably that's a good thing because their earnings were a greater priority to them, above and beyond the issue of customer satisfaction. If you just try to pressure a customer into buying something it's obvious they are not going to be comfortable about the process and that won't reflect well on the brand. Perhaps, over time, we have attracted some people who should not have naturally lived in our business." But the business has been careful to explain the principles of the new bonus system, with Dunstone personally managing email responses from individual employees – keeping close tabs on reactions.

a few high-performing salespeople have 'walked'

In 2008 Dunstone sealed a landmark US$ 1.5 billion partnership deal with Best Buy, the world's largest electronics retailer. Carphone Warehouse will now be involved in the launch of a chain of category-killing electrical superstores across the UK and Europe in the coming years. In this context Dunstone's brand values perfectly embrace Best Buy's vision of delivering a 'truly customer-centric' experience. In their sector, Best Buy predict that customers, when faced with ever-decreasing product prices, will increasingly base their purchasing decisions on service rather than physical product. And to this end, Best Buy is famed in the States for switching to commission-free selling – Dunstone's move in this direction is certainly timely.

Improvements to customer service are vital because of the evolution of mobile communications today, explains Dunstone.

"We've reached a new level of complexity with Smart Phones and iPhones. We are going back to the days when people were really mystified by the product – so we need to go back to having people in our stores who are real experts and can help customers understand what's going on. For a while, mobile phones were not advancing in terms of their functionality as fast as before but that has now changed. We are back, once again, to a stage of really needing consultants in stores to help our customers."

When you truly know what you stand for, decisions are much easier

Dunstone's vision is to prepare a very large retail workforce for how he now sees the future. His programme to remove individual commission and base team (store) rewards on NPS measurement is bold and not without consequence. But here is the learning. When you truly know what you stand for, decisions are much easier. Right from the beginning, finding ways of earning and maintaining a customer's trust was always at the heart of what Dunstone believed would separate his business from the rest – this latest initiative is no exception.

In a market defined by unprecedented technological development – Dunstone is effectively taking his business right back to its roots.

11
Case History

Paul Charron
Former Chairman and CEO, Liz Claiborne

Interviewed May 2008

Seems about right

How did the Washington White House help Paul Charron earn the trust of his retailers by reassuring them that "they were never going to get bitten on the butt by some campaigning consumer purporting oppressive work conditions in a far-flung factory"?

Best practice, modern retailing is the answer.

This dictates that those who work for you are fully respected, rightly acknowledging their contribution to the business. But it wasn't until recently that this included suppliers.

Human rights abuse in garment manufacturing in the developing world erupted as an emotive issue for western consumers in the early 1990s. During this decade, the concept of Corporate Social Responsibility (CSR) came of age. Prior to

Paul Charron, hard at work in a garment factory

that, retail leaders and brand owners were under little pressure to investigate conditions or campaign for improvements for workers in the far-off factories that supplied them.

Paul Charron is a polished individual, quietly spoken, erudite and a celebrated American retail executive credited with effecting real attitudinal change towards overseas manufacturing methods. A former Procter & Gamble executive, it was as Chairman and CEO of the Liz Claiborne stable of fashion brands that he bravely propelled this venerable company into the epicentre of the child labour and 'sweatshops' debate. Instigating change, he campaigned for widespread improvements in conditions for factory workers and their families, raising awareness of human rights violations. As Charron explains, "the company

one of my guiding tenets has always been to try to do what seems about right

and its founders were already trusted and recognized as being philanthropic, progressive and as *giving something back* to the communities they served – this was a natural opportunity to build upon that."

"In 1995, out of the blue, I was contacted by Robert Reich, Secretary of Labour in the Clinton administration. A rigid ideologue, extremely left wing and fiercely progressive on workers' rights, he was avoided by many as being a non-commercial purist. He wanted to get together to push an 'apparel initiative' for human rights. I knew it would be a delicate conversation but one of my guiding tenets has always been to try to do *what seems about right*. And this whole process of taking an enlightened approach to human rights *seemed about right*.... so I saw him!"

"Reich certainly knew his stuff. We obviously knew about overseas manufacturing and sourcing but he helped educate me and my executives on the subtleties of the issues. Very soon he convinced us change was needed and he convinced me that a company like us should be at the forefront. If we seized the initiative and set the agenda we would be in control of change, as opposed to having it imposed on us by someone else, someone probably less enlightened, less commercial."

As a business, Liz Claiborne was ideally placed to influence change. It was responsible for placing enormous orders with countries like China, Saipan and Indonesia. Its lobbying powers were obvious. Over the next ten years, Liz Claiborne executives worked very closely with the White House Apparel Industry Partnership, going on to heavily influence various national trade associations and bodies – regularly meeting governments and factory owners throughout the Far East to promote human rights.

It soon became clear that many countries around the world were heavily reliant on clothing manufacturing but had totally unacceptable production methods. But for Charron and his team, pulling out of these problematic factories was not the answer. "You don't just cut and run and source elsewhere – the people who'd lose out most are the very people you're trying to protect," explains Charron. "So we tried not to exit. We tried to change. Our guiding vision was to make them 'paragons of virtue'. So we put people in to go through the books, to audit things – making sure that sewing machine operators were being paid for overtime. That women did not lose their jobs just because they were pregnant, that dormitories were clean, all things like that. Liz Claiborne introduced rigorous standards of engagement, instigated announced and unannounced tests and visits. And we also spent a good deal of time developing ways to support these businesses as they grew – it's important to get this right too."

But some issues seemed insurmountable.

America's then First Lady, Hillary Rodham Clinton, rang Charron concerned about Liz Claiborne withdrawing from a factory in Macedonia during the Kosovo conflict. Charron told her it was inevitable because of supply chain breakdown. Clinton's work had led her to see first-hand how infrastructure breakdown in war zones was damaging livelihoods and she wanted to protect factory workers in this part of the world. With her intervention and by working with various agencies, Charron and his team were able to keep the factory trading, manufacturing clothes for refugees, funded by US State Department aid. And although the incident wasn't overly publicised, people across Liz Claiborne knew this was happening and it grew their sense of corporate pride.

As Charron explains: "High profile as it may have been, our work with the White House didn't operate in a vacuum. It built on the work of the company's founders and the Liz Claiborne Foundation. We have many initiatives, such as our focus on domestic or relationship violence, and what they do is build a repository of goodwill and trust throughout the whole employee base. Our people feel great that as a company we are not just about making money and enhancing shareholder value, we are also about creating a respectful environment, a thoughtful environment, a progressive environment and to this day this defines Liz Claiborne – continuing to attract people to us and importantly retaining a loyal work force with low turnover. And let's not forget a wonderful secondary benefit. It also gives our customers a reason to trust, value and choose us when things are on parity."

Whether publicity has been sought, word will always get out and Liz Claiborne is now firmly entrenched in the apparel category of the prestigious Fortune Magazine's most admired businesses.

It also gives our customers a reason to trust, value and choose us when things are on parity

Charron's intuitive and energetic lead in what many senior executives would have considered a treacherous field led Liz Claiborne into the highest echelons of US power. As Charron himself puts it: "Espousing the right values is simply good business. It's enlightened management. It's hard to put a price tag on."

And here is the learning for retail empires and corner stores alike. People like doing business with people they like, admire and trust, simple as that. It's not the cynical headline-grabbing profiteering from a good cause but the quiet, genuine expression of a retailer's soul that matters.

By taking the trouble to look after some of the softer issues in the day-to-day cut and thrust of running a shop, a reservoir of goodwill can be built that cannot be bought.

It also nice to know your butt is safe.

Case History

Hugh Harvey
Managing Director, Comet

Interviewed August 2008

Live by

Those in the retail 'know' talk about the supreme difficulty of delivering outstanding customer service with a value proposition.

Those retailers who've come closest occupy a special place in customers' minds, retail folklore and, usually, a retail Hall of Fame or two.

But as managing director of Comet, one of the UK's biggest electrical groups with over 250 large format stores, Hugh Harvey is introducing a radical service-led programme to change the retailer's fortunes and complement its 75-year-old reputation for extremely competitive prices.

Harvey is an engaging individual, clearly very bright and certainly very focused – he just wouldn't offer an opinion he couldn't stand by. In a sector famous for wafer-thin margins (and ever-increasing threats from supermarkets and internet shopping) he says he can deliver success through outstanding customer service *and* competitive prices. Over the last five years he has reduced just about every cost in the business and is now working on the other side of retail's success equation. He is now investing heavily in time and money to deliver exceptional customer service, increasing the brand's appeal as an electrical retailer with a level of service that is differentiated and trusted.

four behaviours that we must live by, and continue to live by

"I'll succeed long term by articulating 'four behaviours' that we *must live by, and continue to live by,"* promises Harvey.

- Firstly, Harvey points to a towering ambition of *superior knowledge.* "The vision here is to be trusted to always have more knowledge than the customer and our competitors. Not just product knowledge but an understanding of everything associated with our market. Training must also recognise *appropriate* knowledge. We have customers looking for uncomplicated guidance and others wanting detailed specifications. For highly technical customers we have specialist colleagues with *deep* knowledge. These colleagues also give master classes to other colleagues. Our whole knowledge ethos is primarily underpinned by 50 or so 'e-learning' modules. Everyone must take pride in their 'knowledge', and role-playing with line-managers on the shop floor hones information and inter-personal skills. We also exhibit our knowledge in-store through appropriate interactivity – meaning seminal technology that, unlike our competitors, is 'always' fully operational on the shop floor."

- Secondly, Harvey talks about a *passion for exceptional service.* "Obviously service is from a customer perspective. We interviewed and listen to thousands of customers – from how they wanted to be approached to the appropriate time for orientation before being approached. From product repair time schedules to delivery time slots. And whether they wanted a phone call just before we deliver or not. We analysed and agreed a *deliberate customer journey* for all key customer contact points from in-store to home delivery and to after-sales. Even discussing call-centre protocol with customers. Nothing exceptional with any of these goals, but we have an ambition to be trusted to ensure our systems truly delivered it! As well as store-based sales, we have an increasing online business too. We deliver into nearly one in ten UK households every year. So to keep our service levels where we want them we have over 1,000 colleagues specialising in home delivery and servicing. We have specialist white and brown goods engineers as well as grey goods engineers (field-based technical support). Our call centres are all UK-based offering help-line support too. I can't think of many other retailers offering all this, especially not in electricals!"

- Thirdly, Harvey explains *care for detail* – underlining its importance when it comes to customer trust. Interestingly, Comet has chosen to break this out from service excellence. "We're selling merchandise that's not instantly consumed. The average life expectancy of products we sell is 7 to 8 years. And occasionally they'll break down and need fixing (under guarantee or extended warranty). All retailers capture information but we've thousands of parts and hundreds of products, so for us accuracy and attention to detail is crucial. With the right information we can, through one telephone conversation, pre-diagnose a fault, even something bought five years ago – meaning we'll send the appropriate parts with the engineer, giving the opportunity to fix it first time. We ensure that our IT systems prompt and facilitate this detailed data capture. We also know our products are researched online so we always provide detailed specifications enabling easy comparisons. We don't tolerate missing product details or 'TBC' notations anywhere. We home deliver about a third of what we sell so we always capture *extremely* detailed information on delivery addresses. If we're delivering to an apartment on the third floor, we need to know if there's an elevator or not. With this information we either send a one or two-man crew. We can't afford to send two-man crews just in case! To me this care for detail is more a mindset than a mechanical process and a vitally important competitive edge."

care for detail is more a mindset than a mechanical process

- Finally, the fourth behaviour Harvey highlights is *individual attitude* in the battle for customer trust. "There's lots of debate as to whether or not you can articulate this as a behaviour, but nevertheless we felt it important to ask each and every one of our 10,000 colleagues, each and every day to consider what attitude they bring to work. We ask they come with a positive, supportive, progressive attitude, one of helpfulness and positivity. Like many organisations we have continuous support programmes to promote this. Back in 2003 our employee engagement score was in the mid-40s, now it's mid-90s. Testament to the mind-shifts now encouraged, heightened engagement is essential for the transformation of our business."

With a focus on service, attracting and retaining the right people is essential. "With high investment in training you have to reconfigure your business to recruit the right people with the right attitude. Older people tend to stay with us longer, it therefore becomes cost effective to involve them more heavily. We've changed how we reward our people too. We now have a non-commission remuneration model. This engages colleagues better and we build on this by including them in decision-making issues like range reviews. It reduces the emotional distance between buyers and shop floor. There's a good deal of sophisticated modelling going into work time scheduling to increase customer-facing hours too," explains Harvey.

But being part of the Kesa Group has also helped Comet. Harvey and his team have learnt a tremendous amount from Darty, another group company. "Darty are the number one electrical retailer in France and on a profit-to-sales ratio, one of the most profitable electrical retailers in the world. They are probably ten years ahead of us with the specialist positioning of being trusted for service and price, but we're catching-up. In the UK we've demonstrated a lot of 'thought leadership' within the category and if you talk to the supplier base or retail analysts they'd accept Comet is out in front, and it's our intention is to stay there!"

Older people tend to stay with us longer, it therefore becomes cost effective to involve them more heavily

Despite their major competitors struggling, Comet claim to be enjoying profitable sales increases through a combination of ruthless cost control and strategic investment to deliver exceptional customer service. It is clear Harvey and his team are emotionally bonding with their customers and trust must be building – a skill-set their parent company has mastered.

But the learning here is as old as retail itself. Giving customers what they want is relatively easy. It's making money when the margins are low that's near impossible.

Case History 13

Charlie Mayfield
Chairman, John Lewis Partnership

Interviewed November 2008

Old-fashioned idea

Businesses, especially those that are customer facing, cannot thrive in today's increasingly demanding and transparent world without integrity and a contented workforce.

A faultless example of this is the UK's John Lewis Partnership (JLP), owner of department stores, upscale supermarkets and remote shopping channels. Its 'employee ownership' model is admired throughout the world and is a rare illustration of 'integrity' driving commercial success, rather than a superficial afterthought.

Coming from a military background, Charlie Mayfield rose to become chairman of JLP in April 2007. A natural leader, he is young, aware and intellectually bright. He has succeeded, just like his predecessors, in continuing to nurture and develop the Partnership's ideals – ensuring they stay relevant and commercially effective in today's demanding environment. At the very heart of these ideals is 'staff happiness'. It's born out of a near 100-year belief that running JLP for the express benefit of its workforce (Partners) will be to the ultimate benefit of its customers, because it becomes the interest of those staff to cultivate the 'long term'.

a rare illustration of 'integrity' driving commercial success, rather than a superficial afterthought

All very well. But what about necessary decisions that make Partners unhappy?

As Mayfield explains, even closing down one of their much-loved department stores became symbolic of the power of being trusted to do things with integrity and care. "It was very sad for everyone when the Windsor store, just west of London, had to cease trading a couple of years ago. This old, cramped building was hit by costly statutory 'disability access' requirements and declining sales. The John Lewis *way* of closing this store was to allow an unprecedented six months between the announcement and the actual closure – giving all 130 branch Partners time to adjust. We drafted in specialist advisers. Support was given to each Partner, helping and guiding them to apply for posts in neighbouring stores or prepare for retirement. We even offered counsel on new career options, and fortunately we found a future for all but two; it was a tremendous achievement."

None of this is new to any retail manager. What is different however is that each Partner is a part-owner of the business and hugely influential with fellow Partners. As Mayfield explains, "It's so sad that we shut that shop but the way it was handled paradoxically embodied everything that's good about the Partnership. People who have given large parts of their working life to the partnership are owed something, and JLP delivered. Taking time and care also helped loyal customers digest the bad news with a gradual realisation, through chatting to the exiting Partners, that everything could be trusted to be looked after sensitively. We had Partners who had been affected by redundancy coming up and thanking everyone for the way we'd handled things."

each Partner is a part-owner of the business and hugely influential

Values this strong take time to penetrate an organisation. Back in 1928, John Spedan Lewis, son of the founder John Lewis, inherited both the stores in central London. He was now in a position to put his pioneering beliefs about *employee happiness*, underpinning and enriching the business, into practice. He set up the John Lewis Partnership Limited and signed the First Trust Settlement in 1929, giving him practical control of the business, but allowing the profits to be distributed among all the employees. In 1950 the Partnership became the property of the people employed within it.

Today as ever, JLP is run to be highly commercial. The company moves quickly and effectively to maintain a leading position in a ruthlessly competitive industry. Yet it's also proudly democratic. Every Partner has a loud voice in the business they co-own. "This combination of commercial acumen and corporate conscience, so ahead of its time, makes us what we are today," explains Mayfield, who spent the first half of his corporate life in FMCG and management consultancy before falling for the *people-oriented* world of retailing. "JLP is about a fairer form of capitalism. It's about a fairer way of running a business which has people and trust at its heart."

And today one of the Partnership's many accolades is being regarded as the UK's retail bell-wether. It turns over nearly US$ 11 billion per annum with 70,000 partners who currently own 27 John Lewis department stores, 200 Waitrose supermarkets, as well as a catalogue and burgeoning online business.

Mayfield believes passionately that JLP's values generate a sense of responsibility in his partners, which instils high levels of loyalty. Staff turnover typically runs at less than 20 per cent, half the industry average. "Too often in big business there's a fundamental separation of ownership and responsibility," observes Mayfield. "But usually if you own something you can be trusted to look after it, you feel responsible for it especially if you can get financial returns from it. The Partnership is totally 'connected' because the ownership and the responsibility for the business is one and the same thing. We have found that responsibility, allowing individuals to be enterprising, can be a very powerful thing in creating a sustainable business."

"There are countless examples of our Partners improving the business at ground level simply because they feel a special empowerment to do so," explains Mayfield. "One of our managers, at the Cambridge branch of Waitrose, recently took the *freedom within a framework* initiative to solve a site-specific staffing problem, greatly reducing attrition rates among time-pressed, part-time working mums. She correctly identified that chronically high staff churn was caused by working mums dropping their kids off at school, rushing to the store just in time to sit at their check-out, doing their 11-until-2 shift, and then rushing out again to collect the kids. The manager realised that there was no emotional engagement between JLP and these Partners. So she introduced a 'paid-for' 15-minute break during their shift. This gave these mums an opportunity to chat to other Partners, embrace our culture, read company material in the staff room and begin to understand the wider benefits of working for Waitrose."

Clearly this initiative overcame a costly rolling recruitment process and was born out the manager's ownership of the problem as well as her ownership of the business. "She is trusted and her responsibility is to do more than just her job – actually her responsibility in this case was to think creatively about how she could resolve a problem locally," explains Mayfield and indeed most retail bosses would expect the same. But he endorses his point to great effect: "The most fulfilled Partners are those who have been able to make a difference. You have to find the right balance between 'anarchy' and 'effective enterprise', but it can be done. *Freedom within a framework* is a phrase used in JLP quite a bit."

Robustly commercial yet delivered with integrity, one of the world's most revered retailers, The John Lewis Partnership, is a 'conviction' brand of the highest order. It's driven by a belief that is as simple as it is effective: the pursuit of staff happiness.

But even though there is much talk about the famous Partners, the JLP ownership structure is not the only thing that differentiates this brand. It has rightly earned its status as one of the planet's most trusted retailers by building a level of integrity with its workforce, suppliers and customers that is the envy of the world.

However, if your business depends on people serving people, it's certainly best if those doing the serving are happy – an old-fashioned idea that chimes remarkably well in a modern age.

14 Case History

Jeremy Hobbins
Director, Li & Fung Limited,
Deputy Chairman, Trinity Limited

Interviewed October 2009

Enviable skill

Entrepreneurialism and huge corporations rarely sit well together.

Find a trusted way, however, and untold riches may lie ahead.

Throughout the cities of Greater China a host of luxury Western menswear brands are reaching the newly cash-rich middle classes through standalone stores operated by Hong-Kong based, Trinity Group. Classic wool suits, silk ties, polo shirts, fashion accessories and beautifully tailored blazers under the international brands: Kent & Curwen, Gieves & Hawkes, Cerruti 1881, Altea, D'urban and Intermezzo. Each designed and manufactured by Trinity and retailed through its network of 350 stores in prime locations in Hong Kong, Macau, Taiwan and mainland China's upmarket malls. It also has a number of joint venture arrangements to distribute imported Salvatore Ferragamo garments in South Korea, Malaysia, Singapore and Thailand.

Eager to tap into this market and adding to its immense US$ 16 billion revenue stream, distribution

a corporate culture that unashamedly makes space for entrepreneurialism

and retail services conglomerate, Li & Fung bought the 150-store Trinity Group in 2006. Doubling the store portfolio and achieving a turnover in 2009 of almost US$ 280 million, it's now focusing on lifting sales in mainland China from 60 to 80 per cent of the business.

Realistic targets have now been set to double turnover every three years – how?

Jeremy Hobbins, a director of the massive Li & Fung company, who was influential in the acquisition of the Trinity Group and intimately committed to its future success, says: "We will dove-tail with entrepreneurialism to drive success."

Hobbins grew up in Australia but is English by birth. He is a confident businessman with an infectious charm and clearly at home in the hectic world of Asia. He knows what needs to be done and has an aura of knowing how to get it. "We intimately understand how manufacturing and distribution works around here. Trinity invests in top design talent and we're proud of a corporate culture that unashamedly makes space for entrepreneurialism." For Hobbins, success is all about developing trust between the creative entrepreneurs and the *intentions and actions* of the corporation.

"The businesses Trinity bought were created and built by entrepreneurs and continued success depends on maintaining this flair. We respect this, accept this and embrace it. And they're incentivised accordingly – it's the Li & Fung 'way'. But what's also important to remember is we're in a very fortunate position. Not only are we retailers; we're designers, manufacturers and trusted guardian owner of the brands, too. We're in control of nearly everything – and that helps enormously," explains Hobbins.

Indeed, with the exception of Salvatore Ferragamo (where finished garments are shipped from Italy), the Trinity Group owns the complete supply chain for all their brands, explains Hobbins. "From the purchase of fabric in the UK, Italy or wherever to product design, manufacturer, finishing and delivery into stores. This means we've a great deal of financial control. We outsource the bulk of the manufacturing to China with the 'cutting' done there to our patterns. We bring everything back for the critical finishing to Hong Kong and can still sell in China under a duty free arrangement."

But unlike many corporations, Trinity keeps the individual brands and associated stores in very discreet silos. Each brand has separate management responsible for design, marketing and the retail experience – this includes the sales force, training, product focus and store design. "The brands are encouraged to ferociously guard their culture. We want the character of our brands to be wholly distinct from each other," explains Hobbins.

Silos may not be the most cost-effective model but they're the very essence of how Trinity operates – without a hint of irony, *Chinese walls* seems entirely apt.

Conversely, the backroom services of supply chain, human resources, finance, EPoS and support IT are pooled to ensure shared benefits. And here the importance of trust becomes apparent. On the one hand, brand individuality must remain sacrosanct, but at the same time maximum value from scale and infrastructure must be extracted. For example, prime sites and rents in the new Mall developments are always negotiated as a 'stable of brands', never individually. But despite the obvious benefits and wondrous solutions, different Trinity brands are never sold or marketed together for fear of blurring boundaries.

Paramount, even under the shadow of this huge corporate trading entity, is Trinity's reputation for design flair. "We're essentially designing in-house. We know our market and importantly we know the fit our customers like. We're selling international fashion. It's crucial our design teams are cosmopolitan and that we are trusted for our deep commitment to creativity. They come and go, but that spreads the word and refreshes the process."

Silos may not be the most cost-effective model but they're the very essence of how Trinity operates

Creativity and empowerment is found in-store too – sales teams are incentivised to be proactive. As Hobbins proudly explains: "The brand teams manage their retail outlets – we don't franchise. We have a two-part VIP customer programme centred on technology and the human element.

- Through Trinity's sophisticated point-of-sale system, customers' spending history, frequency of visits, purchased items, interest in special events and so on, is gathered and readily accessible to every sales adviser.

- And secondly, there's interpersonal skills. Our staff are encouraged to recognise and address customers by name. Nothing unusual there. But it's difficult with our retail model – high margin and low frequency of visit – so it requires discipline and commitment. Incredibly, I'd say better than 80 per cent of customers are addressed appropriately on arrival, even being acknowledged if it's their first visit. Once in, our sales assistants check the EPoS data to deliver a highly personalised service.

Interestingly most of our assistants are female and even in this male-orientated society, we find our customers prefer this. They respect and trust the honest advice from them. We too have to trust these sales assistants not to 'over-sell' especially as we expect them to be very proactive and incentivise them accordingly. They often initiate contact by e-mail or phone to encourage store visits. It's a delicate balance we're looking for but it works well in our entrepreneurial environment. So in store trust flows three ways. The customers respect the advice, the sales assistants respect the integrity necessary for their job and we respect the sales assistants not to abuse their positions. We also pay good base salaries because in China many retail operations are opening up and poaching is rife. But our churn is below the norm."

keep them free and loose, away from the pressures of the backroom

It's never easy maintaining the confidence of people in businesses you have acquired, especially if their behaviours are particularly different. But as Hobbins succinctly puts it, "Li & Fung have a history of celebrating entrepreneurs. They like to keep them free and loose, away from the pressures of the backroom." And naturally that's how his teams are doing things at the Trinity Group.

But getting differing cultures to work successfully with corporate disciplines is an enviable skill. And here's the learning.

It's all about trust – because when it's mutual, so are the riches.

Case History 15

Terry Green
Chief Executive, Tesco Clothing

Interviewed July 2009

Valued customers

Interestingly, success is not defined by what's put into a brand, but by what's taken out.

Many retailers know this – few truly understand it.

Tesco's clothing division is barely ten years old. Yet it has already sewn up nine per cent of the UK's clothing market share by volume, vying with a couple of others for second placing behind Britain's current leader, Marks & Spencer.

CEO of the Tesco clothing brand worldwide, Terry Green has injected considerable muscle into the division since he joined in 2006. Practically doubling fashion turnover to nearly US$ 2 billion in 2010.

Green is bright, intuitively creative and a big personality. He has a voracious appetite for the world of fashion, and very much in line with the Tesco approach has global supremacy as a glittering fashion prize. "We'd have to overtake Hennes & Mauritz, which I think is the biggest by volume currently. But it's within our sights," says the ever-bullish Green.

pleasing the customer so much that they keep coming back for more

His big challenge is to make Tesco's *Florence & Fred* brand stand out in the already congested value fashion market, where price rules and quality increasingly matters – it's already one of the biggest users of Fair Trade cotton in the UK. "Tesco's secret weapon is to offer not just 'quality and value', but to be trusted for 'great quality' and 'unbeatable value'. We've a very clear vision built around pleasing the customer so much that they keep coming back for more. We want to inspire shoppers with great ideas, must-have styles, amazing quality and *impossible-to-ignore* prices," explains Green.

Green may be in the fashion driving seat but he's quick to point out that behind the scenes Tesco's giant machine is powering fashion and design expertise. Both expertly supported by a state-of-the-art technical department testing for quality and a world-class supply chain operation defying deadlines. He is also aware that this particular market depends on driving massive volumes, surviving on wafer-thin margins and reducing the cost base to the absolute minimum. "Take cashmere sweaters," says Green. "They were around £90 in Marks & Spencer and £200 to £300 at Pringle and others. Tesco introduced cashmere five years ago at £48. When I arrived I brought the prices down to £35 initially, and then £30 and £25. Tesco went from selling no cashmere at all, to selling one million pieces a year. Now that changes peoples' perceptions of what quality and value is!"

There are many factors contributing to Tesco's fashion success explains Green. "Besides the almost forensic understanding of our brand, it's the increasing discipline of our buying procedures that I believe sets us apart – how we interpret and how we buy fashion. It's all about being bolder, braver, simpler, cheaper."

Tesco has reduced its fashion supplier base from 400 to 200 suppliers and this number could go down to 100 in the coming years. By feeding bigger volumes to each, Tesco is in a position to expect better prices for the goods manufactured from its nominated leading edge, high-tech factories around the world. "But of course, today price isn't everything," says Green. "We have to be trusted to reject sub-standard factories and with the help of the Ethical Trading Initiative (ETI), something Tesco was a founding member of, and by having an International Sourcing operation in Hong Kong we are in a great position to reinforce this ethical stance. Every factory we deal with is now checked on a very regular basis."

Another strength is Tesco's well-established fashion office in the Far East. Green feels that buying direct, and building up the in-depth market knowledge this requires, has given Tesco the edge over its competitors who traditionally operate through third party agents. Tesco also transports its own merchandise which greatly reduces freight costs.

But although Tesco's economies of scale *with* ethics are world-class, Green is looking for creative ways to differentiate the brand still further.

There's a bold move to drive *greater commonality* amongst the ranges destined for Tesco's globally-diverse stores. Green sees no reason why much of the fashion buying for Europe and Asia can't be the same as the UK. "As the world shrinks and communications grow, as celebrities increasingly dictate trends, we're finding fashion is becoming a universal statement. Our best-selling items are the best sellers around the world. Of course there will be local differences in every region, but we're finding they're over-lapping to a far greater extent. We're developing the necessary skills to have just one 'design, buying and manufacturing' model for the bulk of SKUs internationally – this will massively reduce costs. Currently we have a 50 per cent overlap for the UK and Central Europe but we think we can push that to 70 per cent," says Green. "This model is going to be rolled out in the Far East, Thailand, China, Korea and so on. It's a brave move but one we are comfortable with."

Green's creativity manifests itself in other ways too. From a headline-grabbing kid's school uniform for just £3.75 to an altruistic venture in fashion accessories where he introduced Cath Kidston-designed re-usable shopping bags. Selling at £3.99, with 50p from each sale going to the Marie Curie Cancer Care Charity, they were an immediate hit in-store. The attractive floral bags were made entirely of recycled plastic bottles and sold with no profit going to *we talk about designed by Florence & Fred, priced by Tesco* Tesco or Cath Kidston. Over a million units were snapped up, making half a million pounds for Marie Curie. Adding little or nothing to the bottom line, both added to the value of the Tesco brand – earning a place in the hearts and minds of shoppers.

Selling highly subjective, emotionally-charged merchandise alongside groceries is not ideal. But by creating discreet areas in-store, Tesco cleverly develops the right environment to sell its fashions – but never forgetting its fundamental business model. "We talk about *designed by Florence & Fred, priced by Tesco*," explains Green. "So you get the feeling that this is a designer concern but it's priced so competitively because it's under the Tesco umbrella – which is exactly how it is and why it's where it is – and it works." To Green's delight the profit density growth for fashion is beating the rest of Tesco and his planned web launch, including familiar sports brands, will take Tesco Clothing to a whole new level and audience.

Green's experience spans fashion and department store retailing but he's resolutely a Tesco man now. Seemingly obsessed with breaking new frontiers geographically, operationally and emotionally. "Tesco is relentless. It's always thinking well ahead of the game. No-one works harder for customers."

each of the company 'Values' has the customer as its raison d'être

And here's the learning that's impacting Green's success. Tesco always puts the customer at the centre of its orbit. And not just in word – almost uniquely, each of the company 'Values' has the customer as its raison d'être – but in deed too.

Tesco is trusted to put the effort in so its customers get the most out.

Case History

Jennifer Woo
President, Lane Crawford

Interviewed November 2009

Customer memories

Most would agree, any retailer wanting to stand out from the crowd by delivering great customer service would be hard pressed to find a more difficult region to do it than Hong Kong.

Oozing world-class customer experience wherever you look, Hong Kong, with its fabulously wealthy and highly discerning clientele, is in a league of its own.

But incredibly, Lane Crawford, rather prosaically described as Hong Kong's largest designer brand speciality store group, has achieved sparkling success by being trusted to deliver what many believe to be the region's finest shopping experience.

Bringing together the world's top fashion names from Alexander McQueen and Alexander Wang to Stella McCartney and Yves Saint Laurent, this privately-owned company operates from five outrageously luxurious locations: four strategically positioned in Hong Kong's most upmarket districts and a relatively new addition in Beijing.

Lane Crawford has always been exhaustively service-orientated. But now personally masterminding the ever-evolving 'customer experience' is Jennifer Woo, President of the company and daughter of its owner. Until a few years ago, Woo was mentored by the legendary retailer Bonnie Brookes, who after ten years returned home to Canada. Woo is charmingly modest but clearly very bright. She's an elegant and determined executive, obviously sharing her father's commercial acumen and totally immersed in running the region's ultimate

In Hong Kong helping is normal

fashion empire. Born locally but educated in the UK and USA, Woo observes, "In Hong Kong *helping* is normal. The region is famous for its natural service ethic. So to strive to 'own' the ultimate customer experience we have to be something very special – international standards of service excellence are where we build from, not aspire to."

But like any service industry, Woo's workforce is the key to success. As she explains: "Our people are truly and deeply involved in what we are trying to achieve, intuitively sharing the responsibility of delivering it together – it's in our DNA. But I realise it's easier for us than most. There are only 1,000 of us and I get to have frequent one-to-one conversations, speeding feedback and decisions." Woo realises, however, that there is more to her success than the small numbers in her team. There's a sense of family amongst the workforce and a trusted intimacy that pervades the Lane Crawford brand. It's this 'warm' intimacy that promotes and protects exclusivity, ensuring customers feel personally looked after. "There's a concierge service for all customers, not unusual at this level," explains Woo. She claims offering to park cars, charge cell phones and arrange theatre tickets is the norm for up-scale retailers. But she's taken it to the next level. *Her* customers can request a private room to take tea. It's where friends can meet and relax before or after shopping expeditions, have their hair done and try on selected clothes in privacy.

But for a region that buzzes frenetically Woo talks of the importance to her of 'busy individuals'. How a recent customer service initiative tries to engage more deeply with them. "If a regular customer or, say, a local businesswoman is unexpectedly required to attend a smart dinner, an awards ceremony or corporate ball, she can simply call Lane Crawford and be whisked to one of our private suites. From here she can shower, eat, make calls, and ready herself. We'll ensure transport is arranged. A hairdresser, make-up artist and manicurist will drop by, and of course style advisers will be on hand to seek out the ultimate designer ensemble, complete with designer shoes and accessories." And as Woo goes on to explain in a knowing tone, pitched with just the right amount of humility: "We like to think she can trust us to fix things – even the *unexpected*. We'd like to think this level of service defines what we stand for, we accommodate a great deal for our valued customers, and without charge."

Pushing boundaries and perpetual improvement is the hallmark of any successful brand. In 2004, Woo and Bonnie Brooks shared a dream to develop a *new generation* for this 158-year-old retail business. The heightened delivery of supreme customer service was all part of this, as was a major new physical statement of the Lane Crawford brand. "Hong Kong is tiny but we decided to almost double the size of our flagship store. We moved into an 82,000 sq ft single-storey floor in Hong Kong's prestigious, yet-to-be-established, International Finance Centre. It was expensive, risky and bold. But it was a unique space. Many questioned the wisdom but I saw it as a seminal moment, a one-off chance to forge greater differentiation from our competitors. It wasn't just a physical move, it demanded major adjustments to our business model too." Indeed, borrowing from the science of customer profiling, 80 per cent of the merchandise mix was changed. Woo was particularly interested in how merchandise sales related to each other and how this translated to a specialist store like Lane Crawford. But like most creative decisions, the initial process was proudly intuitive – astonishingly, research was used to 'validate not inform' this leap of faith.

> *true service is not about choice, it's about edited choice*

But unsurprisingly, key to the flagship's success was a wider assortment of brands. This resonated with Woo, who appreciated her main competition came from the discreet fashion houses disadvantaged by offering limited, if not sole, fashion labels. "With increased selling area, our new flagship offered a greater choice of designer brands, a bigger selection of fashion products and accessories, all under one roof," explains Woo. "But as we all know, true service is not about choice, it's about *edited* choice. It's about relentlessly trying to understand, better than anyone, what our types of customers want. They appreciate this, it's part of the trust they have in our brand, and we put enormous effort into making sure we get it right and ensuring our merchandise works in harmony." And here Woo touches on the raison d'être of departmental-type speciality stores. True success is dependent on a series of *related* sales not just multiple single purchases. "We really do carefully edit our merchandise-ranging for both men and women – besides fashion there are shoes, accessories, jewellery, cosmetics, and now, even the home. Our clients can explore the stores seeking advice from the departmental specialists or be accompanied by personal stylists. Or a mixture of both. They might even trust a particular specialist and request they accompany them to other departments – that's not a problem, our training covers this!"

And Woo is succeeding.

By enlarging store footprints, offering greater edited choice and delivering even greater levels of customer service, the *new generation* has paid off. Typically where the selling space has doubled, the sales per square foot has tripled. This brave investment from a young President is the

stands out from the crowd, at the same time as attracting them in – that's not easy

model that successfully launched into mainland China and now informs the rest of her business.

This outstanding level of success is enjoyed by a brand that is now trusted to elevate its customer experience into wonderful *memories.*

And the learning here is how cleverly Lane Crawford stands out from the crowd, at the same time as attracting them in – that's not easy.

17 Case History

Phil Wrigley
Chairman, New Look

Interviewed July 2009

Funding success

Unchecked, fashion brands explode on the scene and slowly die.

That's why the successful ones constantly reinvent themselves to stay relevant – but this takes vision and crucially, the right sort of money.

In 2000, the UK based New Look fashion chain had reached a point where it needed to re-invent itself to deliver a long-term future. Phil Wrigley was brought in as Managing Director and rose to become Chairman having successfully changed a 450-store women's fashion discount chain to a glittering *value fashion* empire, boasting over 1,000 stores.

Wrigley is a mild-mannered individual, a razor-sharp retailer with over 30 years department and fashion store experience. He's a people person who exudes common sense and is clearly a soothing leader in the hectic world of fashion. "Having reviewed the business I *We needed backers more tolerant of change and risk* proposed seismic change. Not only in the product offering but ownership structure too. I convinced founder Tom Singh and the board that the only way forward was to grow the company from a women's discount fashion business to an international chain of huge 'one-stop shops' to include accessories, shoes, menswear, kids wear, and outerwear. For the sort of seismic change I had in mind, we needed a different kind of finance too. We needed backers more tolerant of change and risk. My view was we couldn't remain on the

London Stock Exchange. We needed investors with whom we could build personal relationships. Develop mutual trust. Who bought into our long-term vision and were willing to ride out the inevitable ups and downs of the transitional journey I had in mind."

"To make these changes we needed more space, more designers, bigger and better located distribution centres and money to start laying international plans. We needed huge investment in systems and in the people to get it done. In truth, not one of these things was without risk. And to try and do them at the speed we needed was simply not fair on institutional investors – especially as governance in public ownership doesn't allow 'real time' access to explain the processes, pitfalls and challenges. Imagine, with a business like ours that was doing OK, trying to sell-in anywhere up to 10 major change initiatives to institutional fund managers.

governance in public ownership doesn't allow 'real time' access to explain the processes, pitfalls and challenges

Each initiative capable of derailing the business or at the very least 'disturbing' it – with associated share price drops. You can imagine them erring on the safe side and saying no thanks."

So in 2003 having first got the backing of Tom Singh, the major shareholder, Wrigley set about replacing institutional finance with private equity capital, backed up with bank debt. Immediately, two of Europe's largest private equity houses, Apax and Permira, joined forces and conducted an exhaustive 'due diligence' process scrutinising Wrigley's vision and current business. They eventually bought and, contrary to the widely-held belief that private equity money is only invested to make a 'fast buck', they invested an additional US$700 million into the change programme "Remember new stores and new infrastructures cost money," says Wrigley. "They extended their borrowing to fund our emerging success."

Always mindful of any future plans to revert back to public ownership, Wrigley says the process of going private needed to be beneficial to existing shareholders. "New Look wasn't a fashionable stock at the time. Its market rating was lower than average for retail. The financial markets didn't really value the potential of the business or its quality of earnings, so its P/E (Price-Earnings ratio) was at a significant discount." But the price the private equity investors put to shareholders, combined with market rumours of the company going private, boosted the share price. Existing investors received a healthy 40 per cent uplift on their share price when the company was taken private. "For the future it was really important that existing investors were happy with the sale. More importantly, I knew there were still huge opportunities for the new investors."

In 2004 the company went from having a myriad of investors, difficult to communicate with and disconnected from the day-to-day running of the business, to having a couple of people on the board representing the private equity houses. Wrigley was happy he had found investment partners he could trust and who trusted his judgement.

As Wrigley acknowledges, things worked well. "Unlike before, my new investors had a healthy appetite for change and embraced risk. Importantly, I could regularly meet and engage with them – talking on the phone, every day if need be." As a very personal vindication for choosing investors who shared the 'coalface', Wrigley confesses: "If

'Sweet equity' – a shareholding in the business that's allocated to the management in order to incentivise them

the company had remained publicly quoted during the change process I'm sure I would've been fired! Problems with new logistics systems in particular would have led to several profit warnings. And in truth, it was tough dealing with certain people-management issues during the major upheavals – lots of redundancies. I'm glad we were out of the public eye during this *challenging* period on our journey. That's not to say I had a job-for-life with our new owners. Far from it, but if the worst happened, I trusted it would be for the right reasons!"

'Sweet equity' – a shareholding in the business that's allocated to the management in order to incentivise them – was spread wide following the sale to private equity. In line with founder Tom Singh's egalitarian principles, and to unite Wrigley with the key members of his workforce, 500 people from senior management through to store managers were offered sweet equity. Wrigley reasons, "I knew when I was charging over the hill, so to speak, leading and implementing major change, I wouldn't be on my own. At least I'd have 500 troops alongside me, sometimes even ahead of me, in the charge for success. And success indeed came. It's nice to know most have now paid off their mortgages!"

This success came from an incredibly wide spectrum of change. It's change that created a business now worth nearly US$ 3 billion. In the UK, New look has the third largest market share of women's clothing and is market leader in footwear, denim and a couple of other product groups. Its universal fashion appeal is appreciated by price-conscious customers from Manchester to Moscow and from Eastern Europe to the Middle East. And ironically, the business is now poised to thrive in public ownership again. "Today we have a sustainable business model that offers a platform for growth. It now *ticks* in 2009 the very boxes it didn't in 2004 – so watch this space."

In the ruthlessly unforgiving world of fashion retailing, Wrigley believes he has delivered change and success by carefully choosing where the money came from to fund it.

And here's the learning.

No matter how prescient his vision may have been, Wrigley knew he needed intimate and frequent conversations with like-minded investors if they were to trust him and his team through the difficult transition that lay ahead.

A highly profitable insight.

SECRET TWO – SUMMARY

Trust: Tips for success

- No business can realistically expect to be chosen if it's not trusted.

- And certainly no business can expect repeat business if it is not trusted.

- That's why trust is at the heart of all successful brands.

- Trust must permeate all facets of a business – not just the easy bits.

- Companies must adopt a mindset that views these facets as welcome opportunities to build trust, not onerous tasks.

- In effect, the quest for trust in business must become an ethos, not just a well written company 'Value'.

- Mutually trusting relationships are critical when financing change.

- Be warned, however: marketing has historically been one of the most tempting areas to breach the trust contract with customers.

- As in life, trust in business is hard earned, easily lost – but it's worth the effort. Sustainable profits can't be made without it.

So if you only remember one thing from this section, remember:

No decision is too big to protect your reputation.

SECRET **3**

PEOPLE

PEOPLE

The logic is simple
Around the world billions of customers are served every day. Whether in person or otherwise, it's the most critical operation a retailer performs. There's simply no point getting everything else right if the interface between retailer and customer isn't. My third secret to success therefore, recognises the role of *people* working in retail.

Payroll customers
There are as many ways to acknowledge the importance of the retail workforce, as there are visionary leaders. These days, much emphasis is placed on developing this critical asset and many would argue philosophically that your most important customers are on your payroll.

Trite as it may sound, a happy workforce means a happy customer

Viewing the workforce as customers is a really neat idea. Cleverly, it means that customer happiness, for so long the mantra of retailers, applies to payroll customers too. So besides all the technical skills that need to be continually polished, leaders now earnestly go out of their way to put a smile on the workforce too. Trite as it may sound, a happy workforce means a happy customer – it has unquestionable merit and solid support.

So what does payroll happiness look like?

With much to do with working environment, it has many guises. But central is a feeling of belonging, a feeling of understanding what's going on and a feeling of being able to make a valued contribution.

Across a broad spectrum of the workforce, there's much debate about precisely where pay and reward fits into all this. Clearly it depends on socio-economic issues, but from what I've read and been told, it's seldom at the top!

Learning to belong

Being 'in the loop' is one of the best ways of belonging.

And there's no bigger 'loop' to be in than knowing how your business is trying to win. There's no bigger satisfaction than feeling you're making a positive and recognised contribution. And for all this, I come back to my Secret number One, developing a company mindset of *being chosen*.

I have a very simple method. I ask workshop teams to create a pretend retail brand. As a sense check for the answers, I ask them to explain to each other how the brand they've just created will guide the actions and behaviours of the people working in each department of their fictitious business – simple.

This basic exercise demonstrates the important role of individuals in the workforce in bringing what a company 'stands for' alive, over and above the merchandise or service they sell. How, in their own way, everyone can make a very *real* contribution. How they can appropriately make their company different.

How the brand they've just created will guide the actions and behaviours of the people working in each department

It's empowering for people to know that the business places a huge premium on them knowing exactly what it stands for. Knowing how and why the business does what it does. It means people feel more part of the process, more likely to offer ideas to grow the business. Critically they understand why *they* are important to the success of a company – it develops a sense of self-esteem and belonging.

These people now, as it's all affectionately abbreviated, 'get it'.

Right is good

Interestingly, people who 'get it' seem to develop an unspoken imperative to make the 'right' decisions too.

Businesses with people who 'get it' also tend to have self-selecting workforces. Checks and balances need to be in place to prevent a 'cloned' workforce but successful leaders always go out of their way to nurture cultures that celebrate the right kind of people. It's good for training budgets too. As one boss said, "you can't train the wrong people to do the right thing."

But being able to think the unthinkable, being allowed to shout the unthinkable, is essential too – we must always be talking culture, not cult.

Talent spotting

Depending on size and culture, I have come across businesses with really interesting ways of attracting and retaining what many call 'Talent'. Some throw the rule book away and simply ask lots of questions. Some, as mentioned earlier in the book, talk of *educating* people because 'training' is what you do with animals. Some find ways to 'give' the business to the workers and others have courses designed to take people emotionally where they've never been before.

you can't train the wrong people to do the right thing

But what I've observed is how 'emotional understanding' in the workforce is bringing Human Resources (apologies if you have another name for this) much closer to chief executives.

We all know CEOs have always cuddled up to their financial wizards but now HR is gate-crashing this love-in.

Why the cosy threesome?

Real world

Modern business and modern science now agree that emotions are more powerful than logic in the decision-making process. A critical and potentially profitable customer insight.

We are now seeing enlightened companies encouraging the use of emotional understanding to influence much of their decision-making – indeed shifting their centre of gravity in this direction. Giving softer issues like ethical trading, community or work-life balance substantially more weight. And of course the only mechanism for appreciating and implementing this new phenomenon is an emotionally intelligent workforce. Computers certainly can't. You could even say HR is now the frontline for the battle of customers' *hearts and minds*. Some might say an exciting if not daunting proposition for this function.

But with HR and finance each having an ear of the boss, it comes as no surprise that a new form of business 'speak' has emerged.

emotional edge may or may not be the product of a warm embrace – but I like it a lot

One that appeals to the competitive, logical nature of the finance world and one that acknowledges the softer issues of the real world.

CEOs now increasingly talk in a rather precise confection of words. Capable of calibration, undoubtedly describing the future, *emotional edge* may or may not be the product of a warm embrace – but I like it a lot.

Mugs and mouse mats

In retail organisations, internal communications have become an art form. People bombarded with information. Offices and rest rooms clogged with memos, meetings, magazines and marketing bumf.

People are certainly informed but are they engaged?

Is showing the workforce the latest ads enough?

Much research has been conducted by world-class organisations and it is widely agreed an engaged workforce is a happy workforce and delivers results. Common sense really, and because engagement can now be quantified, the costs associated with generating it are readily sanctioned. And I've seen much evidence of positive engagement in my research.

But my travels have also shown me there is another dimension beyond engagement. There are cultures and behaviours within organisations that you just know *demand* recognition, *demand* success – you can *feel* it.

They are the sort of environments where effective conversations are taking place without anyone speaking.

I have felt this sort of vibe in retailers from Asia to LA. There's an indefinable sense as soon as you walk in that shouts purpose and energy. Maybe the big research companies can measure it but it's nothing I've seen reported – but when you bump into it, it takes your breath away.

It's more osmosis than mission statements on mouse mats & mugs. It *always* starts at the very top of a business and finishes at the very top but includes everyone in between. Something you can't put your finger on but something the boss spends a lifetime fiddling with. Sometimes it's the reason they took the job.

It's more osmosis than mission statements

Often it's the only way they know how to lead. But occasionally you meet a leader who was born to create something very different – with great examples of this being celebrated throughout this book.

It's always easier to do when the business is new or small, but I am seeing increasing signs that really talented leaders are mastering the art of *osmosis* in bigger companies now.

First sign

You've all experienced an *osmosis* business.

But do you know what the first sign is?

It's the first person you see. No matter who it is. Because that person assumes the role of Director of First Impressions – be it at a cosmetics counter or security barrier. Company switchboard or company dog.

Same for the second person you bump into.... and so on. Enough said.

Interesting flip

For me, the chap who put shape around an *osmosis* businesses and Directors of First Impressions is one of the best HR gurus I have ever worked with. Chris Matchan now lectures at the finest business schools, mentors the brightest executives and now seems to dedicate himself to asking and answering the question, do you know your own people as well as your customers?

It's an interesting flip on today's mantra of customer-centricity.

But if your workforce is the mechanism for being chosen, why do few businesses make the effort to truly understand their own people?

do you know your own people as well as your customers?

He is quick to point out that privacy legislation or political correctness can often get in the way but it's an interesting 'people' mindset. To him it underlines the important role of team leaders or managers in breaking down barriers and setting examples by trying to understand colleagues the way they do customers.

He is particularly interested in creating cultures that are powerful enough to allow people to fail. Like *osmosis* businesses, the sort of places where people are bursting to get to work to share new thoughts and ideas, confident they won't be penalised if they fail.

Chris has helped me decode many of the wonderful success stories in this book and I thank him.

A simple finish

Let me now finish this introduction to my third secret of success, with three simple thoughts that speak eloquently to the importance of people in retail:

- The first is from Jack Shewmaker who worked with Sam Walton in the early Wal-Mart days and who simply told me, "You know what, the more we told our people, the more their performance increased and the better we did."

- The second is from Len Roberts who turned Radio Shack around. I am sure he will allow me to paraphrase him when he told me there are only two jobs in retail: serving, or helping people to serve, customers.

- The third is something I heard on morning television promoting a book. (Sorry, I've lost the title.) It's a simple equation: A + B = C. Where A is yourself, B is someone else and C is the relationship generated. They said the only thing you have the power to directly change is yourself, A. Only by doing that can you influence C, the relationship. I am forever surprised how many businesses try to start with C!

So with these anecdotes let me now introduce you to these wonderful examples of successful retailers and their people.

The interviews

- **Starbucks** serves 50 million cups of coffee each week. It is probably the most important global retail success story of modern times and it is driven by a deeply held conviction that the people who serve and the people they serve deserve nothing but the very best.

- **Sainsbury's** was recently crowned the UK's Supermarket of the year. In a ruthlessly competitive sector this business has rediscovered its form by asking its people to talk to each other and suggest better ways to operate. It's been a simple conversation with dramatic success.

- **Myer** is one of Australia's leading department store operators delivering sparkling success through rapid change. With a radically simple idea this geographically distant group has taken internal comms' and built an intimate sense of purpose for its people.

- **JC Penney** is one of America's leading and oldest store groups. With an altruistic vision its 150,000 people have been charismatically led to create a hugely successful and powerfully refreshed brand of 1,100 department stores.

- **Harvey Nichols** is a fashion icon. As a fashion leader in the UK and selected cities around the world this retailer has grabbed success in the challenging world of designer fashion by insisting on doing things and choosing its people, its own way.

- **Allders,** once one of the UK's leading department store groups, fuelled its rapid expansion plans through internal promotions. By taking young executives to emotional and physical places they had never been before, they returned to deliver outstanding retail success.

- **Woolworths** has 185,000 people enjoying a uniquely successful culture in Australia, NZ and India. There is a strong belief in this company that the only competitive advantage in retailing is the ability to attract, grow and retain the best people and it's undoubtedly working for this brand.

- **Draegers** is a tiny American retailer and self-confessed category killer. Specialising in 'pleasures of the table' this highly profitable retailer acknowledges its highly specialised workforce defines the size and future of its business.

- **Bakers Delight** is the most successful bakery franchise in the Australia. Its success is credited to a fundamental appreciation of the very special challenges associated with the people who spend their nights making fresh product.

- **The Chalhoub Group** is the Middle East's pre-eminent master franchisee operation and has recently opened an Academy to help its workforce develop their life skills. A massive and complex undertaking it has seen employees, customers and brands choose this luxury group in favour of others.

- **Pic n Pay** is one of Africa's iconic supermarket brands. In a region often torn by disagreement, this innovative retailer is leading the way to repair old practices by providing huge opportunities for the previously disadvantaged people in its huge network of stores.

18

Case History

Howard Schultz
Chairman and CEO, Starbucks

Interviewed March 2010

The people business

"When people reflect on success they tend to get smart," says Howard Schultz, architect of the Starbucks phenomenon. "We weren't that smart. We had great timing but there was never a doubt that anything we did would always put people first and would always stand for something. I remember in the early days saying I wanted to create the kind of company my parents never got a chance to work for."

As a young man in 1983, full of entrepreneurial spirit and on his first business trip to Italy, Schultz was struck by the warmth and humanity that emanated from the coffee shops of Milan. "I was interested in the whole idea of coffee as a catalyst for genuine relationships." But as a New Yorker who had grown up in Brooklyn's federally subsidised housing, Schultz had developed a heartfelt compassion for the struggling, low-income communities he'd called home. *the fragile balance between profitability and benevolence*

It left an indelible mark that burns as brightly today as it did over 30 years ago. You've got to have a dream, reasons Schultz. "After Italy, I knew I wanted to build a national brand around coffee but I wanted to build it with a different kind of business model – one that achieved the fragile balance between profitability and benevolence."

At the time, Schultz was working as director of marketing for a fledgling coffee retailer based in Seattle. It was called Starbucks (after the first mate in the great American novel, Moby Dick) but only sold coffee beans, not coffee to drink. So when Starbucks didn't share

Schultz's passion for converting to Italian-style coffee shops, he resigned and set up on his own. He had opened three coffee shops called Il Giornale (Milan's daily newspaper) when Starbucks was unexpectedly put up for sale. "It was an unbelievable opportunity but I had no money. It took me a long time to raise $3.8 million to buy the eight stores Starbucks had," remembers Schultz. "But by the end of '87 we had 11 stores, 100 employees and a shared dream to create a national brand around *the coffee experience.*"

Schultz opted to pursue his dream under the Starbucks name. It gave him the essential 'coffee bean' credentials with a blank canvas to paint the customer experience he craved. The rest is history. With 17,000 stores in 53 countries, employing 200,000 people, and serving over 50 million customers a week, Starbucks – despite a proliferation of competitor coffee brands – is the largest roaster of high quality coffee in the world. An empire crafted by Schultz through a quiet, non-negotiable commitment to his non-negotiable beliefs. A polished and clearly intelligent individual, Schultz

We're not in the coffee business serving people. We're in the people business, serving coffee

oozes authenticity. He chooses to articulate the reality of his dream very succinctly: "We're not in the coffee business serving people. We're in the people business, serving coffee."

And the *people* are those who work with him, called Partners, and those they serve.

Schultz steered Starbucks through its most impressive years of value creation. "When we went public in '92 we had a market capitalisation of $250 million. Four years ago it was almost $40 billion," explains Schultz, who stood down from day-to-day control in 2005 but is now firmly back guiding the business after a significant dip in performance. But of all his achievements, he is most proud of the way Partners are treated. "In those early days I wanted to do something that had never been done before in America – give ownership and health insurance to every single employee." And as Schultz proudly recalls, they became the first company to provide these two benefits to part-time workers too.

Ownership came in a very tangible form – a *share package.* Everyone who worked more than 20 hours a week received a minimum amount of equity in stock options, between 12-14 per cent of their base pay. And there was comprehensive health insurance too. "Offering Partners health insurance was linked to what I'd witnessed as a kid. I have to say these two benefits, more than anything else, created a culture, a value system.. guiding principles and a reservoir of trust with a group of very special people."

Indeed, a small group of motivated individuals who started out serving coffee and ended up re-shaping the world of retail – introducing one of the most experiential brands ever.

Everyone knows retail is a people business, but Schultz believes his business is *extra sensitive* to this fact, "The training at Starbucks is legendary. We spend much more money on this than advertising – always have, always will. And it's not just training on technical issues, it's 'educating' people about the values of the company and how we act. For me, the manager of every store 'owns' that store. They're the most important person in the company by far – they set the tonality of that store on so many levels. They hire and fire. We need to recruit happy, 'up' people. It's essential in our type of business, you've got to find people who want to be around people." But conversely he talks of the need to speedily recognise when you've hired someone who isn't right – obviously something every retailer needs to act on – but when Schultz talks about having the courage to say, "You know what, I don't think you *belong* here," you can just feel the polite chill of non-negotiable passion.

Interestingly, Starbucks is not a complicated matrix of global formats. Schultz claims that the experience in each of his 17,000 coffee shops is as consistent as possible, be it Chicago or Shanghai, Polynesia or Poland. "I think we're one of the few western brands that have been able to simply replicate the experience and what we do,

> *They're not just selling a cup of coffee; they're selling a warm, comforting and belonging experience.*

around the world. Fortunately, coffee and humanity are universal." Schultz also talks of the importance of community and when pushed hard on this point recounts: "A regular customer of a US store didn't show for some weeks. The manager couldn't figure why. Something had to be wrong. He does a little research and finds out the customer's wife passed away. The entire store, after closing, finds out where he lives, and they ring the doorbell and give him flowers."

Actions like this can't be taught nor should they. But they are a perfect barometer of the values Schultz holds dear. So when he famously claims, "We built this business one cup at a time," he underplays the considerable emotional depth he has built into his brand to deliver success.

But the true lesson here is how quickly customers recognise and respond to authenticity. For experiential brands there's always a lot of talk about theatre, but that implies acting. Schultz and *his people* are genuine. They're not just selling a cup of coffee; they're selling a warm, comforting and belonging experience – something that can only be effectively delivered by people who themselves have a sense of belonging, feel warm and are comforted inside.

Schultz' mother and father would have loved to work for Starbucks.

Case History

Justin King
CEO, Sainsbury's

Interviewed October 2009

In it together

"The function of leadership is to produce more leaders, not more followers." A remarkably insightful quote from Ralph Nader.

Sainsbury's is one of the UK's largest supermarket chains and when Justin King joined as chief executive in 2004, a top priority was to change the culture. He saw this as key to turning around the ailing supermarket group.

Five years on this judgement has proved spectacularly right. His leadership has brought about success from a company-wide belief that everyone, from check-out to head office manager, is responsible for propelling the mighty Sainsbury's machine forward.

'Staff' have become 'colleagues' acknowledging everyone is 'in it' together. Far-reaching management training and communication programmes have embedded a real belief that everyone comes to work, not merely to do their job but to add real value to the business. Colleagues receive a personal letter from King every month and, unlike the bad old days, are now the *first* to know of new initiatives or financial results. "It's important to me that colleagues are personally informed and engaged. Everyone must feel they contribute at a level that fully uses their skills," says King. "We know they've a choice and I want them to choose us." And they do. Over the first four years of King's turnaround strategy, labour churn shrunk from 41 to 30 per cent. "Every year over 15,000 more people

Staff' have become 'colleagues' acknowledging everyone is 'in it' together

than before choose to stay rather than leave - it's good for them, customers and our bottom line."

King is a confident and likeable leader - approachable, bright and extremely committed. Since arriving he's won the UK's prestigious 'Business Communicator of the Year Award' by creating a sense of *shared purpose* among the workforce. And, unthinkable not long ago, Sainsbury's was crowned 2009 UK Supermarket of the Year.

King's turn-around strategy is 'three-legged', covering operations, customer focus and brand appeal. With almost indecent haste his freshly motivated workforce fundamentally addressed the first two 'legs' by ensuring product was back on shelves, on time. The third was solved principally by the inspired use of one of Britain's most approachable celebrity chefs, setting the brand's vertical path to recovery.

Justin King, presenting coveted Shining Star award

Although considerably more complex than stated here, King has succeeded where predecessors failed. But how?

Overarching everything is colleague alignment and engagement. As King explains, "Though hardly radical, one particularly successful initiative is a 'suggestion' programme. It's designed to encourage colleagues to interact with the business as a whole." Sent directly to King, it's a rich seam of ideas from the coalface. Each suggestion is confidential and intended to offer up ideas that will help the business change and do things better. "It's the depth of enthusiasm for *Tell Justin* that's astounded everyone. Each month I receive hundreds of suggestions which I or members of the board read personally - all ideas are researched with many being put into practice. Every suggestion gets a response and explanation from a Senior Manager personally signed, each with a small memento such as a *Tell Justin* pen."

"Around ten per cent of suggestions are implemented. Save for duplication, the percentage would be much higher. One lorry driver suggested a shorter route into his depot saving £20,000 a year. Another colleague highlighted a data report every store printed-off and never used, saving 50,000 sheets of paper a 'day'. And a great bit of colleague lateral thinking was to reward customers with 'Nectar' reward points for every recycled carrier bag they bring into store and use – rather than charging if they don't – we know customers hate being charged for plastic bags!" In four years, over 25,000 suggestions have flooded in and *Justin's signing pen'* is famous. It's an icon of King's personal involvement in the process. To much applause it was once stolen and thrown into the audience by the MC, American comedienne Ruby Wax, while on stage at their annual conference.

Successful suggestions are rewarded by recognition rather than value. The 'suggestion of the year' however, is celebrated at the annual conference and worth £1,000. The staff magazine publishes all winning ideas and 'Shinning Star' vouchers worth £10 are awarded. But as Kings says, "Many vouchers are not redeemed – colleagues keep them as trophies."

Eschewing 'command and control', King drives the business forward by personally engaging the workforce. He is formally educating and openly challenging the business to work better together – trying to create a close-knit team of like-minded companions not a loose *a remarkably joined-up piece of leadership management with change at its heart* association of individuals pursuing their own agendas. It's a remarkably joined-up piece of leadership management with *change* at its heart. Even the marketing campaign fronted by the chef, Jamie Oliver, encourages shoppers to 'Try something new today.' There's a dynamic ethos of newness throughout the business.

But interestingly, 140 years ago, Sainsbury's earned a reputation as a new breed of retailer by ensuring the food it sold was safe – fit for consumption – by championing innovation in packaging and hygiene. And King has chosen to build on this heritage by talking of 'Corporate Responsibility' rather than a CSR policy. As he puts it, "When we launched our Corporate Responsibility programme it was incredibly important to me that it 'described' our business, not just a set of *worthy social* principles colleagues were expected to remember. What they heard was the story of 'their' business: We sell food, therefore we should be best for food and health. Everything we sell we buy from a supplier, so we must source with integrity. We consume vast amounts of resource therefore we must respect the environment. Our business is not a head office, it's 800 shops trading in 800 communities. We should therefore make a positive difference to those communities. And all this is delivered by colleagues who make the difference to our customers; we therefore want to be a great place to work."

King is proud of the heritage and passionately committed to his Corporate Responsibility. Some may argue it's a fine distinction from the norm but as he describes it, it certainly has qualities of differentiation. King believes his colleagues will proudly engage and align with the story

senior management genuinely wanting to listen and colleagues genuinely wanting to talk

more than a list of social principles. And who would argue with that?

Sainsbury's is a huge and complicated business with 160,000 colleagues and a turnover of US $32 billion. King has worked hard to regain the respect of UK shoppers and his workforce. It's an ongoing process that starts and finishes with senior management genuinely wanting to listen and colleagues genuinely wanting to talk. And that's the learning – King knew he couldn't realistically achieve anything without this happening. And he's succeeded. The aptly named 'Talk Back' surveys measuring colleague engagement have shown significant increases since he arrived.

In large organisations, adopting new ideas is easy, it's abandoning the old ways that isn't. But King's leadership has persuaded the business to do just that.

He's created leaders out of followers and shoppers are falling in love with Sainsbury's again.

Case History

Bernie Brookes
CEO, Myer

Interviewed April 2008

Fast and flexible

Change without communication is like winking in the dark.

You know you are doing it but nobody else does.

And we all know customers love change. Customers love a constantly refreshed offer and love to be stimulated. But the challenge to retail management is how to motivate its workforce to effect this change. To emotionally engage them deeply enough in the process – change, after all, does mean work.

For many organisations the solution is straightforward. Lots of DVDs and videos, lots of voicemail messages, lots of emails, lots of planograms and lots of meetings. But for Bernie Brookes, Chief Executive of Myer, one of Australia's largest department store groups,

Bernie Brookes 2nd left, shooting MYTV

this was simply not good enough. Straight-talking, thoughtful and effortlessly intellectual, Brookes not only wanted immediacy, he wanted frequency of communication. And most crucially, he wanted communications that informed, motivated and engaged a geographically distant workforce.

An experienced retailer,

latterly of Woolworths in Australia, Brookes believed it was "almost criminal" that when he arrived, none of the 63 Myer stores even shared sales figures let alone talk about change. So when in 2006, with private equity backing, the business was split out from the Coles Myer conglomerate, Brookes knew that many things needed to change. And importantly he knew they needed to change fast to meet the ambitious business plans. His solution was to devise an intimate method of communicating directly to his workforce that was as different in style and content as it was radical. He created and fronted a *live* in-house television programme aired every Tuesday afternoon.

Called MYTV, the benefits to the business were as instantaneous as the communication.

"Running for just over 30 or so minutes we produce a TV programme that gets beamed to all our stores weekly. It gives them a trading update and all the latest news. Information on last week's sales, profitability, penetration and most importantly what our plans are," explains Brookes

With 30 people in each store typically watching the broadcast and then immediately sharing the information with their individual teams, Myer has become a very well informed organisation. Brookes explains that in order to keep content accessible and avoid appearing 'preachy', he has purposely retained an almost amateurish feel to the production.

the benefits to the business were as instantaneous as the communication

"You don't want it too polished, you don't want it looking too slick, you actually want it a little bit rough around the edges – and it must be entertaining." A production style playing to his straight-talking persona but occasionally betrayed by personal appearances of gleamingly accomplished celebrities such as the stunning supermodel-turned-fashion-designer, Elle MacPherson.

Clearly in tune with the thinking of legendary author and strategist, Peter Drucker, who popularised if not invented the idea of 'knowledge economy', Brookes says he is now benefiting economically from the enhanced learning and understanding his workforce enjoys. "Throughout the business there's a thirst for knowledge that's being satisfied, and it's translating into figures. We recently delivered a fantastic 350 per cent increase in profitability. Hardly surprising – you can now go into any store and talk in depth about new products, about a new display or about forthcoming promotions *and* the thinking behind them all. As a business we are more consistent and as a workforce we are more informed, more aware. It has raised the bar considerably for what you would call the 'knowledge' of our business."

Interestingly, MYTV has also had wider implications for the business. It has giving the group a platform to talk about brand understanding, brand hierarchy, without making it an intellectual marketing lesson. "How can you expect our customers to understand what we – or our brands – stand for, if our teams don't? We now find the stores want to understand exactly where the various Myer's

Because the benefits of MYTV are measurable we find engaging our suppliers in the process very easy

brands sit within our stable of brands and how they compare to competitors. Now it just seems perfectly logical during a MYTV transmission to re-emphasise, for example, where our designer label or international designer range fit. Talk to them clearly about our mainstream contemporary or private label ranges and how these all relate to each other."

MYTV's reach now extends beyond the internal business to the Myer supplier base too. Manufacturers are made aware of the benefits of this 'communication and knowledge' tool. They soon came to understand its powers. Appreciate how, across huge geographical distances, the business can be fully up to speed with one of their featured products. As Brookes explains: "Because the benefits of MYTV are measurable we find engaging our suppliers in the process very easy. Simply put, everyone knows it sells a lot of product and there's a real value to that. For a $200 dress that would normally sell 40 to 50 a week, putting it on MYTV will see us selling anything up to 150 a week. It's certainly not unusual to see three hundred per cent increases on featured merchandise. Hardly surprisingly therefore that there's a big bank of our buyers trying to get on the telly each week, desperate to talk about their product and events."

For product lines that have short lifecycles, MYTV provides a particularly effective communication channel too, capable of reminding the whole business or highlighting issues immediately. This speed also comes into play when poor sales performances are experienced. "Following a bad week, by Monday we've basically taken all the action we can, by Tuesday we've communicated what we are doing or what we want done, to all concerned. So for the main trading days of Wednesday through Saturday things start happening. It is definitely one extra tool in our armoury that helps our ability to turn things on and off, or revise what we're doing at any given time – it's so flexible and fast."

Through rapid communication, MYTV has helped Brookes deliver rapid and profitable change to this new business and in 2009 deliver almost $3 billion in sales. Exciting change will always be a 'hit' with customers and rapid change is certainly no bad thing when private equity has backed the deal. But if a TV programme has been central to all this change, how does Brookes see MYTV changing itself – what of its own future?

"I think we've got to keep reinventing it. It's a process rather than a programme. We're looking to make MYTV more portable, take it to different locations and add a little more humour going forward – it needs more light and shade, tonally speaking."

Light and shade maybe. But it's clear to see, Brookes never intends keeping his people in the dark.

21 Case History

Mike Ullman
Chairman & CEO, JC Penney

Interviewed June 2008

An engaging chat

In boardrooms worldwide there's a lot of talk, often over a cup of coffee, about the importance of the retail workforce, but few truly embrace this essential truth.

For Myron E 'Mike' Ullman III, forgoing the comfort of retirement to take on the challenging role of Chairman and CEO of the 106-year-old US department store retailer JC Penney, didn't initially appeal.

During a distinguished career Ullman had been the CEO of Macy's, LVMH and the DFS Group (Duty Free Stores). He'd cut his teeth at IBM, run a shipping operation out of Hong Kong, and worked as a White House Fellow under President Ronald Reagan. He certainly wasn't seeking another high profile job when, in 2004, he was head-hunted for the top slot at JC Penney.

"Back then, the company was just starting to benefit from centralised merchandising, efficient supply chain systems, and financial stability after years of problems. And, in some areas, stagnation. Yet the workforce, across our extensive base of nearly 1,100 stores, were still lacking direction and energy. Many were taking sales work as a last resort. They seemed to have no purpose or sense of empowerment." Ullman knew that a demotivated workforce would make taking this business to the next level incredibly difficult.

But during a conversation with Howard Schultz, the chairman and founder of Starbucks, of which Ullman is a non-executive director, he began viewing the proposition from a different perspective. His decision to embrace the challenge has since led JC Penney to complete its astounding turnaround based on the re-modelled attitudes of its army of Associates. "I was challenged by the Chairman of Starbucks to take the job, on the basis that 150,000 people deserved a better fate than just working there because they needed a job," explains Ullman. "Wouldn't it be great if they could actually get up in the morning and feel energised and enthusiastic about serving customers or doing their day-to-day work? I saw an opportunity here to use what I'd learned at Starbucks – where they harness the energy and enthusiasm of their people by fully engaging them in the business."

Ullman is a thoroughly decent sort of chap and a born leader. He is charismatic, approachable and possesses the quality of thought that makes most things seem impossibly easy. It is clear, setting himself this philanthropic challenge gave him the drive he needed for the task ahead and suffering from a neurological condition hasn't held him back for a second. Once installed at the helm of JC Penney, the first thing he did was, "ask the senior managers themselves what they felt needed to be done to take their massive store, catalogue and online business forward?" From this and together with his various teams, Ullman honed the details of a growth plan and fine-tuned the stated mission to become the 'preferred shopping choice for middle America'.

astounding turnaround based on the re-modelled attitudes of its army of Associates

And as would be expected of Ullman, a cogent, cohesive and easily understood four-point plan for long-term success was agreed with all concerned:

- generating an emotional connection with customers,
- becoming an easy and exciting place to shop,
- becoming a truly great place to work,
- and entering the top quartile in financial performance of the US department store sector.

"We believe that if we do that, and do it well, we will be at 12.5 per cent operating profit, which will put us Number One in our industry, so that's our quest."

He knew that this business goal could only be achieved as a result of massive cultural change. "So as a benchmark, we started out by doing an 'engagement survey', asking 50 questions about what people thought of their boss, what they thought about the opportunities they saw for themselves, where would they be five years time, what they liked and what they didn't like. We scored a very average 66 per cent engagement," says Ullman. Starbucks at the time was achieving 75 per cent engagement and leading the consumer sector. So Ullman set a goal of 75 too. "We thought we ought to be as good as the best. We have just finished our fourth-year survey and we're now 80."

To achieve levels of engagement like this, businesses need to empower the workforce to make decisions about how the business is run. Keep everyone informed about strategy and vision. And provide all the elements of a workplace that ensures Associates feel cared for, listened to, valued and understood. "The vision is about sharing in the upside of the business – not only *making the lives of those 150,000 people across JC Penney much, much better* from a compensation point of view but also because everyone can make a difference whether it's in-store, in merchandising or marketing or wherever. Getting everybody on the same page was what it was all about." All this is a good deal easier said than done but with Ullman personally driving the dream, things began to change immediately.

Careful communication across the organisation has of course been key. Ullman and his HR director have spent the last couple of years touring the US, personally conducting two-day leadership courses to the top 650 Associates at JC Penney, and one-day courses are also progressing for 1,100 store managers. "The idea is that change will happen sooner if the people you want to reach have better leaders leading them. We teach these top-performing individuals what it's like to have a vision for their work unit; how to engender trust; how to practice candour and truth-telling because we need a culture where people can admit to mistakes and learn from them."

Essentially Ullman set himself the challenge of making the lives of those 150,000 people across JC Penney much, much better. He wanted to inspire them and give them a reason to bounce into work every day, to do their best. After all, if you can get the workforce of an enormous retail empire motivated and engaged, you can begin laying the foundations for a truly winning business.

Ullman is a truly inspiring individual and having him at the helm has driven the cultural transformation of this $17+ billion business in 2009, from the top down. From JC Penney Associates to their customers alike, more people than know, have good reason to thank the outcome of a chat, over a cup of coffee, in the boardroom of Starbucks.

Staff really are your most important customer.

Case History

Joseph Wan
CEO, Harvey Nichols

Interviewed June 2009

Talent for change

Change is important in retail.

So doing things differently yourself is no bad thing.

At first glance, Joseph Wan is not a fashion retailer from 'central casting'. As head of Harvey Nichols, one of the world's most respected fashion retailers, he is neither flamboyant nor overtly fashionable. He is, however, phenomenally successful.

In a world normally defined by theatrical excess, this quietly spoken, razor-sharp Chartered-Accountant-turned-retailer has transformed a struggling single-store UK operation into a prestigious high-end fashion group. With seven stunning fashion temples across the UK's leading cities and five high-profile overseas businesses run under licence, including Hong Kong and Dubai, the group's turnover has rocketed from around US$60 million in 1992 to fast approaching half a billion dollars in 2010.

Wan's understanding of what it takes to be successful was learnt at KPMG in Hong Kong. Here he honed his skill to question everything, including 'received' wisdom. And in 1992 at Harvey Nichols, one of his first small steps towards success was to challenge the perceived need for the stores' management to be perched above the flagship store. "People thought differently then, but I moved all unnecessary services to a nearby building freeing 23,000 square feet to selling space. Until I arrived, the lighting, air-conditioning and escalators were kept running all night – apparently normal in those days!" Though nothing ground breaking by today's frugal standards, these non-conforming measures were a clear sign of what was to come under Wan's politely challenging drive for change.

But to confuse Wan's success with the single-minded pursuit of driving down costs would be to discount his true contribution. The selection of Talent.

In one of retail's notoriously emotive and sensitive areas, Wan knew that sales success demanded his fashion teams enjoyed exacting skills when assisting customers anxious about the finer points of self-projection. And again, the route he chose was not conventional. With a supremely clear vision of what the business needed to stand for and a self-belief in how to achieve it, Wan created 'Talent' guidelines that allowed the business to engage and retain the perfect people to deliver his vision.

With his three-part vision – fashion authority, exclusivity with accessibility, and a 'feel-good' experience – Wan developed and implemented two guiding principles for selecting and retaining his workforce.

The first was to focus on *attitude and aptitude*, rather than qualifications and CVs. "Previously the process of hiring was very stereotyped," explains Wan. "If applicants worked for M&S or House of Fraser they were considered to have the relevant experience. If they didn't have that experience, the CV went in the bin. Clearly that was wrong. No matter how much training you offer people after they are hired, if they are not the right type of person, of Harvey Nichols calibre, they're never going to have the right aptitude for the job. You're wasting your money on training. We were also rejecting people with entrepreneurial flair, as well as the right customer care attitude and aptitude, just because they'd been out of the business having children and their CV was out of date. This all had to change."

focus on attitude and aptitude, rather than qualifications and CVs

So Wan introduced a process of 'character' selection. Abandoning the concept of focusing solely on paper qualifications. Not the conventional psychometrics of today's huge corporations, but Q&A sessions with detailed role-playing of real-life shop floor situations. "Our interviews are designed to spot people who care about the brand, have done their homework, have a natural flair for living-and-breathing customer service and who suit the Harvey Nichols style of retailing. Candidates are asked how they would deal with an angry customer, or go about helping customers choose a wedding outfit, for example. All obvious things but people who care about the customer and want to offer an exemplary shopping experience soon stand out from the crowd. We know the trigger questions and know what we're looking for."

"And it works. Today, hand on heart, I believe our shopfloor service level is quite a bit higher than our competitors," says Wan, sitting in his office in London's prestigious Knightsbridge shopping district and possibly referring to Harrods and Selfridges. He explains that the regional Harvey Nichols stores excel in customer service because his people are more likely to remain in their roles for the long-term. While the iconic flagship London store is often the victim of its own success, with exceptional store staff being poached by the competition. "We have become quite well-known as a training ground," explains a philosophical Wan.

Celebrating strengths is Wan's second 'Talent' principle. It leads on neatly from his careful recruitment processes and deals with retention. "Quite simply, strengths are celebrated. Line managers are specifically trained to focus on an individual's achievements, making them feel valued and happier in their jobs. We're only human, and everyone has weaknesses. Rather than punish people for their limitations, and focus

Celebrating achievements is now a way of life

on failures, everyone here knows their 'positives' are appreciated first and foremost. We need many types of skills in a business like this, so if you set out deliberately to celebrate people's strengths, and allow them to shine, there will be genuine job satisfaction. I don't know for definite, but when people move here it seems that previous appraisals have tended to dwell on shortcomings – we don't."

Celebrating achievements is now a way of life at Harvey Nichols – from Floor Managers making a point of publicly thanking and praising good work across their teams, to incentive schemes rewarding selling and customer service skills with bonuses. And rightly, multiple related sales are also recognised as an essential skill in this departmental operation.

Satisfyingly, during Wan's 18 year tenure, management churn has dropped to below 15 per cent – almost half the norm. And because of deep brand understanding, many internal candidates tend to succeed in 'open' opportunities for senior management positions. Meanwhile evidence suggests that the sales floors are more loyal too, with churn rates of 30 per cent against an average of 40 per cent for speciality department stores.

Wan draws inspiration from the old Chinese saying: *the universe of knowledge has no boundary*. In his own words, he believes "one must always learn, all the time, until death comes." And true to this, soon after arriving Wan realised that no-one truly understood the 'arbitration clause' in a builder's contract engaged to realise one of his beautiful stores. This situation needed changing too. So leading from the front and showing the right attitude and aptitude Wan, as well as doing his 'day job', went to night school and qualified as a Chartered Arbitrator!

In a business which uncompromisingly demands that creativity works alongside operational efficiencies – not the most natural of partners – Wan has shaped Harvey Nichols into a profitable and world-class fashion authority by surrounding himself with the right Talent. Much has changed; the learning, however, is in identifying what hasn't. It's something his customers love and competitors hate.

This gentleman simply adores doing things differently.

Case History

Stan Kaufman
Former Managing Director, Allders

Interviewed March 2010

Growing conditions

"You can't get on in retailing, if you can't get on with people," believes Stan Kaufman.

A classic retailer and quintessential people-person, Kaufman, until his retirement in 2002, was the formidable Managing Director of Allders – one of Britain's former leading department store groups. He honed his natural skills in various retail positions, ending up running Allders, the publicly quoted billion-dollar business boasting 42 stores. Kaufman is very sharp and, despite a lack of higher education, has always created space in his life to 'develop' those who work with him.

In 1963, as an 18-year-old trainee at Selfridges (London's iconic department store), Kaufman was sent on a course that was to change his perspective on life forever. It was a month-long, intensive 'Outward Bound' training course in England's often bleak, but always beautiful, Lake District. Canoeing, trekking, hunting and orienteering with fellow young retailers in the mountains and lakes, helped Kaufman develop teamwork and leadership skills that would set him on a very particular path. "Outward Bound changed my life. I was *the most important dimension was all about mental agility, analytical skills and leadership* useless at school but for the first time I found things I was pretty good at," recalls Kaufman. "It wasn't just physical; the most important dimension was all about mental agility, analytical skills and leadership."

During his time in the Lake District, Kaufman discovered and understood the power of personal development. It was something he never forgot and eventually led him to create *Allders Achievers*. His own tailor-made initiative, it ran for 13 years, involving thousands of applicants, ultimately testing nearly 200 to their physical and mental limits. "With modern-day pressures I decided *Allders Achievers* should be a highly concentrated week-long course, on a remote part of the South Downs," explains Kaufman. "Participants slept under canvas or in log cabins, getting up at 5.30am and jogging every morning. Under professional supervision, they ate a subsistence diet, sometimes gathered by themselves, and carried out team exercises or individual challenges centred around teamwork, leadership, communication and organisational skills. In the middle of one night they were even blindfolded and individually dropped several miles from base. Everything was designed to take them mentally and emotionally where they don't normally go. It's incredible what people learn about themselves and how they *grow* under these challenging conditions."

Everything was designed to take them mentally and emotionally where they don't normally go

A commercial benefit for Kaufman was how *Allders Achievers* shone a bright light on a very select group of individuals and how it helped identify *and* develop future leaders. "We had gone through a management buyout. We were independent and poised to expand. We were looking to triple in size and double our workforce. Internal promotions were the favoured option – that way we knew what we were getting and didn't have to pay head hunters' fees. The trouble was, we didn't know what sort of Talent we had hidden away in our stores and the 'promising' candidates needed a mechanism to raise their profiles. *Allders Achievers* neatly answered all these points."

The *Allders Achievers* course was well-publicised internally and each year hundreds of hopefuls applied. From detailed application forms, candidates – up to department manager level – with at least two years service, were sifted, identified and then put forward for a rigorous interview by a panel of three directors. This was chaired by Kaufman, with head of HR and another board member. As Kaufman explains,

"This meant three of the most senior and influential people in the business concentrated for one hour on that person." Each year around 12 were finally chosen for the scheme. Kaufman makes the point that he was careful to give full and constructive feedback to *each* unsuccessful candidate to avoid any sense of demotivation.

And speaking of motivation, there was no 'pass' or 'fail' rating at the end of the week-long *Allders Achievers* course. In Kaufman's eyes, everyone passed.

He concedes it's hard to quantify a return on investment, or keep track of the career progress of everyone involved. But he can quantify, three out of four who completed the course stayed and became long-term, successful managers with Allders. "During this time, we opened nearly 30 stores and two major distribution centres – *Allders Achievers* were to the fore in all those developments and we saw our retention rates improve dramatically. We had an increasing pool of highly skilled leaders, fully engaged, driving the business during a crucial era of expansion. Those who didn't stay have enjoyed similar career successes, including senior international retail positions."

Kaufman made sure *Allders Achievers* was a highly regarded and aspirational element of his company – but he believed it was important not to make it overly accessible. "Too many people going through the scheme would have devalued it. So it was important to keep the numbers down, almost keep it elitist. It was a great management discipline too. Just having board members selecting and interviewing aspiring candidates from the workforce was worth its weight in gold – the knowledge the whole board gained about our people and what the candidates in turn gained from the process, was incredible. I loved seeing people determinedly reapplying, having failed the previous year – it was a great check that the system was working and in the right spirit."

Those who had completed the course were celebrated within the business and presented with discreet silver tie-pins, which Kaufman says were worn with pride. "Getting everyone back for post-course briefings was also important. After three months in the workplace we'd ask how they've used their new skills, how they've developed their leadership qualities? The observations these bright young executives made were awesome and very humbling!" Allders also organised and developed Achiever reunions, giving scope for further personal development as well as healthy competition.

Interestingly, as well as creating *Allders Achievers*, for the past 20 years Kaufman has been the Chairman and heartbeat of the BSSA's prestigious Oxford University Summer School. Every August, 250 high-flying middle managers from retailers around the world, spend a residential week being inspired, taught and groomed

judicious and 'creative' education is an investment that has a disproportionately profound effect

by world-class lecturers and speakers. Kaufman has now stood down from this too, but still dedicates time to run workshops on retail leadership and motivation.

But some may ask if *Allders Achievers* was self-fulfilling?

By taking the best of the best and grooming them, successful results are almost guaranteed. Others may argue, and Kaufman himself is a case in point, that judicious and 'creative' education is an investment that has a disproportionately profound effect. Most enlightened businesses argue the latter.

The young Kaufman may not have been a dazzling scholar, but during a distinguished career he leaned enough to know the importance of vocational education. And rather like a schoolboy copying from his best friend, let the last word be left to him: "I borrowed a phrase from IKEA which I heard many years ago: if you want to grow the *business*, grow the people; if you want to grow the *people*, grow the business."

24
Case History

Michael Luscombe
CEO, Woolworths – Australia, NZ & India

Interviewed April 2008

Creating an edge

No-one sells anything that can't be bought elsewhere.

If that's not precisely true, it very nearly is – how then can retailers get an edge?

"There's really only one competitive advantage in retailing and that's the ability to attract, grow and retain the best people." So believes Michael Luscombe, leader of 185,000 people.

"Sure, developing winning strategies and implementing them faster than your competitor is all part of being a successful retailer but none of this is possible without having – and I hate using the word – a great *culture*. But that's what it is, the heart and soul of the people that work in the business." As CEO of the iconic Woolworths brand, Luscombe is responsible for an enormously diverse region that includes Australia, New Zealand, and the subcontinent of India.

Over the last 30 years or so, Luscombe has worked in just about every department at Woolworths. This considered, polite and undoubtedly intellectual gentleman believes he knows exactly what is needed to weld his huge business empire together. "We have a very open and inclusive management style – it hasn't always been this way but *the 'Woolies' culture was so thick you could cut it with a knife* it's incredibly important to me that it is now. There's no doubt people stay with a particular company not just because of pay, but because they feel part of the fabric, feel as though they can contribute, can be recognised and can be part of the decision process. Even part of making mistakes, part of achieving something as a team."

Few would disagree with these sentiments but how does Luscombe achieve this for the world's 25th largest retailer?

His starting point has to be the widely acknowledged truism that modern retailing is all about the engagement of customers. It's no longer good enough to simply buy and sell merchandise and profit from the mark-up. As Luscombe explains, "If you don't make that emotional connection with customers then it's just a little bit of pressure on one foot or the other as to whether they walk through your door or a competitors. It's as simple as that. How then, can a business engage with its customers if it doesn't first engage with its own people?" He might not like the word, but developing the right *culture* has been his answer.

And Luscombe seems to be succeeding. A consultant recently suggested that the 'Woolies' culture was so thick you could cut it with a knife. "They described it as a group of people that when challenged, will come back with how they are going to do it, rather than 10 reasons why it can't be done, no matter what the challenge," recounts Luscombe proudly. "Recently another consultancy doing an engagement survey across the whole business found our emotional engagement score was so high they thought something was wrong – on a scale of 1-10 we're 8.5, right at the top end for any industry. The benchmark for retailers is 5 to 6."

Bosses very often find it difficult to articulate their culture – it is, after all, an innate quality that exists, it's nurtured not manufactured. They find it much easier to express it through examples, or even by what it isn't. So when pushed, Luscombe acknowledged he didn't quite know where it had come from but did say Woolworths has a creed, "*do the right thing*", and gave an example. "A couple of years ago we experienced a category five storm. We had a small store directly in the path of the cyclone. Much of it was destroyed – we had staff members whose homes had been ravaged too. But in the early hours of the following morning they made their way, some walking, through debris-strewn roads, to open their store. It wasn't about targets or budgets or bonuses; they just believed it was the right thing to do. They knew folks would be needing food, water and other essentials."

How has this culture and engagement been fashioned? Luscombe answers, "It's about the business *itself* doing what's right and this manifests itself in many ways. One is through mass share ownership." Although a lofty ambition, it's paid dividends in every sense. Luscombe takes pride in the fact that over a third of the company have become shareholders since the mid-90s. "It's great. People feel engaged, part of what's happening, and they readily embrace the responsibilities that come from ownership. Employee churn is at record lows for the region, especially throughout the management levels – there's such a high proportion of people that feel they *own the place*."

Besides typical staff feedback sessions and the 'closed door' Q&A dinners Luscombe hosts around his region, he is also keen to encourage one-to-ones. "I love speaking to new members of our teams during their first year to ask what's different about Woolworths. Some talk about our customer insights and planning: financial plans, property plans, brand plans or whatever, but almost all, without fail, talk about our

It's about the business itself doing what's right

people plans. We invest massively in our people, at all levels. Annually we currently spend A$50 million on training. We're the largest employer of apprentices, the largest employer of trainees, those without a degree are offered university, and for those with a university degree we have close relationships with the leading business schools. I have also found that our culture is self-selecting. It very quickly sorts out those who are not right for us – toxic staff are soon spotted. Which is great."

Speaking of what's right, Luscombe has a secondary guiding principle: *speed and courage will get you there*. Which in its own peculiar way speaks directly to the company's first principle of trying to *do the right thing*. New team members often talk positively about the speed things get done at Woolworths. And here we see a key learning from a well defined culture, no matter what size of business. You can't have speed without efficient and effective planning but you must have people who feel valued and secure enough to have the courage to change those plans. As Luscombe proudly recounts, "Without being asked, our store-opening team recently opened a new store in just two weeks compared with eight, outmanoeuvring the competition. They hadn't even hired all the staff but reasoned they'd get them from our other stores to get it open!"

And finally, since baby boomers have shaped much of today's Woolworths with generations X & Y refining it in their own particular light, Luscombe has rejoiced in change *speed and courage* himself. There is no head office, only a *will get you there* support centre with 3,000 members. There are only 40 individual offices, none of which have a window with a view. Anyone can have the same company car as the Chief Executive for a small adjustment to their salary. But to dwell on any of these is to miss the point.

Luscombe has built a profitable business through a culture that celebrates the work force, so they can celebrate their customers. It tries to differentiate itself by putting a huge premium on doing what's right.

And regardless of who you are, or what size you are, that can't be wrong.

Case History

Richard Draeger
Joint owner, Draeger's

Interviewed February 2010

Rare ingredients

"At Draeger's finding customers who love our merchandise is not difficult – finding the right kind of people to serve them is," explains Richard Draeger, the founder's grandson and now a joint owner with the family.

Set up in 1925, Draeger's Market Stores operates out of just four locations in the Bay area of San Francisco, with stores ranging from 18,000 to 64,000 sq ft. Each has an impressive food, delicatessen and housewares department *and* cookery school. Two even have haute cuisine restaurants.

Draeger is an accountant by profession. Polite, modest and committed to the family ethos. From his earliest memories all he remembers is family and stores. But with big words for one of the smallest retailers in this book, this mild-mannered individual says his mission is "to be a category killer when it comes to food". In a somewhat softer, *exclusively from cows grazing over 6,000 feet on wild flowers and sweet young grass* customer-facing expression better describing the ambience of the stores, the business is known for *Pleasures of the Table*. It's a company that famously specialises in selling anything, and everything, to do with the finer points of food and eating.

But what category does Draeger want to kill?

Central to Draeger's operation is food for discerning clients – very discerning. "From our specially butchered meats to our celebrated salad dressings, everything we offer is premium. Our olive oils are from award-winning villages, in Italy, France or Spain. We'll have maybe ten different line items within each category, whereas our closest competitors have three or four. We stock gold and silver award winning balsamic vinegars. The gold labels are aged in many more casks than the silvers, giving them much more nuance, and much, much deeper flavours. We offer 3,500 different wines from around the world. From the most select vineyards of France to the great vineyards of the Santa Cruz Mountains, which happen to be in our backyard. We also pride ourselves on the great Alpine cheeses of France and Switzerland – exclusively from cows grazing over 6,000 feet on wild flowers and sweet young grass, each subtle element giving differing flavours to different cheeses. They're beautiful, very rare to find – but we've got the knowledge and history. We've developed a trusted network to supply us and most importantly we've got a sophisticated clientele that recognises and understands these products."

food that requires an educated palate, requires an educated clientele

All retailers understand the importance of location but for the founder of this unique cluster of stores this led to an interesting observation. He believed *food that requires an educated palate, requires an educated clientele*. Since then, Draeger's has taken a conscious decision to place all stores around the prestigious Stanford University in California. "Our customers really need to understand the finer points of our products and if you've got a group of Stanford alumni at your back door, trust me, that learning curve is instant. The further you get away from an educational centre such as this, the longer that learning curve becomes."

But as Draeger explains, even with a highly localised customer base, word effortlessly spreads amongst like-minded individuals. "Our largest store has well over 60,000 SKUs. A very deep assortment for our size, but such depth means we can offer products that are extremely difficult to find elsewhere. Incredibly, our customers are happy to make a 120-mile return trip to shop with us." If fine food is not a big enough attraction for the cognoscenti, the San Mateo store alone has the third largest selection of cookery books in America and

Draeger's was recently voted the country's number two cookery school by the prestigious International Association of Culinary Professionals. But the added benefit of having a quality proposition is that Draeger's has little need to advertise to attract its target customers. "We're looking to satisfy that *one foodie* trying to find that *one item*, and when they do, they're so enthralled they become our word-of-mouth advertising," observes Draeger. "We've also found that classic advertising messaging or promotions can be an affront to their intelligence. We've found POS that talks romantically about provenance can sometimes be received as patronising. It really is a fine line we have to tread but with care you get a feel for what's right. We actually do very well when we keep our wine and cookery school clients informed."

Indeed this business 'turns' on knowing precisely what customers want or will want.

"For us, *getting to know* customers does not simply mean being in our stores; it's being on the sales floor. As owners we're working on the sales floors too. We don't have buyers who just work in an office, just travel to shows, and just study the market. Our *a kind of beachhead for the more esoteric foreign producers into the USA* buyers are on their floors, they do every aspect of the operation from top to bottom. They see how product is merchandised on the shelf, they hear customer comments, they soon know whether something's liked or not, and the reason! They know and understand the velocity of sell-through. It's a point of difference for our buyers, real hands-on, you either like this as a buyer or you don't but it's essential for us. This close relationship with the sales floor has mutual benefits – we're regularly asked to source specific product by our more valued customers. This in turn has meant we represent a kind of *beachhead* for the more esoteric foreign producers into the USA. They're obviously keen to oblige our requests and our customers are delighted we've listened."

Running a fiercely private enterprise, Draeger is protective of figures. He is not comfortable bragging either! But when pushed, he claims to achieve three times more sales per square foot than a typical American supermarket – a significant achievement despite his smaller size. And apart from the dotcom crash in the 90s (Silicon Valley is nearby) and the banking meltdown of 2008-9, the company has mostly enjoyed double-digit year-on-year growth. But he does concede to noticing, recently, a move away from his famous ready-prepared meals towards ingredient-based shopping. But his bespoke cookery courses are booming as a consequence!

So with such a successful formula, why only four stores?

"Service at our level requires a dedicated and highly knowledgeable workforce. It's a resource that's hard to come by and represents a constant challenge. We currently have 600 colleagues, and finding people that are passionate and love this business is the hardest part. In fact, it's why we're not larger."

Successful retailing may be about great customer engagement, location and merchandise but it's all for nothing without great execution. And here's the lesson from Draeger's. Specialist customer propositions demand specialist workforces, it's a simple logic. But specialist workforces are by definition, notoriously difficult to find – a fact that will always stifle expansion. Compromise on this and brand integrity is threatened.

Specialist customer propositions demand specialist workforces

The irony can't be lost on Draeger's – they can source the rarest product but can't source enough of the rarest ingredient, great people.

26 Case History

Lesley Gillespie
Co-founder, Bakers Delight

Interviewed June 2008

Not for everyone

Someone once famously said that they'd like mornings better if they started later!

But for Lesley and Roger Gillespie, mornings – very early ones – mean everything. This dynamic husband-and-wife team founded and still lead the hugely successful Australian-based Bakers Delight, a retail bakery chain with hundreds of stores across three countries, selling bread-based products, proudly catering to local tastes. But unlike their mornings, the Gillespies found *getting going* a major challenge. Not the opening of the first dozen or so Bakeries – that all went to plan – but the next level of store growth.

Lesley Gillespie is an educated, well mannered, charismatic individual who, along with her husband, cares very deeply about their business and especially those she works with. But when talking about the early days of building *"Once our estate reached double figures we faced the law of diminishing returns."* the Bakers Delight empire she admits to a phenomenon that took them all by surprise. "Once our estate reached double figures we faced the law of diminishing returns. Even allowing for stores to mature, each one we opened after about number 12 was less and less profitable – and as you know, profit is the life line. It pays your people and allows you to reinvest back into the business."

After some soul-searching, it was soon realised that two key fundamentals separated Bakers Delight from the normal rules of retail scale – embracing these was essential if the Gillespies were to profitably expand.

- "Number one," as Gillespie explains, "you must understand that bread has a life of its own. Every day we start from scratch. Once the bread starts developing, once the yeast starts growing, if you're not concentrating you'll end up with a poor loaf of bread, poor product and unhappy customers. Unlike normal retail, we can't rely on clever buyers going overseas sourcing fantastic merchandise for us to display and sell – *we are what we make*. With an oven, a mixer, a prover (where the bread is raised), we effectively have a mini-factory at the back of each store and each store manager needs to be a diligent and conscientious baker."

- Number two was easier to understand but no easier to address. Like many service industries associated with food, the hours are anti-social. Only the anti-social element for the Gillespies' operation was somewhat different. When customers were in bed, the baker was in the bakery and when customers were in the shop, so was the baker! Why would anyone want to be a bakery manager?

  Broadly speaking, they didn't!

The answer to all this came from Roger Gillespie, Lesley's husband, a master baker, natural retailer and the driving force behind the solution. In the 80s he'd seen the success McDonald's was enjoying in the Australian market by franchising – he was sure this could be the way to address the two key barriers to their expansion plans.

As Lesley Gillespie explains: "Yes, we had good bakery managers but when they became franchisees, their sales jumped by 30 per cent, they started seeing things as *when they became franchisees, their sales jumped by 30 per cent* an owner rather than an employee. For our type of business to be successful it's so important that we have an 'ownership' attitude throughout, from outstanding customer satisfaction right down to the last loaf of bread."

As always, the test of a good idea is that it becomes obvious as soon as you hear it. In one strategic move, albeit a huge leap of faith, Bakers Delight became a franchise operation and in so doing addressed the two key fundamentals that had stifled expansion and profits. Franchising spoke to the individual managers as retail entrepreneurs. It also spoke to them at an emotional level, ensuring they worried more about the living entity that became a loaf of bread, than when they slept to achieve it.

This fundamental change helped the company grow to over 700 outlets, serving 2.5 million customers every week, delivering an average 20 per cent operating profit – this is even after paying 6.5 per cent royalties and 2 per cent towards marketing. Gillespie readily admits this is "excellent", especially compared with the early days when many company-owned stores struggled to make a profit.

Bakers Delight does not make profits from selling raw materials to its franchisees. This helps protect the franchisee's bottom line as well as the precious emotional bond the Gillespies have famously built. "By law, in Australia, the franchisees must be free to source wherever they want," explains Gillespie. "Instead, we simply negotiate the best

Gillespie family with loyal franchisees celebrating 21 years

possible rates for them, direct with the big flour mills and producers. We never saw it as an income stream."

But as can be seen on their website, the opportunity to join the 'family' does not come cheap. Franchisees have to commit up to A$500,000 to open a new Bakers Delight store. It includes the equipment, fixtures and fittings as well as all the technical *and* emotional support needed. There's also a market for buying existing, very profitable, Bakers Delight stores for up to A$1 million. But ten per cent of the network still operates as company-owned stores. Gillespie says this works particularly well acting as a proving ground for potential franchisees. "For example, here in Melbourne we have several company-owned bakeries. New people come in and can see what a future as a franchisee looks like." And as would be expected from a company that is proud of its business relationships, Bakers Delight has put in place a programme for the *young and keen*. "We can even help finance people into their own bakery. For the suitably qualified this works very well."

Around the world, owners of small businesses work through the early hours serving their communities, delivering the special comfort that comes from locally baked bread. In the classic business sense, the barrier to entry for these family-based independents is relatively low. Rewards coming from hard, anti-social hours. The Gillespies soon found the only way to profitably enter this special retail world was to embrace the unique issues associated with it. For them, franchising offered the solution. It was not an *easy* solution – allowing hundreds of franchisees to run loose with your 'brand', and trying to control them accordingly, is a bit like herding kittens! But with their legendarily honest franchisee relationships and well-known philanthropic attitude to life, the Gillespies have kept a firm hand on the reins and navigated successfully where others have failed. The phrase 'win-win situation' is often over used but this truly is a

a bit like herding kittens

winning formula for both the franchisees and founders alike. Franchising is not for all businesses. But surely the learning must be: if a retail model succeeds when small, but fails when bigger, or when the prerequisite for success is long hours calling for huge emotional engagement, then franchising is worth a consideration.

The British have a saying, 'the early bird gets the worm'. And you'd certainly have to get up very early to beat the Gillespies. It wasn't easy becoming Australia's most successful bakery franchise but letting their managers share what early mornings can bring was an inspired decision and a great wake-up call for the business.

Case History

Patrick Chalhoub
CEO, the Chalhoub Group

Interviewed February 2009

Hardwired

To be a great retailer, you need a great team.

To deliver a great retail experience, you need a great team.

And to be a great team, you need individuals who know how to engage with customers and each other.

So believes Patrick Chalhoub, CEO of the Chalhoub Group - a prominent organisation specialising in the retail, distribution and marketing of luxury fashion, beauty and gifts in the Middle East. As a senior franchise partner to a host of major global luxury brands, Chalhoub says he recognised some years ago that to be chosen, his people must become a major point of differentiation for the business.

Not the first retail executive to acknowledge the importance of his workforce, Chalhoub is certainly one of the very few to create a bespoke solution specifically to deliver *engagement skills*.

A charismatic individual, steeped in the business founded by his family over 50 years ago, Chalhoub not only talks about the importance of engaging an audience but personally delivers it with a charming intensity that is hard to resist. "To new franchise partners and luxury brands, I wanted my company to be able to promise *people must become a major point of differentiation* fully engaged, fully trained, fully motivated people who are extremely loyal to the organisation because of the training they receive - I had a vision of how to deliver this and created our own Retail Academy."

Based in Dubai, recruitment and training is complicated by the region's mix of people and their varying capabilities. "You have almost 200 nationalities from different origins – from those with little formal education to engineers from Sri Lanka and professionals from Syria or Australia. In fact it's a mix from all over the world including Europe and Africa, some even qualified as teachers or as doctors looking to repay their student debts. It's a melting pot and retail is very accessible to them, they need us and right now we also need this resource."

It's particularly important for the types of brands represented by the Chalhoub Group to deliver first-class retailing skills. "We need to elevate the level of engagement and customer service delivered by our diverse mix of people," explains Chalhoub adding. "The aim of our Retail Academy is *not* to give an induction to our brand, our partners' brands or products – that's done elsewhere – but to try to develop the 'retailing' skills of those people who come to work for us. We identify their core competencies, develop their natural talents and work with them on any weaknesses. At the Chalhoub Retail Academy we are effectively talking about the 'hard-wired' lifeskills relevant to retailing. It's a fascinating journey we take our learners on and they love it."

coaching the understanding of how to persuade and influence people

From 24 different criteria, each entrant undertakes 18 modules focusing on various skills depending on their occupation or position within the company. "Besides the necessary communication and leadership skills, unlike most retail courses we cover subjects as diverse as 'conviction skills' – coaching the understanding of how to persuade and influence people – or 'psychology', where they are taught the dynamics of how to better understand and handle the moods of customers and others. And rather than just teaching the classic visual merchandising skills, they are taught how to appreciate creativity through the 'association of colours and shapes' together with the 'analysis of design trends'. And for those who are not naturally gifted, the 'interpersonal' unit gently coaxes the skills necessary to engage customers more effectively."

The courses at the Chalhoub Retail Academy are part-time and typically take 12 months to complete. After an initial assessment, each individual receives regular 'knowledge and performance' assessments for all 18 unit qualifications. "We are obviously looking for entrants to achieve a minimum acceptable level by the end of the course but we are also particularly interested to identify and encourage their natural strengths – this is a hugely important element of the course."

Upon successful completion of the course, a fully recognised Level 2 NVQ qualification is awarded for Retail Skills. Since the initiative was created just two years ago, over 700 qualifications have been presented. Chalhoub says there has been a "total shift in the mentality and the spirit of the organisation," adding, "they really feel they have achieved something which has a value, *a doubling of the customers who have 'purchased-and-revisited'* wherever they go in the world. The qualification undoubtedly proves a recognised level of ability – we take them on a journey and by the time they arrive at the destination they understand the benefits to themselves and the business of everything they have learned."

The measuring of the many different competencies has also helped the internal promotion process too. "We look not only at an individual's sales results, but also at their competences. Our Academy has also been beneficial in terms of hard numbers – stores where the team have achieved the award, or are working towards it, enjoy a measurable 20 per cent sales increase. There's also a doubling of the customers who have 'purchased-and-revisited' when benchmarked against other outlets." These figures are indeed exceptional, but so is the whole region; they certainly acknowledge the power of engagement. As Chalhoub says, "We're also delighted there's been a 'word of mouth' effect, with the company now specifically attracting people who want to go through the Chalhoub Retail Academy."

Building on the effectiveness of his academy in Dubai, a second is planned to open in Saudi Arabia by the end of 2009. There are also ambitions to open a third, providing an induction capability before people join up and go through the Chalhoub Retail Academy.

While Chalhoub doesn't believe his academy to be unique, he does passionately believe it represents a key element for the future of his business. Not only does it develop a great retail resource delivering better sales; it also provides global brands with another reason to choose his company to represent them in the Middle East.

And choice is what this initiative recognises. We live in a society of plenty, which means plenty of choice. It is rare for any retailer to sell something that can't be bought in another shop or in another city. So most customers choose to shop, and return to shop, where they most enjoy the process, with the individuals who serve them being a hugely critical factor. It's as simple as that!

Any retailer can teach individuals about product knowledge; any retailer can impress upon them the importance of 'closing' a sale or good 'housekeeping'. But unlike Chalhoub, very few retailers have the *develop the softer retail* vision and commitment to develop *issues 'hard-wired' into* the softer retail issues 'hard-wired' into *an individual's lifeskills* an individual's lifeskills – which, when you think about it, is strange. Because doing so is as rewarding for the customer as it is for the business and the individual.

And that's an engaging thought.

Case History

Nick Badminton
Chief Executive, Pick n Pay Group

Interviewed February 2009

Something bigger

The local 'corner shop' holds a romantic vision of retailing at its purest.

With the world's grandest retailers emulating this simple model through complicated technology to engage their somewhat anonymous customers.

But Pick n Pay, one of Africa's largest and most respected food, clothing and general merchandise retailers is trying something different. Through a 'positive affirmation' initiative, it is paving the way for black entrepreneurs to run their own local grocery stores – fully embracing the wider principles of South Africa's post-apartheid social system.

With almost 800 stores, part franchised and part company-owned, The Pick n Pay Group is quoted on the Johannesburg stock exchange and controlled by the philanthropic Ackerman family from Cape Town. Under Group Chief Executive Nick *fully embracing the wider principles of South Africa's post-apartheid social system* Badminton's stewardship, the company is identifying and training promising new franchise partners from South Africa's *previously disadvantaged* (principally non-White) population.

Joining the group as a young trainee some 30 years ago, Badminton is now passionately committed to this seminal initiative. He is clearly a talented retailer, very approachable and disarmingly down-to-earth – almost knowing every store manager by their first name. Pick n Pay was recently voted 'International Retailer of the

Year' by the world's largest retail trade association, America's prestigious National Retail Federation.

"In recent years South Africa has been moving away from the old black/white social divides. Things are really starting to normalise," explains Badminton. "Empowerment is one of the big issues redressing the past; we feel strongly about it too." As Chief Executive Designate in August 2006, Badminton was concerned that out of 200 franchise partners running Pick n Pay stores, less than 10 were black. "Traditionally our franchise stores were very 'white', many being former corporate Pick n Pay divisional managers," says Badminton adding. "Things needed to change!"

At the same time the Pick n Pay group operated an underperforming specialist brand called 'Score', catering exclusively for the poorer, typically black neighbourhoods in townships and cities like Soweto and Johannesburg. "We did a lot of research and soon realised that the black and lower income people were angry. Score was

not seen as a specialist store designed for their specialist needs but as an inferior brand aimed just at them," explains Badminton. "I asked Chris Reed who had previously run the Score chain what he'd do if he were King-for-a-day. That's easy he said – convert Score to Pick n Pay, run by black franchisees. And that's what exactly what

Famous 'Mokete' store launch celebrations at Marble Hall

we are doing. Now we effectively have one brand, Pick n Pay, for all. We've also set a franchisee recruitment target to match the population profile too."

"Before all this started, we were already associated with an Academy building the business skills of black students. We now use this facility to fast-track our new generation of franchise partners. The calibre of people coming through the training is outstanding. Individuals possessing solid values, raw enthusiasm and unbelievable levels of natural talent. These fast-tracked entrepreneurs undertake two years of theory and practical training – they're then placed with an experienced franchisee until qualifying for a store. When the necessary financial loans are secured (often helped by government agencies and overseas aid) these 'new' franchisees take on their stores with the inevitable goodwill from the local communities."

"The community support is incredible. There's always intense pride at the graduations and again at the store openings. Floods of tears from friends and families. Each store opening has the local mayor and our HR director, Isaac Motaung, present. Isaac has become something of a father figure. He introduces the new franchisee but also makes a big point of acknowledging the parents too. It makes everything so personal. There's even a *Mokete* – a traditional ceremony where a bull *It must be the ultimate form of customer engagement* or calf is slaughtered and barbecued. The event often draws the whole community, sometimes numbering thousands of people, celebrating, eating and dancing. Very quickly, everybody knows this place is special – it's Joe's or George's store. It's a great way to launch a business. It must be the ultimate form of customer engagement."

"After the launch we keep a watching brief to ensure things don't get out of hand. Encouraged by us to keep it personal, it may be Vince's or whoever's Pick n Pay, but they must be mindful of our brand values. It's a fine line, an important line, but with proper mentoring problems rarely happen – but it's retail at its honest best."

Unsurprisingly, this visionary strategy is delivering huge success and engendering deep brand loyalty. The first 30 stores to be converted to black franchisees have doubled their sales in less than a year. And in the spirit of the Ackerman Foundation, community links extend further with emerging black farmers encouraged to supply the stores with their produce, and in return, buy their animal feed and materials from the outlet.

"Experienced white franchisees are embracing this inclusive ethos too by partnering with our new entrepreneurs," explains Badminton. "They are part-investing in them, holding their hands through the first couple of years – many doing it because *they now see the building of South*

Africa like this. A white guy called Chris who owns 49 per cent of a store is thought of in the local Shoshongowe community as George's 'brother'. He'll sell the shares back once George is established. Another such franchise in Meadowlands is flying, achieving a three-fold increase in turnover when compared to the old 'Score' format. High-margin hot food is 'done' particularly well here; they know exactly what sells. New and old retailers learning from each other!"

According to Badminton, "126 Score stores struggled to achieve annual sales of 3 billion Rand, but when the programme is completed we will have converted almost 80 to black franchisee Pick n Pay stores (the rest will be sold), with turnover from these alone expected to be over 6 billion Rand, that's over three quarters of a billion US dollars." Whether, in the prevailing political climate, the customer resentment experienced by the 'Score' format should have been forecast is now academic.

This franchise model allows all this 'engagement and localness' to be underpinned by huge economies of scale

What's important is the birth of an initiative that profoundly acknowledges a basic retail doctrine – the more you emotionally engage your customers, the more secure and successful you business will be.

And it doesn't get more engaging than local people, running local shops, relating to their local customers with their local needs, on a personal basis (no franchisee can own/part own more than three stores). It's competitive, too. This franchise model allows all this 'engagement and localness' to be underpinned by huge economies of scale – which unfortunately is more than can be said for most local 'corner shops' around the world.

But in a book dedicated to seemingly parochial issues, the last word must be given to the 2008 International Retailer of the Year. It's a timely reminder of the power of retail.

Previously disadvantaged individuals running profitable stores is just the tip of a mammoth iceberg, observes Badminton. "If you've got lots of black entrepreneurs, not just a few, sorting their future out and their families out, I think you've got a much better model for something bigger."

SECRET THREE – SUMMARY

People: Tips for success

- To be chosen, a business needs a talented workforce who intuitively understand what the business stands for.

- If the people who work in a business don't 'get it', how can their customers be expected to?

- People turn strategy into action – when inspired by managers they deliver operational excellence.

- More often than not, the attitude and aptitude of individuals is more important than their knowledge.

- Successful businesses always communicate internally before externally.

- Creating the right culture in a business not only helps self-selection of the right people; it's the unspoken imperative that encourages a work force to do the right thing.

- Neuroscience tells us emotions in the decision-making process are more powerful than logic. It's hardly surprising, therefore, that the businesses being chosen, being trusted and being visionary enjoy success by putting emotional understanding at their centre of gravity. Something that can only be appreciated and delivered by 'people'.

- Your most import customers are on your payroll.

So if you only remember one thing from this section, remember:

Your people are your mechanism for being chosen.

SECRET 4

VISIONARY THINKING

VISIONARY THINKING

Agenda for the future

"It is not the strongest of the species that survives, or the most intelligent. It is the one that is most adaptable to change."

Standing the test of time, and ever-improving scientific scrutiny, this remarkable insight from Charles Darwin best introduces Secret Four.

In a world where people's lives are changing faster than ever before, it's undeniable that successful businesses have a self-imposed agenda for change.

Always reflecting and often championing change, I have found that the most successful retail bosses lead from the front, to stay in front. They believe *being chosen* is not only important for today, but for tomorrow too. In the backward-looking world of like-for-like figures, the truly successful bosses are never deflected from looking forward.

a profitable status quo is no place to hide

And as common sense dictates, a profitable status quo is no place to hide.

In a ruthlessly competitive industry, it's the quality of forward thinking that literally decides whether a retail business has a future or not. I have therefore made visionary thinking my secret to success number four.

Let's be clear

I am *not* talking about the sort of grand vision that normally goes with mission statements.

I am talking about the visionary day-to-day thinking I have experienced from the world's retail leaders. The sort of thinking that delivers the right goals and strategies for their journey to success. I am talking about how they adapt, how they *actually* capture a spirit of tomorrow and translate it day in, day out. How they capture the excitement of change, galvanising their organisations to move with, and ahead, of the 'times'.

That's the sort of visionary thinking I'm talking about here!

A fragile thought

Of course everyone agrees the future is important – nothing particularly visionary there.

But just for a moment, let's consider what changing nothing looks like for a business. As the rest of the world adopts new ideas and society demands new ideals, any business that doesn't move with the times is going to be left behind. Indeed, any business that stands still is, in effect, going backwards. And you don't need me to tell you how *unattractive* that is to customers. Wooden tennis rackets stand proof of this or even, dare I say it, tie manufacturers in an increasingly casual world – some change is obvious.

But why would any business want to go out of its way to change things when it's doing its numbers, making a profit?

The answer is simple. To the great retail leaders, success is fragile and is always regarded as such. They know their customers are notoriously capricious, sometimes categorised as promiscuous. I remember a piece of research showing that nearly a third of British shoppers chose which supermarket to shop based on the nearest one opening with free, non-multistorey car parking! Things have changed since then but whether it's revolution or evolution a business must constantly strive to stay 'in tune' with its customers. If it's

half a step is an exciting thought that's designed to challenge an entire business to be in permanent visionary thinking mode

revolution, drastic measures will call for drastic actions, allowing customers to 'feel' drastically differently, but if it's evolution, this calls for something altogether more subtle. The boss of M&S always talks about being half a step ahead of his customers – not a full step, that's too much and would risk losing them.

But for me, half a step is an exciting thought that's designed to challenge an entire business to be in permanent visionary thinking mode. Permanently acknowledging the fragility of its relationship with customers. An easily understood thought process to keep customers from straying.

Who is the competition?

Larry Hochman, former European Business Speaker of the Year, is one of the most inspiring speakers I've ever heard.

Not the sort to make me walk across hot coals. But the sort to inspire wonderfully simple and logical thinking. For me he's particularly good at the kind of thinking that unlocks the seemingly complicated relationships businesses have with their customers. I wonder if Voltaire had Larry in mind when he famously remarked: "Common sense is not so common." Certainly, other people's thinking seems oddly lacking when you hear Larry's brand of common sense.

In a profound section of his recent book, *The Relationship Revolution*[*], Larry simply implores that you know who your biggest competitor is. I first heard him ask this question at a conference. The answers ranged from Wal-Mart to someone's brother-in-law. But Larry soon put his audience into a head-banging frenzy of nodding approval by explaining that it's themselves! As he puts it, "Your biggest competitor is your own view of the future."

He's not talking and writing about limiting beliefs; he is simply acknowledging that unless *you* have the vision to adapt for the future, *you're* not going to survive. He then goes on to explain exactly how you might do this and underlines his point by drafting in the Darwinian quote I used at the beginning of this introduction.

But as I say many times in this book, success is all about mindset. Whether you're a leader or aspiring leader, please remember and

* Larry Hochman, *The Relationship Revolution: Closing the Customer Promise*, John Wiley and Sons. Ltd

understand the mindset of successful leaders. Most I've interviewed take the view that *they* are their biggest competitor and that *they* must constantly challenge themselves and their businesses to understand and adapt to what's happening in the world around them. They understand and adapt to what's happening to their customers and their lives. At its simplest, they make every effort for their business to be as relevant as possible to their customers. It's worth drawing your attention to the Macy's case study in Secret One, where individual 'city intelligence units' have replaced regional offices in order to be geographically more relevant.

Obstacles

Interestingly, barriers play a very big part in visionary leadership.

As Henry Ford once said, "obstacles are those frightful things you see when you take your eyes off your goal." And I can't tell you how many times overcoming seemingly insurmountable problems has formed the centrepiece of an interview for this book.

Budgets are often the biggest barrier to visionary thinking, and so too is the fear of additional workload on an already busy workforce. Bureaucratic nonsense also protects the status quo, as do worthy opinions unencumbered by fact – people speaking on behalf of other people to stop something from happening. But as you may read from case studies in this book, well articulated payback models, eloquent lateral thinking and determined engagement programmes, amongst other things, prevent most obstacles from gathering traction.

worthy opinions unencumbered by fact

I've often heard the cry that if it were easy, others would have done it. An interesting *aide-memoire* when pushing boundaries on the lonely leadership journey. Counter-intuitive and visionary thinking has regularly taken my interviewees where others feared to tread.

Although new, exciting and, in the modern idiom, 'random', the point often made is that visionary thinking is never impulsive. It's always a determined process that is grown from a culture that encourages, celebrates and facilitates a series of well thought-out steps, each pointing precisely along the path to a successful future.

Self imposed

In one guise or another, every retail leader I have interviewed has expressed the fear of complacency within their businesses. It somehow informs change.

Some put it more strongly and talk about the need to avoid the curse of arrogance, so often a by-product of success. But what has struck me on my travels is that not one retail boss, no matter how big and successful, has ever given the slightest hint that they take customers for granted. Again an obvious statement, but nevertheless a strict, self-imposed mindset that helps shape a retail leader's agenda for the future.

Indeed, if I had to generalise, I'd say the more successful a leader is, the more humble they become in their search for customer understanding and customer relevance. Sometimes as with Hot Topic in Secret Five and HMV in Secret One, major change has been brought about through critical necessity. Other times, as with Best Buy in Secret One, it's a rolling programme of ever deeper customer-centricity. But for the most successful retailers, this humility has meant visionary thinking being elevated to an ethos everyone *feeling* and *embracing* things need to change to be successful.

Research can't help

I always said in my own business that when you give customers what they want, they end up not wanting it. Whenever we diligently gave our clients exactly what they said they wanted, they'd be happy until they fell in love with something completely different that a competitor had speculatively showed them. Mine was a particularly creative world, but like retail, my customers wanted to be surprised and delighted. The

All research can do is refine not create

trouble is, they didn't know what they wanted until they saw it. Just like retail customers. And the trouble is, research can't help either. All research can do is refine not create.

Of course, really good quantitative researchers can *listen* between the lines of what's said in research groups. But when you think about it, nobody would have actually said they wanted a motor car to replace the horse and carriage. Or could we please have an aeroplane, ships take too long. No-one specifically asked the owners of Zara fashions featured in Secret One, that they wanted stock replenishment twice a week to all 4,300 stores.

The great leaders I've interviewed purposely go out of their way to grow cultures that do the right thing by encouraging change. Fortunately, retail is well placed to do this. The day-to-day contact with customers is *free* research. Most other businesses have to pay to speak to customers. If the workforce is appropriately motivated they can be a wonderful conduit for feedback.

The boss of Sainsbury's, featured in Secret Three, places huge importance on colleague feedback and has a highly successful initiative for this. If a workforce feels they're genuinely listened to, they become a wonderful source of ideas. Never forgetting they are 'customers' too. I talk about *Osmosis* brands in Secret Three – these are particularly good at all this, their leaders are great at creating powerful cultures where visionary thinking is not only encouraged and valued, but expected. They are companies where everyone feels it's worth 'sticking their head above the parapet', so to speak.

Growing tomorrow

Another interesting dimension of visionary thinking is sacrifice. Much of the thinking I experienced can be paraphrased as 'giving a little today for a lot tomorrow'.

While aware of day-to-day results, the really successful leaders practice what I call *brand husbandry*. *never allowing short-term decisions to become long-term strategy* Keeping with the farming analogy, they resist ruthlessly harvesting their brands, favouring visionary thinking that makes space to 'put' something back. They are effectively feeding their brands and businesses to ensure strong future growth – never allowing short-term decisions to become long-term strategy.

I have found these successful retailers have moved with the times and understand that 'modern value' is no longer simply about quality and/or price, it's about what customers get, for what they pay –

acknowledging the role of emotion in the equation! These retailers avoid being hooked on the discount drug. They simply use it judiciously, always avoiding opportunistic profiteering that damages the long term.

Being first

The truly gifted leaders seem to possess an indefinable blend of prescience and counter-intuitive thinking. Customers love this, growing to appreciate and 'valuing' a company that offers them things that are different and never knew existed.

creating a culture where it's everyone's role to open the 'box' so others can think outside it

We often talk about *first-mover* advantage and its appeal to customers. It's a particular area of visionary thinking that effortlessly says more about your company than the company can ever say about itself. Sports Authority in Secret Six is a prime example of this when pioneering giant formats.

Unfortunately, prescience and counter-intuitive thinking are qualities that can't be taught. You either think like this or you don't. Something the truly great leaders recognise. They insist on creating a culture where it's *everyone's* role to open the 'box' so others can think outside it! A particularly creative illustration of this is Saks Fifth Avenue in Secret Five, where they won over the hearts of the famously hardened and sceptical New York shopper.

Thinking successfully

You will have noticed that in this introduction I have tended to refer to examples from other secrets in the book. Besides encouraging you to read these (if you're simply dipping in and out), I accept their centres of gravity are elsewhere but I have chosen them to highlight the role of visionary thinking. To show how it specifically informs the detail of success. It is also further evidence that none of my secrets are mutually exclusive.

So along with my final thoughts, let me introduce some world-class visionary thinking from highly successful retailers.

The interviews

- **Wal-Mart** has proclaimed China as its next big frontier. With visionary thinking it is claiming to make the lives of millions of new customers better and skilfully helping hundreds of thousands of small farmers to be more effective, to mutual benefit. This retailer has two case studies in this book as befits its pre-eminent status as the world's largest.

- **Kingfisher Group** is a truly international home improvement retailer. It was one of the first retailers to successfully persuade millions of customers of the importance of sustainability. Visionary thinking that is saving the planet and delivering commercial rewards.

- **The Aldo Group** is a huge fashion shoe retailing empire in 55 countries. It has successfully grown internationally by evolving a remarkably visionary thought process that quantifies how much the business is allowed to 'flex' when crossing cultural boundaries.

- **Spar International** has 13,000 stores across 30 countries. This food retailer has achieved international greatness through the remarkable prescience of its founding fathers. And to this day protects its unique status with visionary thinking that sets it apart from all others.

- **New Clicks** is a drug store business with 350 stores throughout South Africa. With some prescient thinking that's taken almost forty years to be realised, this group now has permission to dispense competitively priced pharmaceuticals and clinical services to a needy population.

- **The Warehouse Group** is New Zealand's foremost general merchandise retailer and market leader. With visionary thinking, the group has been led to greatness, reinventing its business model in the face of necessity and in the process become one of the regions iconic retailers.

- **Al Ghurair Retail** is based in Dubai. With some outstanding counter-intuitive thinking this huge company is developing a cosmetic and toiletries retail format that challenges the normal business model of the region. With visionary thinking, this business is bravely and successfully opening a whole new market.

- **The Robinsons Group** operates several world-class brands throughout Singapore and Malaysia including its own iconic department stores. With considerable visionary thinking, these department stores were saved from obscurity with the help of a brave and strategic glance backwards.

- **Dairy Farm** has 5,000 retail outlets in ten countries throughout Asia, predominately specialising in food and health & beauty. The company is driving substantial growth and profits with some visionary thinking that has embraced company weaknesses as a positive influence and a huge opportunity.

Case History

Rob Cissell
Chief Operating Officer, Wal-Mart China

Interviewed November 2009

Local understanding

In the world of commerce there's much talk of thinking globally, acting locally. That's because it not only makes sense, it makes money.

And for the global giant Wal-Mart, the local opportunities are phenomenal in China.

With retail sales growing at roughly 15 per cent a year during the 2000s, it's not surprising that this vast country is viewed by Wal-Mart executives as the ultimate export destination for Sam Walton's famous Every Day Low Pricing (EDLP) merchandising model. It now has 170 huge stores currently delivering a seemingly small, less than two per cent share of an unbelievably large market of 1.3 billion people. "We don't divulge projections but we've been here ten years and we intend to continue growing organically and through acquisition – we're already one of the largest foreign owned retailers in China," explains Rob Cissell who, since 2007, has been the regions COO for Wal-Mart.

Cissell has an engaging personality. A typically dynamic corporate executive, but clearly a very natural retailer. As soon as he arrived in China his President and CEO, Ed Chan, sent him on a mission. "It was clear everyone here was doing a great job but needed to somehow, step up a gear – it was obvious to Chan we needed more clarity," says English-born Cissell, who previously held various senior posts with the UK's Kingfisher and Argos retailing empires. "Things got done but no-one was really sure how – they'd leave a

EDLP needs to be fed and funded by Every Day Low Costs

room not knowing, 100 per cent, who was accountable. It happens in new businesses with an entrepreneurial 'new frontier' spirit – especially when they're driven by a small number of individuals at the top. But to deliver our big aspirations we needed the entire business to develop a real understanding of 'purpose'. An understanding of what Wal-Mart wants to stand for globally and to ensure all local 'arenas' were aligned to their particular challenges. So the first thing we did was re-engage the whole business in Wal-Mart's easily understood global mission – to enable its customers to save money, so they can live better."

By taking the business back to basics, Cissell and the team demonstrated how the economic model performed and how it must be focused. "EDLP needs to be *fed and funded* by Every Day Low Costs

Farmers from the Wal-Mart 'Direct Farm' programme, China

(EDLC), we call this the 'Virtuous Circle'. Its net effect is to emotionally engage everyone with the idea of ruthlessly cutting out anything in the business that doesn't ultimately benefit the customer."

With an easily understood 'purpose', making the right decisions locally became easier for Cissell's teams. Accountability was a natural response and the business instinctively knew what 'good' looked like for their market. Wal-Mart executives jetting economy class long haul and staying in budget hotels is legendary. But in the Shenzhen head office alone, $1 million a year was saved by making individual executives accountable for their photocopying. With energy efficiencies, LED lighting and by switching-off unnecessary lights, there was a 30 per cent cut in the stores electricity bills. Office elevators were programmed for maximum passenger flow and minimum energy use.

But as Cissell explains, "Doug McMillon, our International President, acknowledges we need the China version of EDLP, and the China version of EDLC. We must give the China customer what they want and obviously that'll be different to other countries." And here Cissell is both proud and coy about Wal-Mart's tough negotiating prowess. "Sure we expect big discounts to match our big volumes but there's a genuine fear you only get lower costs at the *expense* of suppliers. But that is not the Wal-Mart principle. When it's done right, it should be a win for the consumer, a win for us and a win for the vendor – but that's providing we can keep our costs down and get the supply chain to work as efficiently as we would want."

There are many vendors around the world who may beg to differ with Cissell's rose-tinted view of the negotiation process – but true to his boss's wise words on finding the China solution, it won't be Cissell's ever-growing band of 250,000 small farmers in China.

Supplying Wal-Mart with vegetables, fruit and rice these Chinese farmers have been able to increase productivity and reduce waste by working in supportive co-operatives set up by Wal-Mart under its 'Direct Farm' programme. With huge importance placed on freshness, customers are typically drawn from a two-kilometre catchment area. They expect to shop their local 200,000-square-foot Wal-Mart hypermarkets three or four times a week and are delighted to see packaging detailing which local supplier produced what. By accepting world-class agricultural advice, and by tapping into the retailer's legendary supply chain expertise, the farmers have eradicated their normally accepted 35 per cent 'produce wastage'. Ambitious and much welcomed plans are in place to increase these programmes through 'central distribution' for other areas of food and general merchandise.

the farmers have eradicated their normally accepted 35 per cent 'produce wastage'

Cissell is enthusiastic about these China-based achievements and talks of improving lives at both ends of the supply chain and winning customers. "Take wine, there's another example of our win-win principle. We're now tapping into Wal-Mart UK's wine contacts in

Chile. We're helping develop the wine market in China by keeping prices down and opening a huge new market for the producers."

But Cissell's executives rightly monitor their qualitative performance amongst shoppers too. Interestingly, in China, Wal-Mart is famed for its product quality and customer service ethic. It's also becoming a hugely trusted brand – particularly beneficial in a country with high profile, food and hygiene scares. But there is a downside as Cissell admits: "We're not perceived as being as competitive on price as we would like. Research shows our customers refuse to believe we can offer high standards at low prices. But according to our sophisticated price comparison data, we know we do. Delivering our desired *cheaper price* separation from all our local competitors – even over-delivering at times. Fortunately none of this affects our most important measure – Net Promoter Scores. This measures the degree our customers would recommend us and they're ahead of target and unbelievably positive. But paradoxically, given Wal-Mart's well earned global reputation for price, in China we're having to work on price perception as a priority."

Like most well run businesses Cissell's team also measures internal rate of return. By resolutely reducing operational costs and by increasing efficiencies he can *the more products sold, the more the 'Virtuous Circle' turns in China* proudly boast that many smaller markets are now viable, which weren't just a couple of years ago. Another self-fulfilling benefit of EDLC. Of course, the more markets entered, the more products sold and the more the 'Virtuous Circle' turns in China.

But world-class visionary thinking can only be delivered with world-class understanding. And individual regions will always need individual solutions.

And here's the learning. From the biggest ideal to the smallest detail everything works best when local understanding is at the heart of the delivery.

30
Case History

Ian Cheshire
Chief Executive, Kingfisher Group

Interviewed August 2008

Saving the planet

As Bill Shankly, former manager of the UK's Liverpool City FC famously said, "Football's not a matter of life and death, it's more important than that."

The ultimate big thought maybe, but there's one international retailer thinking just as big.

Prescience is an essential retail skill and a key part of success. Visionary thinking with the ability to introduce ideas to customers before they know they might need them, want them or eventually buy them, is fundamental.

Putting all the environmental sceptics to one side (otherwise known in United Nations Global Compact speak as flat-earthers), we see from Kingfisher Plc, the international home improvement retail group, a quintessential bit of retail prescience: sustainability. Ian Cheshire, Group CEO believes retailers are in a particularly important position concerning this issue. "They can *a quintessential bit* be very powerful in the mix between their *of retail prescience* supply chain and customer base. They can be the leaders on sustainability and, importantly, get some competitive advantage out of it too."

For several years Kingfisher has been developing a business strategy based on sustainability. "While the environment might be at the forefront of everyone's minds today, when Kingfisher had the vision to chart this course back in the late 1980s it was very much on its own. One of our first initiatives helped create the Forestry Stewardship

Council, ensuring that the wood used in leisure furniture and tables came from a sustainable, certified source. Sounds familiar now but when we did that, we were pretty much alone. Today we are seeing a very profound shift in the demands of consumers. It's something retailers must now embrace – they are uniquely positioned because they touch so many people."

Ian Cheshire, with iconic low energy light bulb

Ian Cheshire is one of those charismatic individuals with a towering intellect whose thought processes seem to effortlessly translate into words that make common sense. A quality many appreciate. Besides his day job, he is one of a very select few advising the British government on sustainability.

But retail prescience needs to be as commercial as it is compelling.

"Over the last two years our low-energy light bulb sales have doubled and insulation has trebled. We've found that around 45 per cent of our customers are actively considering some form of green credentials, while a further 20 per cent pay some attention to it. That's 65% of our customers who are engaged and it's only going to get bigger! There are probably two or three things you can easily do to make the most difference in a home. Usually it starts with light bulbs and insulation. But with these two simple steps, what we've found is that people tend to get increasingly interested. Understandably going on to do additional things, becoming ever more engaged."

Cheshire goes on to explain: "Now customers are not only looking for help on sustainable products and services, they are looking at retailers much more critically and asking 'what are you doing and how are you behaving'. For our part this has meant new emphasis.

- First, we must put our own 'house' in order, dramatically changing the way we operate, setting ambitious targets. Over time we're after zero carbon, zero waste etc.

- Secondly, we must better engage our workforce to effect this change, so they can better inform our customers.

- And thirdly, we must address the speed at which we make these changes – time is not on our side!"

Simultaneously, Cheshire says his vision must also include challenging each of his businesses around the world "to be the customer choice for sustainable products and services."

But is sustainability a sustainable proposition?

Some might argue that everybody is catching up with the Kingfisher's thinking. Cheshire believes there is considerable competitive advantage to first-mover advantage, being deeper into the thinking than his competitors. As he puts it, "We are always going to the 'next step' forward and we are determined that Kingfisher can continue to stay ahead of the chasing pack. If you are further down the track thinking about *First, we must put our* sustainability and inculcating it, you *own 'house' in order* will constantly be leading the process. And yes of course, some of those things will become standard. We started selling low-energy light bulbs many years ago and now a lot more people are selling them too. But now we've already moved into the next generation of bulbs and fitments. By being on the leadership front foot you will always be driving 'change' to the next level."

Even the most insightful insights need to move on.

B&Q, one of Cheshire's international DIY retail chains has recently and significantly raised the bar on sustainability. In association with the WWF and BioRegional it has embraced a new development called 'One Planet Living'. Justifiably Cheshire is excited about this new initiative. He believes the focus it brings will more efficiently and effectively articulate the issues, giving greater clarity to the challenges, better informing his business and its customers. "This latest initiative really takes quite a simple idea that if we continue to consume resources at the same rate as today, then we will need three planets. So the world needs to make sure it's got a more sustainable model going forward."

As management thinker Peter Drucker once famously said: "All good ideas degenerate into hard work." And besides their normal duties, it's the Kingfisher workforce who have to implement the company's good ideas. "Because we deal with the very down-to-earth business of home improvements, when we first started really focusing on 'One Planet Living' we thought our people might find it a bit too extreme and not engage. Actually we've found quite the reverse. They are really proud and keen to work for a business that is trying to push-on in this area."

So there you have it. Sustainability - a profound piece of prescience whose retail time has come.

With the paradigm shifts caused by world banking in 2008/9 no retailer can guarantee financial success but here we have a company with a true strategic vision of the future and bringing it alive with some outstanding thinking. Taking the chance to emotionally engage with its workforce like never before and emotionally bonding with customers to such an extent, their competitors are running hard to keep up.

Not only helping save itself energy and therefore money – but helping save the planet too

If the imperatives of sustainability in general, and 'One Planet Living' in particular, are fully embraced and embraced immediately, the company believes it can help deliver a sustainable future. Not only helping save itself energy and therefore money – but helping save the planet too.

Save the planet? Makes Shankly's comment seem oddly parochial.

31
Case History

Norman Jaskolka
President, Aldo International

Interviewed June 2008

Limits needed

When expanding internationally, more retailers fail than succeed – why?

Xenophobia or corporate intransigence – well, maybe.

But according to Norman Jaskolka, President of International Operations for Canada-based Aldo Group, which operates 1,400 young-fashion footwear stores in over 55 countries, if you change more than 20 per cent of a business model when developing overseas, the culture and the format will likely be lost and the business will fail. In effect he is talking about over-dilution of the brand essence, as he calls it, the *fibre* of a business – the very thing that created the success of the business at home. Some might even call it the soul of the business.

Everyone realises a business with international aspirations needs to adapt to local cultural, socio-demographic and climatic imperatives. But what is so interesting here is how Jaskolka, a chartered accountant and ex-partner of Ernst & Young, has amazingly quantified in his own mind just how much 'flex' he is prepared to allow his business to undertake when developing overseas. Whether he is right or wrong, and evidence would suggest the former, it does represent a useful aide-memoire. It is a kind of sense check for management when the immense pressures come thick and fast to adapt a retail business for entry into a new market. "Besides merchandise, there's a component of the business – you might says it's between 15 and 20 per cent – that can be adapted for different markets. If you have to do any more than that, in my mind, you don't have an exportable concept," says Jaskolka.

But he is clear that the 20 per cent flex does not include changing the brand in terms of how it informs the business, the culture, or the values of the organisation. "These aspects must be kept firmly in place. They are non-negotiable. They are the components that make a business unique, everything thing else is up for grabs, but only to a certain extent."

Jaskolka loves travelling and loves experiencing new cultures. He is highly intelligent and clearly enjoys the challenges of understanding the global customer. He has a creative demeanour not normally enjoyed by 'numbers' people. Appropriately the failures of others, in their efforts to expand internationally, do not faze him either. "In today's world with the internet, magazines, social networking and the capability of people to communicate instantaneously with each other around the world, the idea of a 'globalised concept' is much more relevant than it was in the past. So when you ask 'can I have something that's going to successfully work across many countries', maybe it was much harder years ago. But back then, you have to remember engrained local tastes were the *the idea of a 'globalised concept' is much more relevant than it was in the past* norm. Look around, today people are more open to change, they are exposed to experiences of other countries and tastes."

As Jaskolka explains, the path to successful international development is born out of a few of simple questions and thoughts.

- "First, ask why you want to develop abroad? If it's chasing success from scale then it's probably the wrong answer and doomed. It has to be because you believe in what you've achieved so strongly and enjoyed so much success, that you have a natural need now to satisfy your stakeholders' dreams. To dare to say, we have just got to take this 'thing' to the next level. It's not an expansion process, it has to be all about: *let's get over there and share it with them!*"

- "Second – and this is related to the first question. Have we been incredibly successful in our home country? If the answer is no – stop right there. If the answer is yes, ask what is it that made us successful and is that, in itself, transportable. Not always easy to define but essential!"

- "Third, having understood what makes you special, go to whatever country you're interested in and see how much of it you've got to change to have a fighting chance of success. If it's more than 20 per cent, it's almost certainly too much. Adapt the merchandise sure, but keep a close eye on the things you're told *need* changing. Keep a close grip on the things you know make you special. It sounds obvious but you'd be surprised how many influences start chewing away at your very *fibre!*"

- "Fourth, decide how you are going to keep control, and I mean control, of what makes you special. Decide whether you can afford to do it out of your own money – this gives you the best and total control but is a slow process – or whether you can find a partner that intuitively feels so right they immediately become part of your family. And family is an important emotional word, because if they don't immediately feel like family, it's going to be very tough indeed. For us the golden rule is, when we choose the partner route, we only ever have one master franchisee for a whole region – that way you have immediate standardisation of execution and that means I know I have a franchisee execute things in the same way I execute it. In our opinion if you have multiple franchisees in the same country you've taken it one step further. That means one step further for our *fibre* to have to travel – and that'll be the same for most businesses!"

As with all great ideas, they sound simple when someone else has already thought of them. But it is hard to see a flaw in the logic, especially when practised so effectively by a globally successful brand in the cut-throat world of fashion.

If it's more than 20 per cent, it's almost certainly too much

But on a more prosaic note, if you have international aspirations, not only do you need Jaskolka's talent for quantifying what's important, you also need his boundless energy – and an embarrassing love of airports. International development is up-close and personal.

But here the visionary thinking and insight is obvious. If you are going to change your *fibre* in order to cross international borders, you'd better make sure you have some limits. He says 20 per cent. It might be more, it might be less. But at least his numbers should get you thinking.

Change too much of your *fibre* and you are not developing a retail business internationally, you're effectively becoming a multinational owner of several foreign businesses. And as anyone might argue, why would you be able to run a retail business in another country, better than a local?

why would you be able to run a retail business in another country, better than a local?

History is littered with examples proving his case.

32
Case History

Dr Gordon Campbell
Managing Director, Spar International

Interviewed August 2008

In the DNA

In modern retailing, innovation is key – nothing new or different there!

But for the central management of Spar International, whose chain of nearly 13,000 independently-owned supermarket and convenience stores spans more than 30 countries, innovation is achieved rather differently.

"It is important first to understand the foundation and ownership structure of our world-wide business," explains Dr Gordon Campbell, Managing Director of Spar International Stores. "In the early 1930s, having seen the successful emergence in Europe of international retail chains such as Woolworths, our Dutch founder, Adrian Van Well, realised that wholesalers like himself and the independent retailers he served needed to combat this growing threat. His visionary concept was to work with the local retailers to a common aim. He persuaded them to buy all their product from him and in return, use his new-found scale to buy better – guaranteeing to pass the benefit on. Together, through the creation of a Guild, this 'organisation of partners' elected a committee to run the joint venture, each contributing funds for the greater good. Eventually the retailers even saw the wisdom of changing their names to 'Spar' – allowing budgets to be created for marketing, the production of own-label goods and even supported by contributions from suppliers."

Today, through various incarnations and ownership structures in individual countries, the Spar brand has become a confederation of independently-owned retailers, which has grown into the largest chain of food retail stores in the world. It is primarily a business that fiercely caters to the local needs of its local markets. And here lay a particular challenge for this global brand.

The vision for most multinational retailers is to introduce local thinking into a global structure but for Spar, with its unique ownership, it is the reverse. Central management has sought to introduce best practice into the international operation while continuing to give store owners the freedom to do what they do best – serve their local markets. Accordingly, Campbell's team see their role, in his own words, "not to be deeply involved in national activities but rather to champion business initiatives that will benefit the 13,000 stores in general and the brand in particular."

an environment and process where store owners are 'tempted' to embrace new initiatives

As with all retail, innovation is a key driver in the business and Campbell's influence in this manifests itself in many ways, not least in the group's Flagship store development initiative. His remit is not to implement a one-size-fits-all global strategy but to create an environment and process where store owners are 'tempted' to embrace new initiatives.

At the heart of the Flagship store programme, started in 2002, is a worldwide process of 'best-practice' achievement. For each country and each store format, a Flagship store is created. Whilst this ultra-inclusive style of management may appear convoluted, it has certainly had the desired effect. Around the world, Spar has managed to slim down its number of store formats from over twenty to just four: hypermarkets *Inter Spar*, large supermarkets *Euro Spar*, local supermarket/convenience stores *Spar*, and for high footfall locations, *Spar Express*.

"Retail needs to change to move forward. The big breakthrough for us came when we set ourselves the target of working with each member country to produce its own Flagship for the particular formats they operate. Each specifically acknowledging local needs. In China for example, it's not unusual for customers to shop three times a day. They're very price-sensitive, spend an average of US$3 and demand extreme freshness. Whereas Russian shoppers are not so motivated by price but by choice and variety. So we have very high sales and yields per square metre but the issue there is expensive build and fit-out costs. Having tailored each Flagship store we then assist and encourage other Spar owners in that country to adopt and adapt these prototypes. As a Spar owner, there's nothing more attractive or compelling than having something specifically designed for your market! We now have a central team capable of working at a very high level in each country and that's made the whole thing click. Where appropriate, we're able to transfer best practice from one country to another as well as from one store to another – there's no point re-inventing the wheel each time."

At an emotional level the success and willingness of member countries to embrace the Flagship development process has helped lead the way for other initiatives – hugely important as Spar drives to achieve international best practice in all aspects of its business. "For example, we're progressively implementing store design protocols. From Australia to Africa or Maastricht to Mumbai, you have the large branding of Spar, big red portals, open-glazing if possible, and on entering the stores we always start with *fresh*."

the Flagship development process has helped lead the way for other initiatives

Nothing ground-breaking here for the uniform compliance of most international food retailers. But as Campbell explains, "Cost effective international promotions and our long-standing sponsorship of the European Athletics Championships have given Spar very high TV coverage with associated high brand recognition. It's essential therefore that the branding visualisation on TV is replicated within the stores. A successful example of this being re-branded stores showing up to 45 per cent like-for-like sales increases in tourist areas compared with half that for non-tourist areas."

Unsurprisingly, Campbell refutes any speculation that with so many individual owners the Spar organisation lacks cohesion. "Over time, the store owners have found it's in everybody's interest to go in one direction and show one face to consumers and the industry." This is a simple statement loaded with implication, echoing the vision and sentiments of the individual 'founding fathers' who bravely changed their name to Spar 80 years ago!

But Spar is proudly an 'organisation of partners' with its internal processes successfully differentiating it from most global corporate doctrines. And here the learning from this case study can be found.

As recounted many times in this book, differentiation is at the heart of every successful brand. The more emotionally based the differentiation, the more sustainable it will be. Spar proudly protects and cleverly guarantees its own brand differentiation by its very structure and operating methods. To this day its Guild, where possible, ensures local people run, control and emotionally engage on their own level with their own customers. Leaving central management to add a persuasive global perspective – promoting change by showcasing world-class retail best practice, all compellingly laced with unbelievable economies of scale. The beauty of Spar's visionary thinking and business model is how it skilfully celebrates and delivers the emotional benefits of 'local' with the tangible benefits of 'global'.

every action within the business is informed by a deep and profound understanding of itself

The 2008/9 banking crisis has affected retail worldwide. But Spar continues to innovate and grow. It is now the largest food retailer on the planet with an ever-expanding presence in mature and emerging markets.

Innovation and change continue to play a central part in Spar's development. And like all great visionary brands, every action within the business is informed by a deep and profound understanding of itself – being different, after all, is in its DNA.

33 Case History

David Kneale
Chief Executive, New Clicks Group

Interviewed February 2009

Three dimensional

Change is not only a necessary part of retailing; it's a massive opportunity to refresh the brand and the business.

Get it right and customers will love you – but get it wrong and they'll feel alienated.

A new store format is one of the most immediate and authoritative statements a retailer can make about change. Although a serious commitment, it gives new and existing shoppers permission to *feel* differently about the business. Used with care, and provided it's loaded with substance, it offers the retailer an opportunity to send powerful brand messages, and at the same time improve the customer experience.

In early 2006, David Kneale became Group CEO of New Clicks Holdings, a publicly listed company trading in South Africa. This dynamic retailing group is predominately a drugstore business called Clicks. But it has other interests in wholesale pharmaceutical distribution, music retailing and is the master franchisee for Body Shop in the region.

A new store format is one of the most immediate and authoritative statements a retailer can make about change.

Kneale, who is English, has spent his entire career in retail both home and abroad. He's a passionate retailer, extremely bright, technically very astute, and loving the challenges of his new career in Africa. He's unbelievably well qualified for his role, having spent 26 years in various management positions for Boots, the UK's premier chemist, health, beauty and general merchandise retailer.

Similar to legislation in other parts of the world, until recently, retail pharmacies in South Africa had to be 'owned and run' by qualified pharmacists. Though understandable on grounds of safety regulation, this meant the economies of scale promised by corporate retailing could not be passed to the needy population of the region – a vision the founder of Clicks cherished. So, recognising the need and social benefit, the South African government changed the law in 2004. Enjoying first-mover advantage, Clicks is now at the forefront of dispensing prescription medicines at cheaper prices.

"Even though our founder had the vision this day would come, Clicks had to wait nearly forty years to cease being a drugstore-not-selling-drugs when it was eventually allowed to sell prescription medicines. With the huge footfall associated in being market leader for cosmetics, vitamins and toiletries everyone expected the change would be an instant success," says Kneale. "But the dispensaries were simply bolted on at the back of the stores. Suddenly you had these people in white coats pitching up and keeping themselves to themselves – it certainly wasn't an integrated experience."

The founder's daughter's idea in the early 70s of naming her Dad's store chain Clicks, because it clicked so well, was proving a woeful misnomer.

Kneale was brought in after a couple of years to sort things out. "It was immediately obvious customers didn't understand what was happening. The changes that had been made were disruptive, customers were lost and feeling 'what have they done to my shop?'" So Kneale and his team set about creating a blueprint for a proper integration process – putting pharmacy at the spiritual heart of the store with a new layout where existing products flowed naturally. "This was obviously a seminal opportunity for the business and my vision was that it shouldn't be viewed as just an incremental *putting pharmacy at the spiritual heart of the store* revenue stream. We needed to engage our customers and present a more cohesive 'offer' – everything had to speak to this vision and our thinking had to more accurately reflect this. A new over-sized entrance, framed by a bold and welcoming design feature called the 'goalpost' allows people to see right into the stores. It's a signpost of change as well as being used to advertise what's in store."

The new store layout features a 'customer journey' acknowledging pharmacy as a destination not just a department. "Not unreasonably, we kept the pharmacy at the back of the store – it's low margin, labour intensive but attracts huge footfall. Naturally, we wanted pharmacy customers to see everything else we sold. And it's worked. 90 per cent of our pharmacy customers buy other merchandise on each visit. Importantly we always build a clinic alongside the pharmacy. It's staffed by a nursing practitioner offering a range of primary healthcare services like blood pressure monitoring, cholesterol testing, baby immunisation, family planning, etc. We don't have to do this but it's a wonderful opportunity to engage deeper with our customers. Building meaning and value into what I want the Clicks brand to stand for. It's not a free service but is quicker than the State system – so less wages are lost and our customers appreciate that. We're about accessibility and approachability too. We now present self-medication by therapeutic classification. Given literacy levels, it's very patient-friendly. Most competitors use the alphabetic method."

"There's a blueprint for how we staff our pharmacies," explains Kneale. "With our training and systems, the balance between pharmacists and assistants has moved from parity to 1:1.5 – making dispensing more viable in much smaller markets. We have our own Academy and even train pharmacy assistants for the State. In addition, a clever little communication system has been installed to enable pharmacists to use a discreet radio buzzer to contact healthcare assistants on the shop floor when pharmacy customers require

valuing the authority and trust that comes from the pharmacy 'halo'

something specialised from another section."

But offering pharmacy is not only a huge financial investment, there are hidden costs too, as Kneale explains. "There's a heightened customer service expectation in stores with pharmacies. They expect the same level of knowledge and professionalism throughout the store. Now we have to be particularly aware of our skill levels everywhere." But proof customers are valuing the authority and trust that comes from the pharmacy 'halo' is evidenced by a near doubling in sales of Clicks own-label goods to 20 per cent. It was an expected, but nevertheless welcomed, additional profit stream and further evidence that the Clicks brand is benefiting from its pharmacy credentials.

In 2010, around half the 350 stores have pharmacies, 100 of them to Kneale's new blueprint – interestingly, the limiting factor primarily being qualified pharmacists. But clearly Kneale's visionary thinking has many fans. Pharmacy stores now enjoy 12 per cent better than trend growth over non-pharmacy in the first year of conversion and go on to deliver a healthy differential. To August 2008, Clicks had achieved a three-year compound growth of 32 per cent in earnings per share and built an impressive market-leading 11 per cent share of the dispensing market. "What has surprised us is the rapidity of customers taking up our pharmacy offer, normally people tend to be loyal to their pharmacies."

A critical part of a retailer's armoury is the three-dimensional quality their brand offers

Increased footfall could have been achieved by simply offering cheaper drugs. But with an injection of some fine strategic thinking and executional excellence, Kneale has used this historic opportunity to change the Clicks' business forever. And his customers, both new and old, love it.

A critical part of a retailer's armoury is the three-dimensional quality their brand offers – overlook this in your thinking and you won't change very much.

34
Case History

Stephen Tindall
Founder, The Warehouse Group

Interviewed June 2008

Success form failure

A celebrated American humorist once said, "You've got to go out on a limb sometimes because that's where the fruit is."

More than fifty years on from Will Rogers' famous quote, Stephen Tindall gave up a very successful job in department store retailing, cashed in his pension and insurance policies, sold the family caravan and went out to buy a very expensive computer. So began, in the early 1980s, a journey that would elevate Tindall to be one of New Zealand's most revered retail icons and a billionaire.

Retail is in Tindall's blood. His great great grandfather emigrated from England and along with a brother created one of New Zealand's

Stephen Tindell celebrating in 2001

largest department store groups. But this was not how Tindall saw his future. He saw an opportunity and was prepared to risk all to realise it.

What was the vision that helped Tindall become New Zealand's foremost general merchandise retailer and create the market leader? How did this charmingly intelligent and philanthropic gentleman use lateral thinking to thrive in the highly competitive world of value retailing?

In his own words: "It seemed pretty obvious at the time. Ever since the Second World War the New Zealand government had operated import quotas policed by licensee agreements (to protect local manufacturing). Potentially they were a license to print money. But in the early 1980s, the Government of the day decided to re-tender these import licenses, on a purely transparent basis. This meant the highest bidder won. But that didn't mean the winner had the necessary retail expertise. In many cases it led to poor sourcing, resulting in distressed merchandise being offered to retailers at ridiculous discounts.

For Tindall this was an absurd situation and his visionary thinking kicked in with a charming logic. "I decided to approach the import licensees, who were mainly wholesalers, with a business proposition. I knew up until then retailers were buying this distressed merchandise from them at anything between 10 and 20 cents in the dollar – then selling it on at over 50 cents in the dollar to their customers. My proposal was to open dedicated stores taking in this distressed stock from the wholesalers on 'sale-or-return' and being paid on a commission-only basis for what I sold. My plan was to offer the merchandise at *under* 50 cents in the dollar to customers, with me taking 20 per cent commission. This meant the licensees won and the customers won – and yes, I won too. And if it didn't sell at this price, we'd agree a lower price or the wholesalers could have it back – which never happened! They simply loved the whole idea and I called my first store 'The Warehouse.' It opened with just under half a million New Zealand worth of stock and it hadn't cost me a cent – within five months I had three similar stores and never needed an overdraft."

> *For Tindall this was an absurd situation and his visionary thinking kicked in with a charming logic*

A key element that gave his whole proposal credibility was the computer he had bought. It was programmed specifically for the wholesalers. Impressively, it gave them a fortnightly statement detailing exactly what had been sold and at what price – all very remarkable for the early 80s. And better still, statements were always accompanied by a cheque for what had been sold! The computer was expensive and had taken three quarters of the start-up costs, the balance being spent on a rent deposit and store fit out. But this piece of technology mirrored the quiet efficiency of Tindall's lateral thinking – he knew it gave his venture the necessary credibility for people to part with stock without being paid; it reassured them.

The Warehouse was booming.

But Tindall knew it wouldn't last. He had heard on the grapevine there were plans to phase out import licenses. For many, a fundamental threat like this would have signalled the end of The Warehouse and its unique business model.

Building on what he had learned, Tindall set about taking advantage of the planned end of restrictive practices. He used his current profits to successfully bid for some of the remaining import licenses. Not because he saw this as a short term chance to make more money during the death throes of import licensing but because it allowed him to go straight to the source of products: China, India or wherever. As predicted, the licensing arrangements were progressively disbanded, but Tindall now had all the overseas contacts he needed. His visionary thinking was about to pay off for a second time.

perfectly placed to take advantage of New Zealand's retail renaissance

Tindall re-established contacts from his buying career, capitalised on contacts from his licensing career and instinctively knew exactly what customers would want from his retailing career. He was perfectly placed to take advantage of New Zealand's retail renaissance. As Tindall explains, "We knew that the whole thing was going to be about speed-to-market. This meant we needed to open more stores, be the first to offer new product, be first for lower prices, and based on our shop floor feedback and computer system, know which products were selling and repeat them fast."

Ever the strategist, Tindall created his own brands. "Because so many of our products were unique or represented tremendous value, we decided this would be a key differentiator for us. We created our own in-house brands and to this day they account for around 60 per cent of sales and help us achieve superior operating profits.... typically between 8-10 per cent compared with between 2-6 per cent for most other major general merchandise companies around the world."

Ownership in the early days was co-operative in style, with 50 per cent owned centrally by Tindall and each major region of stores part-owned by two directors with 25 per cent each. In 1994 the business was floated – this provided money for ambitious expansion plans and repaid the directors for their commitment. Tindall has seen off many imitators from home and abroad and he, in turn, has been seen off when dabbling overseas. The Warehouse now operates 85 stores in New Zealand and 46 Warehouse Stationery stores – in all giving a 47 per cent share of the sector or 7 per cent of the country's entire retail market.

This case study is an example of the raw power of lateral thinking. When executed with elegance and precision it has the potential to deliver success from failure and profits from opportunities – it is a business tool to be revered and encouraged.

Stephen Tindall has now retired from management but retains a seat on the group board. He is a much loved local hero who now spends his time working for the good of his beloved country through his Foundation. Interestingly, he has also turned his thoughts to encouraging future exports and invested in over *the potential to deliver success from failure and profits from opportunities* 100 start-up businesses which demonstrate "Kiwi" innovation and knowledge.

With some astute thinking Tindall went out on a limb to build an empire clearing up after other peoples' mistakes, effortlessly moving on to define *value retailing* in New Zealand.

But it takes real vision to swap a caravan for a computer just to get it all started.

Case History

Keith Flanagan
Head of Al Ghurair Retail, UAE

Interviewed February 2009

Where's the future

It's well known in retail, if you can't innovate, imitate. With much time spent doing just that.

Not so much time, however, has been taken practising the delicate art of counter-intuitive thinking.

During the recent banking crisis, most well-established markets faced testing times. For the Middle East too, the economic downturn meant its frenzied retail growth was finally abating. But for some observers, even before all this, there were signs that this particular market was becoming saturated. Just about every western fashion brand and department store were represented in the palatial, air-conditioned malls of the region.

So when, in 2000, British retailer Keith Flanagan was recruited to head up Dubai-based Al Ghurair Retail, he realised it wouldn't be long before some fresh thinking would be required. Flanagan, a natural retailer, intelligent, approachable and exuding common sense, started his career as a graduate trainee at Marks & Spencer. He has since worked in various retail management positions including Al Shaya in Saudi Arabia. But as most will agree he's risen well to the challenge he set himself. In a land of opulence and luxury, Al Ghurair is now, under Flanagan's leadership, also appealing to an element of Middle Eastern society untouched by indulgence.

appealing to an element of Middle Eastern society untouched by indulgence

Flanagan's visionary thinking was to specifically cater to the untapped sub-strata of 'service workers'.

"They want lipsticks, blushers, toners, moisturisers, the 'basic necessities in life' but just cannot afford to pay department store prices. This workforce of chambermaids, cleaners, kitchen staff is typically made up of Filipinos, Indians, Sri Lankans and Nepalese – and now we're seeing a lot of Africans and Eastern Europeans coming in too." These hardworking immigrants, many of whom send most of their money home, have little disposable income. But their vast numbers suggest there's a viable market worth supplying with low-ticket items.

Flanagan has opened cosmetics and toiletries outlets specifically targeting this new market and it is fast becoming a new business proposition for Al Ghurair. Through a franchise agreement with a Korean brand, *The Face Shop,* he believes he has the blueprint for a chain of stores that will prosper right across the Gulf.

The Face Shop is huge in Korea and although yet to enter Europe, operates nearly 1,000 shops worldwide. Under Al Ghurair's franchise agreement, after six months, five stores will open in UAE by early 2009 with 12 units signed for further openings. Flanagan expects to have 30 franchise stores trading by the end 2011 but given the brand's enthusiastic welcome sees potential beyond that,.

Flanagan has exciting plans. He is keen to introduce 'barrows' and 'kiosks' anywhere his target audience gather. "There are countless opportunities wherever money is tight," says Flanagan. "For instance, Dubai has an all-female university, so I will test a small kiosk there. Also as 'unexpected' space comes up and rentals get more realistic, we will be ready." Customer data also suggests there's interest from the better-off elements of society too. "We've

There are countless opportunities wherever money is tight

discovered that the brand generates a feel-good factor," explains Flanagan. "People come to the malls but currently there's not much money around. So instead of spending on prestige brands they will pick something up from our store. And at our prices, it makes them feel good – this is an unexpected secondary effect and an added bonus of our core proposition. We must then make sure they stay with us."

"In the past the only real alternative to top-name brands like Chanel, Dior and Clinique has been unbranded toiletries and cosmetics for sale in Carrefour and the like. But buying these products with your groceries in big anonymous stores or hypermarkets is clearly unappealing – it doesn't satisfy that all-important emotional element. So what we're giving our shoppers is a branded product and branded experience for a fraction of the price. It's certainly working for them and we are delighted with the brand loyalty we are building."

For obvious financial reasons, the notoriously difficult part of value retailing is delivering the right customer experience. But the compact format and well designed 'budget' fit-outs offered by *The Face Shop* across the world has meant huge economies of scale. This has made new markets increasingly viable. According to Flanagan, "this also means there's adequate margin for the all-important 'good level of customer service' too." And once Al Ghurair has a network of stores to justify mass media advertising Flanagan insists this will happen. But to date, word of mouth has been working well. "We say to people, 'Try it. If you like it tell some friends. If you don't like it, tell us why.' That's not meant to sound trite, we really *do* go out of our way to get feedback. Our female customers are not the 'vocal' type. They're not that confident. They'd prefer to walk away and not come back. With gentle coaxing, we make a point of learning exactly what's going on in their minds – we encourage a very friendly and open relationship. "

Each shop is provided with a company mobile phone so store managers can SMS customers. Certainly not the most sophisticated relationship marketing programme but importantly it does keeps things very personal. By gently asking for customer phone numbers Flanagan's team explain it is ideal for new product launches, special offers and notification of re-stocked popular items. All very personal. And there are small discounts available to customers who sign up to the loyalty card. It's simple, cost-effective initiatives like these that are helping to build a loyal customer base, generating healthy sales ahead of budget. While Al Ghurair normally expects 18 months to pass before the capital investment in a store shows a return, *The Face Shop* outlets are impressively delivering ROI three times faster.

What next for Flanagan's visionary thinking?

"Value fashion and underwear are already well provided for in this region and homewares are not an option because our typical customers don't have their own living space. Interestingly, cheap ethnic fast food, although a 'sure winner', would be too complicated to set up," says Flanagan. "But competitively priced footwear could be a huge market and may be our next big venture. Everybody needs footwear. We're still scouring the world for the right brand and format. It's going to be a challenge on logistics but I am confident we have the expertise – we'll find another winner."

But the important learning from this case study is as obvious as it is essential. Counter-intuitive thinking needs bravery.

challenged the 'evident and accepted' to identify a totally 'new' market

Flanagan is not simply catering to the lower end of an established market. His visionary thinking challenged the *evident and accepted* to identify a totally 'new' market. And such was the leap of faith required, Flanagan admits to being asked if he'd put his job on the line!

Hopefully this was just robust management technique. Because businesses need to create a climate that encourages, celebrates and manages these types of risk – otherwise, counter-intuitive thinking will remain wholly counter-intuitive.

And where's the future in that?

Case History

John Cheston
CEO, Robinsons Group

Interviewed June 2008

Look back

Most would agree visionary thinking tends to suggest looking forward. But this is not always the case.

When, in 2004, John Cheston became CEO of The Robinsons Group, one of Singapore's oldest department store chains (formed in 1858), he seriously questioned the company's long-term vision.

Known for much of its life as the Harrods of Singapore, Robinsons had since the early 80s become a discount department store focusing increasingly on deals-of-the-day and Sales. "When I took over we were on Sale for 225 days a year. Things had gone so far that the business was leasing additional space in big 'expo' halls near the airport, making its numbers by having cheap additional space that could be filled full of sale-or-return goods."

Robinsons heyday
(from James Song Collection, National Archives Singapore)

Although this discount positioning had proved necessary and indeed highly successful during the severe economic downturn in

Asia, Cheston says the company had now allowed itself to turn short-term expediency into a long-term strategy. "Robinsons had become addicted to discounting. Almost as if the brand had forgotten what it stood for. But you can only motivate by price for so long – not forever."

With so many days on discount, Cheston admits there were only a limited number of 'ways' or 'days' the business could drive comparative sales increases. Something radical had to be done and for Cheston there was only one place to look. It involved taking the company back to its roots. Unashamedly going back to its upmarket, exclusive roots – a brave move celebrating everything that had previously made Robinsons an iconic brand, revered and respected around the world. "We were going to have to walk *you can only motivate by price for so long – not forever* away from short-term profit while we detoxified from the drug of quick financial fixes. I was determined to recapture the essence of the Robinsons of old – high-quality merchandise, exclusive products and an outstanding shopping environment."

This, of course, represented a seismic shift in thinking, not only for the business but for customers too. "Over the last 15 or 20 years Robinsons had concentrated on catering to the very local population. Something it had not done before in its distinguished history," explains Cheston. "I realised returning the business to an upmarket position would mean disenfranchising the very people who were keeping the business going. And equally importantly, I realised how difficult it would be to reposition the brand in the minds of the wealthier customers who had abandoned us!"

Trading a brand downmarket is easy – returning it upmarket is near impossible.

But for Cheston going upmarket was the only strategy. Staying down was unsustainable, moving to the middle market wasn't differentiating and so he boldly 'looked back' for inspiration. It meant a huge capital expenditure when sales were falling. And perhaps more daunting, it meant courting new and exciting brands back to his own tarnished brand, particularly difficult during a period of upheaval. It also demanded the company faithfully recreated the ethos of a bygone era by travelling the world sourcing exclusive products. And it meant finding a communication strategy capable of convincing a precisely defined target audience that things had changed to their liking.

Cheston cleverly chose to centre his vision on authenticity – many older customers remembered Robinsons of old, so his efforts to reposition the brand upwards chimed with their affections and offered him an appropriate relaunch platform for the younger market too. Inspiration for all this was found in the archives – wonderfully evocative images were used to great effect for marketing activities that celebrated change, both internally and externally.

Not surprisingly this sudden shift from bazaar to upscale department store resulted in the company taking a big hit on its numbers. "Profits nearly halved in the first year whilst investment increased several-fold," confides Cheston. But this incredibly bright and straight-talking executive from the north of England knew he had to hold his nerve. Honing his management skills at Marks and Spencer, Cheston knew the time-frame to achieve his dramatic turnaround was incredibly tight. He openly agrees he needed to act immediately, capitalising on his honeymoon period. "Change would be expected because of my newness. Whether the sort of change I had in mind *was* totally expected is a moot point!"

But as he admits: "In large part I was pushing on an open door. Selling my strategy upwards was in many respects easy. A growing number of board members felt it was time for change. The workforce was also really supportive, if for no other reason than they were absolutely shattered. The first day I came in I sat down with a group of our people and asked them: if I could do *anything* for them, what would that be? They said stop so much discounting. We're exhausted, we put the bins in, then we put the bins out again."

Good retailing is about change but great retailing demands you take the business with you

Good retailing is about change but great retailing demands you take the business with you.

As Cheston explains, "I knew I couldn't do anything without the workforce being on-side – it's all about being straight and sharing the vision. We hired a hotel and ran six sessions for over 1,000 staff where we shared the 'journey we were going on' and what we wanted to do. We told them there and then that it might impact on their bonuses for a year, but explained the choice was whether they wanted to have a one-year bonus or whether they wanted 10, 20, 30 years worth of bonuses. Everyone in the business eventually bought into the vision, and fortunately so have my customers."

Turnover continues to rocket and profits are at record levels, but more importantly, Cheston believes he has created a business model that is sustainable. The workforce is happy and aligned. "Everyone at Robinsons is now proud to work for the organisation again. They don't feel like they're part of a *passamalan* (Malaysian term for a market stall) any more. We are all engaged and re-energised which is great we're more productive."

And as Cheston explains, Robinsons has its famous brand back too, "which is very important. It helps us make the right decisions – not just the big strategic decisions but the little ones too. Last Christmas we hired a Santa Claus all the way from the USA. A proper white-bearded Santa rather than someone with cotton wool stuck on. We all intuitively knew it had to be a real *more about wrestling the needs of the short term with the wisdom of the long term* Santa for the real Robinsons – word spread, kids were queuing to have their photos with him."

Cheston will undoubtedly reflect on this particular 'turnaround' fondly. The business doctrine of looking back was, for him, the only way forward.

However, the learning for retail leaders, especially the new ones, is that winning thinking is not about whether to look back or not, but more about wrestling the *needs* of the short term with the *wisdom* of the long term.

Get it right and the rewards are immense – get it wrong and a short honeymoon soon ends in divorce.

37

Case History

Michael Kok
Group CEO, Dairy Farm

Interviewed October 2009

Identifying weaknesses

Only seven per cent of the leaders interviewed in this book were internal promotions.

Arguably this is because all businesses need to change over time. Received wisdom implores a 'new broom' is best at sweeping away the past, making room for the future. The strengths and weaknesses of this argument play both ways – not least the fact that internal candidates know what needs to be fixed, but may well be part of what needs fixing!

But with almost 20 years loyal service, no such hesitation was apparent when Michael Kok was promoted to group CEO of the Dairy Farm retail empire based in Hong Kong. Boasting over 5,000 outlets in ten countries throughout Asia, this company is a complex machine. From China and Hong Kong to Singapore and India, it was felt the business needed visionary thinking and *insider* to unleash its potential.

internal candidates know what needs to be fixed, but may well be part of what needs fixing

"I arrived in the role with a big question, 'how do we drive this company forward?' – for me, it lay in addressing our weaknesses," says Kok. "I think weaknesses are the low-hanging fruit; it's usually where the opportunities are and you'd be surprised how far up the tree they go." Dairy Farm is a huge, US$8 billion business with 76,000 employees spanning supermarkets, hypermarkets, health & beauty, convenience stores, home furnishings and a joint venture with a chain of restaurants. Throughout the region its store brands range from Wellcome to Giant, from Mannings to Guardian and from 7-Eleven to a master franchise for IKEA.

Born in Singapore and appointed Group Chief Executive in 2007, Kok is extremely bright, polite and operationally very astute. There's an urgent honesty about his need for change. For him, "a positive mindset within the organization is imperative; I don't want our weaknesses to be viewed as problems, but rather as huge opportunities. Change had to be embraced not feared."

As well as being a point of pride, Kok is aware that being market leader, or number two, in each of his particular markets is a strength that sometimes leads to complacency. So not unreasonably and to kick start his role as leader, he organized an off-site meeting with regional directors and operational heads. As he explains, "We agreed a wide-ranging ten-point plan that supported our strengths but fundamentally made a point of identifying our weaknesses." This plan simplifies into three central themes:

- One, to maximize opportunities and ruthlessly turnaround or divest underperforming businesses.
- Two, to review and invest heavily in IT and intelligence.
- And three, to grow own-label.

As an example of bringing to life the first of his central themes, Kok built on his predecessors' efforts by honing still further Dairy Farm's international presence. "Our strategy is now clear, we'll focus 100 per cent on Asia," says Kok. "The opportunities there, especially places like China, Indonesia and Malaysia, are colossal. We know the market and have the portfolio to succeed – in China and Indonesia we are only scratching the surface." In truth, Kok readily admits Dairy Farm missed a great opportunity several years ago by not being among the leaders to open hypermarkets in China. "But with our proven expertise, I'm now driving a massive and hugely successful roll-out of convenience and health & beauty stores. 7-Eleven is now market leader in South China."

Lateral thinking is core to Kok's approach. "We had a non-performing business in Indonesia. We didn't close down; I changed the entire management team and converted the majority of stores from up-scale supermarkets to our lower-end hypermarket brand, Giant. We're now highly profitable."

Closing non-core countries, developing convenience and health & beauty stores in China and the swift banner/format change in Indonesia. All examples of Kok's vision for eradicating weakness by acknowledging and harnessing the company's inherent strengths.

IT and intelligence is the second major theme to receive Kok's attention. "Historically we haven't invested as much as we should in IT. To grow a company you've got to have embedded processes and infrastructure. But despite much of the region having a reputation for cutting-edge technology, Asia's investment in front-end retail IT is minimal. Previously it was all back-end, financial and firewalls – we didn't even have hand-held terminals for ordering stock in some of our businesses!"

But Kok has approved huge investment in IT and is bringing standardisation across his stable of brands. With his top ten suppliers accounting for 35 per cent of business, Kok now has the tools to collaborate on issues like forecasting, inventory control, supply chain efficiencies and service levels. As he explains, "We're not just demanding bigger discounts; we're genuinely looking for better ways to work together. We've introduced balanced scorecards for suppliers, quantifying key performance indicators and holding them accountable."

But as Kok explains, intelligence is not only externally focused. "We're breaking down 'silo mentality' across our brands. In Hong Kong we have three dominant business units – Wellcome, Mannings and 7-Eleven. In the past they didn't view each other as healthy competition to raise standards but only as competitors. They didn't work together, review suppliers together or share information.

We're breaking down 'silo mentality' across our brands

Astonishingly, in some cases we bought the same merchandise from the same supplier – at different prices. Even though we're in the same building! That's changing fast. Progressively we're *benchmarking* everything within the entire business. It's had a dramatic effect and brought everything into the open. Underlining to people, emotionally and operationally, both internally and externally, that we are *one* business." You can almost feel Kok's frustration at how such strength was allowed to be a weakness for so long.

And the third of Dairy Farm's central imperatives is to grow own-label sales. Kok's normally inscrutable expression positively beams as he recounts how the business is now fully engaged with this. "Previously, own-label had represented just two and a half per cent of total sales. There was no ownership, no leadership – that's changed. In just two and a half years own-label penetration has nearly quadrupled and with the world banking crisis continuing to bite, customers love the value. But we must encourage and educate our customers to appreciate own-label even when money is less tight. In this region, however, it's all *skilfully used weakness to drive a business forward* about product safety and quality. Quality assurance is fundamental, we must expand our own-label at a careful and deliberate pace – one day I'd like 20 per cent of sales." Not an outrageously ambitious figure by international standards but considering Dairy Farm is a non-customer-facing name, it's certainly a challenging target. Kok uses *benchmarking* to negotiate scale economies on behalf of individual formats – further evidence of the group's latent strength overcoming evident weaknesses.

On every dimension, Kok's vision and masterplan enjoys success. Since arriving, profit growth has been around 17 per cent a year, exceeding previous performances. It's all work-in-progress, but the lesson here is surely the skilful way Kok has used weakness to drive a business forward. Not dwelling on negativity but promoting the opportunity it presents.

Maybe something best suited to an insider?

SECRET FOUR – SUMMARY

Visionary Thinking: Tips for success

- Understand and appreciate visionary thinking is not always the same as a Vision.

- Visionary thinking is about capturing a spirit of tomorrow and actually translating it day in, day out. Galvanising businesses to move with, and ahead of the times.

- The most impactful visionary thinking tends to be a subtle blend of counter-intuitiveness and prescience. Delighting customers by satisfying their needs that hadn't existed before.

- Unfortunately, research can't create this type of thinking, only refine it.

- Paradoxically, visionary thinking can either embrace or eschew the past.

- Not unreasonably but often ignored, visionary thinking that involves crossing cultural boundaries demands empathy, with unspoken rules needing to be heard.

- And as Nelson Mandela famously said, "The most elusive, and therefore the most desired, quality of leadership is vision." Managers with aspirations must take heed.

So if you only remember one thing from this section, remember:

Your biggest competitor is your own view of the future.*

[* with thanks to Larry Hochman for this quote taken from: The Relationship Revolution: Closing the Customer Promise Gap, John Wiley & Sons, Ltd]

SECRET 5

IDEAS

IDEAS

Key part

I am often asked about the executives I've interviewed.

Often asked if there's a retail gene. I think there is, but maybe that's for another book.

Without exception however, I have enjoyed the creative energy of each and every leader. After the initial, well-rehearsed 'company line', their individual love of creativity always shone through. Wide-eyed and excited by the power of 'ideas', each has enthusiastically shared anecdotes of how creative thought processes, intuitive or intellectual, have helped them win.

all the leaders featured in this book talked excitedly about the power of a creative thought

Of course this is hardly surprising given the other retail secrets to success. Ideas will always be the leap that brings to life the thinking and processes for *being chosen.*

Founder or financial wizard, marketing or merchandise guru, whatever their background all the leaders featured in this book talked excitedly about the power of a creative thought. In acknowledgement, I have made the pursuit of ideas my fifth secret to retail success.

Desired action

You would think it obvious that executives love ideas.

But in my thirty or so years in advertising and marketing, I have found this is not always the case.

To some, ideas were threatening. To them, ideas had the power to threaten the status quo. And there were many who simply found more comfort in the 'known'. Ideas are also snuffed out by people playing to their own agenda – often known colloquially as 'well-poisoning'. This type of negativity is a particularly insidious science. It means the whole process of ideas and decision-making starts from a negative stance, needing to be cleansed before positive action can move things forward. And I am not talking about rigour; rigorous thinking is good. I am talking about people who are energy sinks. They put unnecessary and time-consuming pressures on those who champion creative thought in pursuit of winning. I was once told that *profit is the reward of risk,* and I find this a particularly effective thought when dealing with energy black holes and well-poisoners.

But let's be clear, all the executives I interviewed for *The art of being chosen* were tingling with creative endeavour and loved the whole idea of ideas.

Indeed the leaders I spoke to celebrated ideas as the process to translate rigorous thought into actionable and powerful influences. Appreciating how great ideas neatly engage audiences into desired actions. Understanding the core purpose of an idea is to disrupt patterns, that need to be disrupted. And they saw how creativity was a vehicle to allow a 'thought' to punch above its weight.

A great idea

Not everyone can create ideas. Not everyone can recognise good ones from bad. Indeed it takes a particular skill to recognise the power and potential of an idea.

As Carl Jung, the influential Swiss thinker claimed, "everyone is in love with his own ideas." This may or may not be cynical but the difficulty of creative thinking is knowing if you've just seen, heard or had a good one!

From experience, retail businesses with a well defined and well articulated understanding of how they are *being chosen,* certainly appear to recognise great ideas quicker than others.

But interestingly, ideas that fail often educate as eloquently as raging successes.

The boss of Draegers, from Secret Three, soon realised his discerning customers felt patronised by normal advertising. This led to a more refined marketing agenda with phenomenal success. And I remember working on a campaign idea for a chain of retail bakers in the UK. Research unsurprisingly told them that people hated waiting in line for their products. So not unreasonably they adopted a self-service option. The trouble was, this bakery chain enjoyed a market point of difference by freshly baking and making up many products on the premises. Self-service meant they were effectively defaulting to the competition – where product wasn't freshly prepared.

interestingly, ideas that fail often educate as eloquently as raging successes

The better idea was to create a store format where customers were encouraged to value the 'preparation' time, celebrating what made the brand unique. This insight was a huge success.

But what I have found is that successful leaders seem to have an effective process in place for ideas, particularly creative ideas. As well as trusted lieutenants and 'filtering systems for well-poisoners', some have developed bespoke tests for ideas. HMV, in Secret Two, has an interesting combination of magnetic north and a funnel. And Bunnings, in Secret Five, leans very heavily on a business process and idea from an American academic institution to test what 'good' looks like on a day to day basis.

Sweet thought

It is clear that great ideas are the lifeblood of great retailing. They fluently bring to life creative thoughts and visionary thinking and are the reason every case study in this book boasts wonderful examples.

The most creative thoughts are seemingly simple. Betraying complex thinking, each always has a single essential thread that pulls many issues tidily together to help people absorb information. I remember a presentation when someone grabbed a handful of sugar cubes from a coffee tray and threw them at a poor innocent, challenging him to catch them. The recipient didn't catch any. But as was explained later, if only one cube had been thrown, the chances are it would have been caught.

As I picked the sugar crumbs off my jacket I reflected on what a great lesson I'd just had, one I would never forget. When loading information into an idea, it's only one central thought that can really be caught by the audience. Interestingly I'd read about this sugar cube demonstration in a marketing textbook but it still took me by surprise – I also decided to make a 'career decision' and declined to point out to my superior that ideas are at their most powerful when original!

However, for the clever and ambidextrous amongst us, a secondary thought to support the core message of the idea is sometimes allowed!

Sticky is best

To work, ideas have to be memorable. Ideas must stick.

No amount of visionary thinking can help a business to be chosen if the audience can't remember what they've been told. And when decoding how the great retailers get their ideas to work, I simply can't think of a better idea than borrowing from the most wonderful book, *Made to Stick* by Chip and Dan Heath.[†]

I have read many books on communication, marketing and advertising in my time but this is simply the best ever. *Made to Stick* is a remarkably user-friendly book where the reader glides effortlessly from page to page unlocking the secrets of how to get ideas to stand out, be understood and remembered.

there's no set formula for a sticky idea but they have unearthed a set of traits common to the really great ones

Chip and Dan claim there's no set formula for a sticky idea but they have unearthed a set of traits common to the really great ones. I paraphrase the broad outline below but urge you to buy their phenomenally authoritative book on the subject.

Unforgettable

Naturally I love their first idea to use the acronym: SUCCES.

[†]Dan Heath and Chip Heath, *Made to Stick: Why Some Ideas Take Hold and Others Come Unstuck*, Arrow Books Ltd

It not only acts as a perfect checklist for ideas, it cleverly prioritizes the elements as far as I am concerned – a complex thought process easily digested:

- **S**implicity. They talk about finding the essential core of what's trying to be communicated. Flying sugar cubes spring to mind!

- Unexpectedness. Here counter-intuitiveness is the key with a goal to violating people's expectations. Getting them to sit-up and take note.

- Concreteness. This is an imperative to explain things in terms of human actions, in terms of sensory information. Things we can imagine.

- Credibility. This is instrumental in keeping scepticism to a minimum. Information should be presented in a way that allows the audience to test the thought – to mentally 'try before they buy'.

- Emotions. The whole idea of emotion is central to an idea that sticks. The aim therefore is to make people feel something – we are wired to feel for people not abstractions.

- Stories. People remember stories better than information. They can't act on anything if they don't remember what's been said.

Joined-up

What has impressed me most is how the really successful retail businesses totally grab hold of an idea and run with it. And how *being chosen* always informs this process.

Be it strategic or tactical, internal or external, every idea I have had recounted permeates as many parts of a business as possible. It might be about

Successful ideas seem to demand that there are no boundaries

change management or simply about suggestions. It might the mechanics of delivering an idea or a compelling thought for institutional investors. Successful ideas seem to demand that there are no boundaries.

Creative thinking has been shown to be at its most effective when it is joined-up throughout the businesses.

Varying proportions

Let me finish this introduction about ideas with three personal favourites. It would be wrong to single out any from my travels so I'll share these with you to specifically demonstrate how a simple idea can inform a business in varying proportions and intensities.

- *Business:* I once heard the boss of the enormous American retailer, Home Depot, talk about a profound business thought. Whether or not this is a classic 'idea', in terms of Dan & Chip's observations, I've personally never forgotten it and I suggest most retailers shouldn't either. It was: to *not* let the few dictate to the many. In his business he wasn't going to let the two per cent of dishonest customers set the agenda for the other ninety eight. It was in response to a promotion that had the vague possibility of being abused by some of his customers. It struck me as a really simple thought, resonating well and effortlessly galvanising the business around a great customer service ethic. He was subsequently proved right. Very few abused the promotion, everyone else adored it.

- *Merchandise:* what's in a name? A golfing buddy, Alan Bradley, made a fortune in the cut-flower retail business, eventually supplying London's largest and chicest companies. He started out selling from a barrow in the Portobello Road – one of London's fashionable markets. On one occasion he was struggling to sell some beautifully lush fern plants he'd speculatively bought from his wholesaler. In desperation he tried bundling them up with exotic flowers and even slashing the price. But customers still wouldn't accept them. He then realised he wasn't giving his customers a reason to value the ferns and so he came up with a simple idea. He decided to re-brand them 'love leaves'. This immediately aroused curiosity and when asked, he claimed he didn't know why they were called love leaves but he was certainly putting some in his own bedroom. Those who buy from market stalls expect the truth to be stretched, enjoying 'caveat emptor'. But with this creative idea the fern leaves became a huge success. Customers coming back weekend after weekend to refresh their wonderful talking points in the bedroom.

- *Marketing:* I sit on the expert judging panel of the World Retail Congress and was recently asked to judge advertising & marketing entries. JC Penney went on to win the digital category with 'Beware of the Doghouse'. Fundamentally they came up with some fabulous lateral thinking culminating in a simple idea. People who had bought so-called 'bad gifts' were consigned to a doghouse. An incredibly engaging website was created where dissatisfied recipients of gifts were encouraged to send 'significant others' to the JC Penney doghouse. The only way out was to start giving good gifts. Exiting the dog house wasn't easy – often involving harsh subjective reasoning. But jewelry from JC Penney was a sure-fire winning method. Having worked on many department store accounts, I know just how hard it is to *own* the gifting sector at competitive times of year and what particularly impressed me was the simplicity of thought disguising really complex, emotional insights. It was executed beautifully with a viral campaign complete with click-through links to the social network sites. This was a hugely successful and simple idea loaded with nuance, demanding ownership from every Associate in the business. I am glad the other judges agreed with me on its quality.

Just because

I start my specific introductions to the case studies for secret five with Holt Renfrew of Canada. Andrew Jennings specifically asked that he be first and when I enquired why, he said why not? It seemed an odd *a disrupting thought when* request and the only time I've been *he made the request* asked. But that's the idea. He wanted it and he knew how to get what he wanted. It was a disrupting thought when he made the request and I haven't forgotten it in two years and a hundred interviews. It's an honour to put him first, and as you will see the honour was eventually all his.

The interviews

- **Holt Renfrew** is one of Canada's foremost specialty store groups. With a simple idea to 'wake up Canada' this 165-year-old retailer achieved phenomenal success by punching considerably above its weight. With a set of five golden rules, the business was led to successfully redefine itself.

- **Desigual** is the fast-growing irreverent young fashion retailer spreading throughout Europe. With a wickedly unconventional personality this brand needed a simple idea to engage and inspire it's ever growing army of customers. Paint and parties were the hugely successful idea.

- **Bunnings** is Australasia's number one home improvement retailer. What an executive heard on a business course has laid the foundations for a change management programme that has effortlessly galvanized the entire business. An idea so effective it's helping deliver record profits and a new internal shorthand.

- **Saks Fifth Avenue** is one of America's iconic department store groups. With a flagship store in New York City this retailer captured the imagination of savvy local shoppers and hard-nosed media with a compelling piece of creative thinking. A profitable idea so simple that others have tried to copy it – but all have failed.

- **Peter Sheppard Shoes** is a magnificent statement to the Australian market of how to offer comfort and fashion. A small retailer by global standards, the success enjoyed today is down to a simple idea, ruthlessly executed and uncompromisingly delivered.

- **Radio Shack** now has 7,000 electronics stores throughout the USA and is understandably a formidable retail force. It took a simple thought, by a brand new boss, to save the business. An easily understood idea that gave the business a purpose – immediately turning it around and opening up incremental revenue streams to secure a profitable future.

- **Titan Industries** is an enormous Indian company with a watch and clock retail division. With a remarkable piece of thinking this company challenged one of retail's oldest conventions. It was a simple idea convincing customers across a network of 8,000 outlets that it was time to change habits of a life time.

- **Hot Topic** is on a new journey with its brand and near-700-store estate. With a compellingly simple idea born out of necessity, this American young fashion, music and entertainment retailer is now offering its adoring customers something really new. With access to celebrities that money can't buy and showcasing highly localised music, this dynamic retailer is looking to break the mould.

Case History

Andrew Jennings
Former President, Holt Renfrew

Interviewed April 2008

Nessun cliché

In recent years the term 'retail theatre' has been over-used.

But every so often an idea raises the bar so high that 'theatre' hardly describes it – how's it done?

Andrew Jennings is a polished individual. One of a rare breed of truly global retail executives – to date, he has worked across three continents running iconic brands including Harrods, Saks Fifth Avenue and now Woolworths South Africa. But it was during his time as President of the Canada-based specialty store group, Holt Renfrew, that he devised and delivered *Viva Italia*. An in-store event that not only achieved the objective of igniting interest for all things Italian across Canada but almost single-handedly gave his target audience permission to re-think their views on Holt Renfrew stores in general and the brand in particular. In Jennings'

the idea was to own words, "When I took the business over
'wake up Canada' it was an iconic, 165-year-old Canadian brand that was underperforming and failing to deliver a holistic customer experience – today it is one of the most successful and vibrant speciality retail businesses in the world."

However it is described, *Viva Italia* was an incredible bit of theatre.

As enormous as it was extravagant, this three-week spectacular celebrated all things Italian, from food and wine to fashion and home. "I was very certain what I was trying to do, the idea was to 'wake up Canada' and create a one-of-a-kind lifestyle event positioning Holt Renfrew at the forefront of global retailing. My sponsors came from the great Italian fashion houses including Armani and Dolce & Gabbana with a host of top designers such as Roberto Cavalli and James Ferragamo making personal appearances at the gala evenings. I even persuaded Sophia Loren to join the celebrations as Patron of Honour. Viva Italia enjoyed record sales, accounted for an increase of over 20 per cent in customer traffic and enjoyed domestic and international media coverage worth more than US$7 million."

Jennings is certainly not a person to think small. When anyone sets a goal of wanting to 'wake up Canada' to Italian products with a bit of retail theatre, they had better know what they are doing and certainly know how to go about it. "My focus in everything starts with the customer and ends with the customer. The

Andrew Jennings greeting Sophia Loren – Patron of Honour

customer needed to understand that we had magnificent international merchandise, merchandise they'd hardly ever seen before and that our business was now very, very different – we needed to do something so grand we'd literally wake up Canada and have them say *wow*." With a vision punctuated with the occasional cliché, Jennings delivered his success with some original thinking and tactics.

Throughout the process Jennings insisted that he and his team never accepted 'no' for an answer. Literally never accepting 'no' as a response, literally developing a mindset that found 'no' unacceptable. From the beginning, he developed a potent sense-check of what was needed and what was needed to be done to get it.

For this, Jennings had five golden rules beginning, sensibly, with giving sufficient time to complete a project. "From two years out we started developing relationships, talking with the Italian government and then with the fashion designers and various suppliers," he recalls.

The initial stages were taken up with convincing the rest of the business of the merits of the event and never missing an opportunity to advocate the benefits at all levels. As Jennings explains, this leads onto the second rule – creating a committed team. "They must be strong, optimistic individuals, who can absorb the

literally developing a mindset that found 'no' unacceptable

day to day pressures without losing enthusiasm or focus. Critically they must be 'naturals' at re-building confidences and supporting members of the team who have taken setbacks."

What should not be forgotten is that beyond the core team, an enormous amount of enthusiasm is generated within the rest of the organisation from such events – the halo effect. Not only because it represents a big opportunity to sell more products but because it engages and excites everybody. "Everyone wants newness and everyone wants to be part of a winning team, this enthusiasm must be harnessed. Never forget, done well, events such as these always elevate the reputation of a business and, on an on-going basis, help attract a better calibre of staff."

Without support from employees and the core team it would be incredibly tough to adhere to Jennings' third golden rule: avoid obstacles. His proven strategy is to be pretty single-minded: "Sometimes I will just say, this is how it's going to be and *you find* a solution, find me someone who can walk through that wall."

Truly big promotions mean truly hard work, so be ready for the budget keepers. Nine times out of ten Jennings reckons people hide behind budgets. Be prepared and have a plan for this, and the walls will begin to crumble. "For big retail theatre the wall-breaker is sponsorship." And amassing plenty of it is his fourth golden rule. With *Viva Italia* sponsorship came, impressively, from the Italian government as well as suppliers. "For signing-up the really big names like American Express it's a case of strong belief in your plan and a very well rehearsed, very well articulated payback," explains Jennings. "Anything is possible. It's all a matter of just putting a plan together and then finding solutions to that plan – they're always there if you look hard enough!"

Jennings and his team certainly 'walked through many walls' for *Viva Italia*: He negotiated with suppliers, who'd heard it all before;

negotiated with credit cards, who'd heard it all before; and negotiated with the Italian government, who'd *never* heard it before. And succeeded, all for just a 12-store speciality store group in Canada!

And just in case Jennings' methods were sounding rather logical, his fifth golden rule is to start at the end!

Or as Jennings puts it: "My plans always begin with the end in mind, the vision. This is the picture I'd like to paint and everyone says 'wow' (there's another cliché), how are we going to do it? I simply set up a critical path and then crucially involve and engage the right people in the detail of building the plan."

Jennings believes that if you think small you'll deliver small, so he's never done that. Besides the hugely successful numbers this piece of 'retailing' delivered, and besides all the glitz and glamour it took to do so, what is *if you think small* remarkable is that *Viva Italia* was an idea *you'll deliver small* that truly *did* wake up the Canadian public – and in the process completely redefined what Holt Renfrew stood for, how people *felt* about the group. That's big retail theatre.

And the President of the Republic of Italy awarded Jennings the *Onorficienza of Grande Officiale al Merito,* its highest civilian award for his endeavours. 'Wow' – nessun cliché.

Case History

Manel Adell
CEO, Desigual

Interviewed May 2008

Very conventional

It's not rocket science. If a business's roots are sown in *unconventionalism* then its brand should reflect this.

And for retailers there's no bigger visual expression of a brand than their stores.

One of Spain's newest and most unconventional young fashion brands is the fast-moving manufacturer and now fast-growing retailer, Desigual. Boasting a proudly irreverent collection of garments aimed at youngsters desperate to make a statement, Desigual stores have done the same by differentiating themselves through quirky interiors.

An amiable and charismatic individual with a glint of steely commercial fun in his eye, the brand's unquestionably Spanish chief executive, Manel Adell explains: "We sell jeans and urban casual wear, they are very graphic with edgy messages, and when we expanded into retail we wanted to translate this philosophy into our store environment."

someone who would break the rules of architectural convention

Eschewing the conventional route of simply transferring the gritty statements onto the walls of their new stores, the company's Swiss founder, Thomas Meyer, along with Adell, commissioned a famous Spanish industrial designer Marti Guixé (who refers to himself as an ex-designer!) to create an appropriate environment for their first store. They wanted someone who would break the rules of architectural convention. "Guixé's big idea was to leave the shop's interior finish white and throw a party with a disc jockey, serve red wine and traditional Spanish ham. We'd then choose a colour palette and invite artists to decorate the walls in an event that will last no more than two hours. And that was it." Adell adds, both metaphorically and literally, "By the end of the party the company had a unique store."

Street-artists, classic artists, graffitists, painters and graphic designers were invited to decorate this first store – but they were all friends of the company. Adell intuitively knew that while it was a great idea, they had missed a great opportunity.

Great retail is about engaging local audiences and

Typical store opening 'painting party'

the customer base. With this in mind Adell revamped his second store launch. "This time we invited around 100 ordinary people, virtually off the street. We just welcomed them in, gave them a paintbrush, a glass of wine and a slice of ham. I arrived 10 minutes late and was shocked, it was such a strong emotion that hit me. A real positive energy. People couldn't believe what they were seeing or indeed, creating. What it achieved for us was to create something completely different, a different kind of fashion destination. What a special way to announce our arrival. It was so us, so 'on-brand'. And best of all, something people felt part of. This store can still be seen today in Barcelona."

Adell's subsequent research affirmed his intuition and the faith he had put into this wholly unconventional launch statement. "The first thing a customer buys is the shop – and the second is the product itself. We managed to create a very strong identity as a fashion retailer from day one, and sell a lot too. We all know brands are built over many years and over many details but we couldn't have dreamed of a better start."

This style of launch and decoration continued for the next 40 or so stores. However, such was the diverse mix of artistic styles involved that Adell decided to refine the process to achieve some cohesion. A three-colour palette was introduced until eventually, through a series of refinements, the 'decorators' were given only two minutes to work on the store using spray paints. None of these refinements seemed to dull the excitement for the brand. But if engaging the target audience was important to Adell, getting buy-in from his teams was crucial. As he explains, "We definitely succeeded in this. Some employees became addicted to the parties and attended each opening. It set the tone of our retail identity, of our brand, as well as the sort of people we now attract and retain."

People couldn't believe what they were seeing or indeed, creating.

Having impressively engaged both his customers and teams, Adell was aware of the need to create and maintain what PR executives refer to as 'mo' (momentum). For this he turned next to the press, inviting them to decorate an area of the store as they filmed themselves. "Not unnaturally, it received massive coverage and helped fuel the continuing brand development process."

Ultimately, successful ideas are measured by profits. With a universal appeal to the young and a clear understanding of what they stand for, Desigual has detailed plans for global expansion including the emerging markets. This young company is now Europe-wide and has grown 20-fold in six years with turnover over of US$150 million. Year seven, 2009, is forecast to show over 50 per cent growth with more than a quarter of a billion dollars in sales, derived from 130 company-owned stores, 250 shop-in-shops in major department stores worldwide and over 4,000 outlets served on a wholesale basis.

Like the first young audience Desigual was designed to appeal to, the company is growing up too.

And although the parties with radical painting are no longer part of a launch programme, the fundamental principles of being individual and different are still a strong guiding influence. "Because of the many openings across borders, the local painting parties were more difficult to implement and like any brand, especially a young fashion brand, we've had to move on, evolve. But the new stores still feature hand-painted graphics done in a very spontaneous manner. Currently, our new format replicates the famous market of Boqueria in Barcelona – the concept is based on the vibrant merchandising techniques of a local market environment, not what you expect of a fashion store, it's unconventional and so I am excited!"

There are many who talk of the importance of engaging customers but few can match the commitment of Desigual. It's always easier for smaller companies to embrace radical ideas, but the learning here underlines how success comes from a deeply held belief of what the brand stands for. It's then just a simple matter of *allowing* this to inform and guide decision making.

Sadly for some, Adell and his team have put aside the paintbrush and in a move that at first appears to celebrate Spain more than unconventional thinking, they now only launch their stores with a party, guitar-playing and Spanish ham. They have well reasoned arguments for this, all *Letting youngsters loose with a paintbrush and a glass of wine 'beggars belief'* claimed to be on-brand and centred on the need for the company *and* its customers to find new ways to express themselves during store launches. But for the purists, the ham will be a constant reminder of the company's healthy appetite for quirkiness.

Letting youngsters loose with a paintbrush and a glass of wine 'beggars belief' and is certainly not for everyone, but that's the point of this idea. Flamboyant store interiors is *not* what this initiative is all about.

It's about a brilliant idea, a brilliant piece of unconventional thinking born from the strict disciplines of good branding – all very conventional.

Case History

John Gillam
Managing Director, Bunnings

Interviewed June 2008

It's academic

There are many phenomenally successful retail executives who could never be accused of being academic.

Historically, retail has prided itself on intuitive prowess. Executives proudly seduced by the immediacy and simplicity of tills delivering their clinical verdicts. But as the expectations of customers become more sophisticated, academia is playing an increasingly important role in modern retailing.

John Gillam is a deliberate, eloquent and highly intelligent individual. As Managing Director of Bunnings Australia, he is fashioning a very successful metamorphosis of his huge home improvement business with the help of an academic model imported from the USA.

The need for change in retail is nothing new but as Gillam explains, "what helps the process significantly is having a signpost that consistently points you in the right direction, ensuring everybody within the organisation stays onboard during the journey."

seduced by the immediacy and simplicity of tills delivering their clinical verdicts

And signposts are especially important when dramatic change is planned. In the early 1990s, having seen the success enjoyed by others around the world, the management of Bunnings made the decision to move their long-established hardware/home improvement store chain to Big Box formats.

While many in retail use the measured efficiency of change management consultants, others rely simply on their sheer force of personality to steer them through the hazardous waters of 'change'. But Bunnings has successfully chosen as its navigator the 'Pentagon and Triangle'. Originating from the William & Mary Mason School of Business in America it's a business model (and study course – where it was discovered by a Bunnings executive) that represents the eight ways to win in retailing. According to Gillam the idea is, "the pentagon defines *how you're going to win* – it's the five key points of a retail offer that a customer can see - location, product, price, people and promotion. And inside the pentagon is a triangle which graphically details the logistics, various systems to deliver success and, along with this, a productivity model, too. Which all means there's a framework that ties in what the brand stands for, with what the buyers are doing and what the stores are supposed to look like. You end up with a business language that's also your operational language which is all about delivering a winning offer."

a framework that ties in what the brand stands for, with what the buyers are doing and what the stores are supposed to look like

Initially, the Pentagon and Triangle helped provide the Bunnings team with a framework around which an 'offer' could be defined. This involved looking first at location. "We worked out what the customer attributes were concerning location. So we chose to focus on physical and geographical convenience. We chased three-hectare standalone sites in order to have lots of car parking. We then looked at range. Big Box meant width and depth, so a strong position was built around each of our specialist categories. For value and promotion, we went for EDLP (Every Day Low Pricing). Customers want products when they need them, not just when things are on Sale. And for our people, we believed that an ambition to deliver the best service was essential – when you're doing something around your house, more often than not you'll need advice and help".

While much of this thinking falls under the heading of *classic retail* insight, the key benefit of the programme is executional direction.

"We'd known all these attributes from the business we were already running but we used the methodology of the Pentagon and Triangle to help us clarify our thinking. The whole idea is user-friendly and undeniably inclusive. It helped the business understand and communicate what was needed for a successful transition to Big Box formats. It was a tool that enabled us as a business to collectively agree and define our offer and bring it to life every day. It also gave us a shape for how to think about the market and our competitors – define a way of going to market with clear points of difference that customers valued."

One of the most important aspects of the methodology was that it provided a framework to talk about the company's offer in a style the merchants and store managers could understand. "It gives you a language, a vocabulary and a shorthand to tie everything together and articulate what we are trying to achieve. It allows lots of people who are coming at things from very different angles in the business to 'click' and talk to each other. The beauty of this particular model is that it's not bogged down in jargon. It's very accessible to all concerned yet rigorously keeps everyone moving in the same direction – whether they're 'born and bred' diehard retailers or young graduates pushing the boundaries of retail convention. For me the test of a good business model is whether it's self-policing, whether the various teams know what 'good' looks like and feel they know how to act accordingly."

a tool to collectively agree and define our offer and bring it to life every day

Gillam is very keen, "to make space for the business to keep innovating within this framework. I never forget we've always got the challenge that customers love consistency but if somebody has got something new, they're going to love that too. The question always is, how can you be consistent *and* change? The answer is, welcome to the challenge that is Retail. For me a good brand is like an old friend that always behaves in a predictable way. Customers must understand and expect that part of your predictable behaviour is being new and innovative. So my desired customer response is: I'll go straight to Bunnings because they'll definitely have it. And when they get to us, I want them to say hey, isn't that great they've got this too!"

Change is all about progress and development. And rather like a shark, retailers will die if they don't keep moving forward. Successful change therefore is the lifeblood of any retail operation with effective communication at its heart. And here must surely be the learning from this case study.

Bunnings used the Pentagon and Triangle method to define how the company wanted to start playing as a Big Box operator. Gillam and his team now use this idea to challenge themselves on consistency and innovation. And it has worked to devastating effect. Over the course of 14 years Bunnings has grown nearly 30-fold and now operates 170 big store formats out of a total estate of 230. The group *understand and expect that part of your predictable behaviour is being new and innovative.* is now ranked as the region's number one home improvement retailer and generates a profitable turnover over US$5 billion across Australia and New Zealand.

There are many who would choose a different method to effect change. But that's irrelevant.

As a retail leader, the skill is to find an idea and process that identifies and delivers the necessary change. In fact any process will do – so long as it works for them, their customers and most importantly their internal audience.

That's what's important – the rest is academic.

41

Case History

Steve Sadove
Chairman and CEO, Saks Fifth Avenue

Interviewed June 2008

Lifting the lid

Retail lore dictates the higher the floor, the lower the sales.

Not unreasonably, people become progressively indifferent to what's going on, the further they have to climb.

How then did America's Saks Fifth Avenue get the hugely popular and prestigious *The Today Show* to broadcast live from the opening of a shoe department on their eighth floor?

"I believe this was just one big example in a whole series of others, that have gotten people to notice Saks as a company that's really out there, trying and doing different things and getting noticed," says Steve Sadove, Chairman and CEO.

Sadove joined the iconic department store group as Vice Chairman

in January 2002 and was promoted to CEO in 2006. He is relatively new to retailing, having spent the previous 25 years in FMCG with prominent successes in creating household brands. Under his various stewardships, Clairol achieved pre-eminent

Steve Sadove left, with celebrity look-alikes at 10022-SHOE launch

hair care status and Herbal Essences Shampoo was launched and became a billion-dollar business in the US alone. So for this savvy, cerebrally dynamic and measured executive, thinking big is just a small part of his repertoire.

When Sadove arrived at Saks he viewed staff motivation as a key issue to be addressed – throughout his executive career he has always seen this as the engine of a business. His solutions at Saks were, "to encourage innovation from within, work hard at internal communications, scrupulously let staff know they were valued, and celebrate ideas." And it was this change in management ethos that led to one of the most celebrated PR scoops in the history of Saks and a master class in creative thinking.

A wonderfully simple and highly effective idea.

Encouraged to think freely and innovate, Sadove's teams came up with an idea that had New Yorkers talking about the launch of a shoe boutique in a department store, gasping at the audacity of the venture. While some sceptical commentators might *one of the most celebrated PR scoops in the history of Saks and a master class in creative thinking* have argued it wasn't the most compelling bit of retail news to hit town, the fact that most people did was testament to the power of creative thinking and eloquent execution. And certainly an acknowledgement that Sadove's new regime was working.

It was August 2007 that saw the opening of what Sadove claims to be the world's largest luxury shoe department, taking up the entire 8,500 sq ft of selling space on the eighth floor. An instinctive marketing man, Sadove was convinced that only an idea of the highest order would be enough to generate the kind of footfall necessary to make this stunning new department a success – especially given its elevated position. He set the business the challenge of capturing the imagination of New Yorkers and their media.

"Terron Schaefer, Senior Vice President of Marketing had the idea of going to the US Postal Department and requesting a Zip code," explains Sadove. "Every home and business address has one, but never before had a Zip been granted to a floor. Nor had the normally redundant four characters at the end of Zip numbers ever been used as a letter suffix."

Schaeffer's team came up with the inspired idea of creating '10022-SHOE' – this meant the near billion-dollar turnover flagship store could boast a shoe department *so big it has its own zip code*. The US Post Department eventually agreed (Nike and Coke have since tried to copy the idea without success) and this eccentric piece of US history became the basis for a relatively cost-free marketing campaign. A bona-fide series of limited edition 41-cent stamps also commemorated the event, with brands like Gucci and Prada featuring their product on the stamp faces.

Thanks to the new can-do, cross-departmental corporate culture, and stiletto-sharp marketing, the '10022-SHOE' department was born, attracting incredibly high-profile media coverage. "As soon as we started talking about it everyone wanted to know more," says Sadove. "It was instantaneous in terms of PR. *The Today Show* decided to broadcast its opening live, *The Oprah Show* wanted to cover it, we were everywhere, you can imagine. The *New York Post* dedicated a two-page spread to the opening, detailing the layout of the floor, again not costing Saks a cent. The promotion went phenomenally well, creating a buzz right across New York and instilling a real sense of achievement in the staff at Saks!"

a shoe department so big it has its own zip code

10022-SHOE was an ingenious piece of marketing but the reality had to live up to customer expectations. Here Sadove played his part too. "Nothing gets the various teams' creative juices flowing like a bold investment decision and I authorized an express elevator from ground floor direct to level eight, making access simple and speedy." The innovative culture encouraged by Sadove was clearly delivering results with the retail team succeeding in creating a vast, stunning, head-turning sales space of genuine *destination* status. As well as presenting a seemingly endless display boasting an incredible range, supported by a 10,000-pair inventory, the department was designed with sociability and interaction in mind.

"The idea was to create a more of a living-type room; a conversational place. As part of the design, seating is arranged so that customers trying on shoes are sitting right opposite each other. Being New York, banter strikes up with people complementing each other's choices." The idea is that the customers are essentially selling to each other.

"With a special space like this, there are countless great stories of the kind of interaction that goes on. On one occasion a couple out shopping got chatting to a fellow customer who told them she was a chorus line singer on Broadway. The singer loved two pairs of shoes but said she could only afford one pair. They chatted for some time and the husband says: 'Tell you what. If you sing me a song, I'll buy you a pair of shoes.' So she got up in front of the entire crowd, sang a Broadway song, and the guy whipped out his American Express card and bought her the shoes."

The idea is that the customers are essentially selling to each other.

Most experienced retailers would baulk at the risky manoeuvre of transferring a core, high-margin, department from the relative safety of a low floor to the dizzying heights of the eighth. But by inspiring and encouraging his management teams to think creatively as well as laterally, Sadove has overseen another career success by launching 10022-SHOE. Posting an impressive sales uplift of over 50 per cent in its first year.

Sadove and his 'can-do' team created a world-class idea that resonated with its audience. It also confounded hardened sceptics by persuading a government department to do something really different. They had the motivation and drive to turn an audacious idea into a profitable reality.

Besides celebrating some truly creative thinking, the learning from this initiative is clear. Big success needs big thinking. But this can only be achieved by people who talk to each other and feel valued 'big-time'.

In the three-dimensional world that is retail, encouraging these people to think outside the box takes leadership – someone who is big enough to lift the lid.

Case History

Peter Sheppard
Founder, Peter Sheppard Shoes

Interviewed June 2008

Given the choice

If you're going to open a shop, why not sell what people love?

And women love shoes. By their own admission they have an almost unfathomable relationship with these essential accessories. Hugely emotional and often irrational, the special bond they have with shoes is well known.

Why then would anyone running a shop selling shoes choose to make things more difficult?

Step forward Peter Sheppard, an outstanding shoe retailer headquartered in Melbourne. A typical antipodean, he is open, forthright, extremely likable and utterly competitive. And when it comes to matters of the female foot, this passionate retailer knows his subject so well he chooses to give his customers something his competitors find difficult to equal – comfort!

Sheppard's incredibly profitable achievement is centred around one big idea. He offer ladies' shoes, not just in an impressive range of styles, colours and half sizes, but in a range of five width fittings as well. Although stock control skills are a crucial element of his

The idea is, we openly learn from them – they openly trust us

particular business (launched in the 1970s), he believes his success goes beyond this. "Anybody can develop a stock control system but it's the execution that matters," explains Sheppard. "You've got to be able to read between the spreadsheet lines of what's reported and understand what it means. For me it's having the patience to build a business slowly, brick by brick so you understand it inside out. Understand the history and individual elements of its success. Build with the solid tools of knowledge and success, not dreams and investment. Offering consistency is crucial too, these customers come to us again and again. The idea is, we openly learn from them – they openly trust us."

Putting the vagaries of style, colour and self-projection to one side, for one emotionally-charged shoe purchase, the SKU logistics are breathtaking. "Buying for multi-width is a big investment," says Sheppard. "If you buy one pair of every size available you're looking at 104 pairs. But obviously in the average sizes you've got to buy more than one pair. So to offer just one popular style, in one store, you'd probably need to buy around 200 pairs as an opening order."

When multiplying these figures by style and by colour the enormity of the logistical challenge emerges. How and why does he do it?

Sheppard is relaxed on these points. "80 per cent of the job could be done by a monkey, as long as it's paying attention. As always, it's the remaining 20 per cent that's important. So I'd say 40 per cent of the job is managing buying risk. And for this we study purchase histories – we know that a higher heel or pointed toes will sell well in narrow fittings but not so well in wide fittings. 40 per cent is proper stock control. We know where every SKU is in the business and we never take our eye off a single pair – we have a system where the computer will automatically generate stock

80 per cent of the job could be done by a monkey, as long as it's paying attention

refills from one store to another. And the crucial 20 per cent is gut instinct. There's that feeling you get when you're talking to customers, chatting to sales teams, listening to designers, reading the stats. What's right, what's wrong and what's going to happen."

And it's this 20 per cent that characterises the way Sheppard stays in touch and engages with his market.

He defines his customers as ladies aged 45-plus who now have a focus on family, live a healthy lifestyle and no longer wish to punish their feet with ill-fitting shoes. "Giving these customers time and care in store, and even when they ring to make orders over the phone, has helped us build meaningful relationships. On average, I expect our loyal customers to buy three pairs of shoes each year for the rest of their lives!"

"My idea, and it's now a mandatory rule in the business, is that anybody who wants to buy a pair of shoes from us sits down and our sales staff sit on a foot stool too," says Sheppard. "And unlike other retailers, we always remove *both* their shoes and measure *both* their feet. Firstly, this gives the sales assistant the chance to check for anything out of the norm, lumps and bumps, etc., and ascertain the perfect size, for the perfect fit – customers often remark it's the first time both feet have been measured since they were kids. And secondly, there's a certain psychological shift the minute both those shoes come off. Somehow a relationship develops. A barrier is removed and well-attuned sales assistants can pick up subtle signals that we can use to improve our offering. Interestingly, because our *Direct department* (Mail/phone/ internet) sales teams are all from the shopfloor, they build similar relationships, often recommending new styles that will fit and be comfortable based on a customer's purchase history – a critical brand-building exercise when dealing with those who live far away. Australia is huge!"

But Sheppard has realised this '20 per cent' gut instinct may be the limiting factor for his business expansion. Not the size of turnover, but the numbers of stores. "It's the critical level of personal feedback that we need to sustain our edge – it's the sheer logistics that I believe puts a ceiling on our portfolio." Consequently there are just three Peter Sheppard shoe shops in Australia, located in Sydney, Melbourne and Brisbane. But they're large, magnificent, exquisitely fitted emporiums. Each a homage to fashion, each becoming a well-known destination for thousands of Australian women who love the product and trust the brand. Indeed, being a destination means Sheppard can afford to position them in prime areas, but in secondary locations – a real saving on rent. He talks about testing third-tier locations next, such is the pull of his brand.

it's the first time both feet have been measured since they were kids

The Sydney and Melbourne stores each turn over around US$ 10 million a year, and the smaller Brisbane store about US$7 million. Sheppard equates the total figure with the typical turnover of a chain of 25-30 small shoe shops. "But we could never manage that many stores," he says. "The close-knit culture that we need would not allow us to do it. We would never have the control we've got now."

In commerce, there's an age-old philosophy to view problems as opportunities. And this is the learning from Sheppard's illustrious career. Unlike his competitors, he soon realised there was a 'gap' in the shoe market that couldn't be served by conventional retailing models. Rather than accept this, he set about understanding what the limitations were, why they were there and how to overcome *view problems as opportunities* them to his advantage. Lateral thinking led him to increase the size of each individual store rather than the estate, driving scale and substantial profit. And his burgeoning telesales operation speaks to this point – with this particular channel to market they don't remove shoes when they serve customers but they do find ways to remove barriers. The idea here, is to deliver a level of personal service that belies the huge distances involved in this huge continent.

According to Sheppard, with the exception of the USA, there are few markets, if any, that do what he is doing. But given the choice there are few women, if any, that wouldn't *love* it.

So why has no-one else stepped forward?

43
Case History

Len Roberts
Former CEO, Radio Shack

Interviewed March 2010

Dirty forks

"I want you all to do me a favour, find your job description and tear them up. They're irrelevant. From this day forward there's only going to be two jobs in this company. One, you either service the customer directly or two, you serve someone who does."

With these sentences, Len Roberts ended his get-to-know-you chat with 160 directors and senior personnel at the head office of the iconic American retailer, Radio Shack. It was all within 55 minutes of his arrival as CEO – having never worked in retail but fresh from running a chain of restaurants!

Clearly Roberts is stranger to self-doubt. And rightly so.

In a glittering catering career that culminated in him being named youngest ever CEO, running a chain of 2,000 roast beef restaurants, he had become famed for turning huge losses into mouth-watering profits. But in 1995 he was the 'shock' choice to save Radio Shack, the

Len Roberts, waiting on a different type of table

failing giant electronics retailer – his chairman, however, would soon be proved to have made an inspired appointment. By the time Roberts stepped down eight years later he had arrested the company's downward-spiralling profits and increased them 500 per cent to just under half a billion dollars a year. He'd added 1,000 outlets to the existing 6,000-store estate, delivered annual sales of US$5 billion, but most importantly had given its 40,000 workforce a commercial raison d'être.

It usually takes an outsider to recognise when a business is looking at itself through the wrong end of a telescope and Roberts was quick to see this, as he explains. "People loved Radio Shack because of its knowledgeable associates. People go there to figure out how to get their TVs connected up, what cable they need, find out why their remote gate-opener or security system has failed, get special batteries for gadgets, ask why their camera keeps blinking. But this trusted consumer franchise was not seen by head office. It certainly wasn't being leveraged and truth be told, not even talked about in my interview. Which was odd, because it was all there in black and white in the dozens of research documents that I'd asked to read before I accepted the job. Or indeed on every occasion I'd *Nobody remembers anything good, if the fork is dirty* 'needed' Radio Shack as a customer. The business seemed fixated on merchandise and its phenomenal buying power – important as that was, it's not what the business was all about."

Roberts is charismatic. He is a human dynamo. A likable and natural leader. There's a sense he does what he says he's going to do, and for those brave enough, even listen and act on their dissenting thoughts. In marketing parlance he is fiercely customer-centric, totally customer–sensitive. In restaurant parlance he points out, *"Nobody remembers anything good, if the fork is dirty."* But he intuitively understands modern retailing. "If you operate 6-7,000 small, 2,000 sq foot stores, you can't compete effectively by selling bulky, high-tech merchandise. You leave that to Best Buy or Circuit City, they're the big box category killers. I've always made a point of fighting for customers on my terms not my competitors'. So when I arrived – and cutting a very long story short – I re-orientated the whole business. What we did attitudinally and operationally was best summed up and succinctly described by a new advertising strapline at the time. We changed from *Radio Shack – the Technology Store* to the fabulous line, *You've got questions, we've got answers.* And from that point on, everyone in the business knew exactly what was expected each and every minute of each and every day – no discussion!"

The internal knock-on effect from this repositioning thought was huge. Store associates became prouder of their role within their communities and with only four or five in each store, a strong sense of family quickly formed – Roberts claims there were few of the negative corporate issues normally found in larger stores. And because the 'core' SKUs (parts, batteries and accessories) enjoyed gross margins around 80 per cent, the business averaged out with an impressive 50 per cent. So even with the high labour content necessary to deliver Roberts' service ethos, the business achieved a very credible 13 per cent net profit at the store level.

fighting for customers on my terms not my competitors'

Roberts' simple idea was to move the centre of gravity of the company from a merchandise organisation to a service business.

Underlining this shift of emphasis, stores were remodelled. Service counters at the side of stores were removed and as Roberts explains, "circular counters were constructed and strategically positioned, acknowledging we knew customers were coming for help and advice. And talking of advice, after my first couple of days, I literally spent the next three months out of my office. I said there's nothing more you can teach me here, I'm off to learn from customers and stores. That may sound theatrical but most service initiatives and operational excellence emanate from the front line. And just like a restaurant, I wanted to be a very visible *maître d* – out there supporting my teams."

Over time, Roberts worked hard refining and broadening the 'offer' within the confines of his stores' small footprints. He soon realised the brand enjoyed a remarkably broad customer demographic. He believed this could be harnessed to other service-led business opportunities. The first he identified was a natural development. He was already selling home security units but it struck his entrepreneurial nature that having sold the equipment on behalf of the manufacturers, these same manufacturers then recruited *his* customers for highly lucrative 'monitoring' services. Roberts suggested these recurring annual revenues might be shared as he'd done the introductions. "It took a while, but they eventually agreed, we had 7,000 stores and they knew it. I called these revenues, *residuals*."

Next up was the TV satellite business, which ultimately opened the market for Radio Shack to sell mobile phones. "At the time there weren't dedicated phone stores as such, so we started selling phones, a lot of phones, cordless phones, regular phones, eventually mobile phones," recalls Roberts. "Just imagine, we'd developed a reputation for knowing what we were talking about with complicated technology and then along come complicated phones, with complicated tariffs, complete with a bunch of self-serving phone networks. It proved to be a lucrative business stream. Not only was the demand for mobile phones exponential, but we started selling own-brand devices with great margins. Oh, and I raised the subject of residuals with the networks. Again, a lot of squealing but by the time I retired, the residuals represented nearly a quarter billion dollars a year.

Too many retailers talk about listening to customers but fail to respond. And this is the learning here. There's absolutely no point doing research if you don't act on it. Or as Roberts puts it: "Listen hard, choose *your* agenda for the fight and come up with an idea that resonates."

Wall Street may have been shocked by his arrival and saddened by his departure – but Roberts was only ever interested in how his customers felt. Bon appétit.

move the centre of gravity of the company from a merchandise organisation to a service business

44

Case History

Bijou Kurien
Former COO, Watch & Clock division,
Titan Industries

Interviewed May 2009

A little soul

Giving a discount is as old as retail itself. Unquestionably effective, hardly differentiating.

It was this retail truth that led Bijou Kurien, former COO of the Watch and Clock division of India's huge Titan Industries, to create a discounting idea with a difference. "Bring in your old watch, broken or not, and we'll refurbish it, donate it to a deserving cause and give you a 25 per cent discount on a new one."

Product recycling is no longer unique in retailing. But when launched several years back, this simple-sounding proposition from Titan took the Indian market by storm. It gave their customers permission to change the habits of a lifetime and created a real bond with an emotional legacy that's been hard for competitors to copy.

A marketer by training, Kurien is an engaging individual, bright with

Could we dare to dream that our proposition was strong enough to override sentimentality?

an insatiable appetite for the *customer* – excited by challenges, animated about the opportunities retail promises. Along with its retail interests, Titan Industries is India's biggest watch and jewellery manufacturer enjoying a 25 per cent share of the Indian market. It sells its branded watches through an enormous network of over 8,000 shops and dealer showrooms.

Kurien and his colleagues actively strove to find marketing messages that would resonate and more importantly, 'stand out' in a crowded, discounting market. "The harsh and obvious reality is, for things that don't wear out or have built-in obsolescence there isn't a natural lifespan, they don't *need* to be replaced. Understandably, research also told us that disposing of old watches, even if broken, is felt to be wrong, especially if they were a gift – no matter how small. Retailers who sell shoes or clothes are lucky, their products either wear out or go out of fashion but a watch can last a lifetime. So the temptation for retailers like us is to lapse into discounting to encourage sales. It's quick and simple to administer but as we all know, can only motivate so far."

To stimulate sales Kurien realised he needed to find an idea that excited, and then engaged, his customers at a deeper level.

"We wanted to find a way to give value for something they no longer needed – if we did this, we could *strike a chord* with them, we knew we could grab their attention. And if we then refurbished the old piece and promised to give it to a deserving cause, we could not only grab their attention but capture their imagination. Our goal was to engage with potential customers to such an extent that we could persuade them to change their normal ways. Persuade them, so to speak, to question if there wasn't something better they should be doing with their old or broken watches. Get them to question why they were cluttering up drawers and cupboards. Could we dare to dream that our proposition was strong enough to override sentimentality?"

Compared to Titan's normal discount promotions, the 50 per cent increase in sales, during the first of many 'recycle' watch campaigns, proved Kurien and his team had created a winning idea.

Essential to the success of this promotion, Titan's advertising was tasked with *disturbing* people's existing relationships with time pieces as well as sowing the seeds for repositioning watches as fashion items. This helped fuel a fierce viral campaign to drive home the overall marketing

One of 8,000 stores dressed for the 'Exchange Offer'

proposition. In store a huge transparent box acted as a graphic centre piece where the 'traded' watches were deposited to act as a tangible focal point for the whole promotion.

According to Kurien, "quality of execution had proved the undoing for competitors trying to 'rip-off' our promotion and despite our huge scale, it was essential we distanced ourselves from these imitators. For example, huge logistical issues were overcome by ensuring that every re-cycled watch was precisely credited against the discount on a new-purchase watch. Sounds easy, sounds obvious, but much time and effort was spent policing this! We also found our competitors underinvested in marketing support when speaking to customers before they entered the shops – we didn't!"

all about a really big idea – the redistribution of property

In PR terms, striking the right balance and tone was critical for Kurien to make sure his customers and the enormous population of India fully understood how these refurbished watches were accounted for. "This is all about a really big idea – the redistribution of property and trust is essential. We were, so it worked well in contemporary India. But it's an idea that could travel to any trusted organisation committed to a CSR agenda."

Indeed there are now many examples of this philanthropy throughout the retail world as 'sustainability' climbs the planet's agenda – ever-pressing imperatives make similar schemes more compelling. It's interesting to hear Marks & Spencer eloquently quoting a successful promotion with Oxfam in the UK, with people who donate old M&S clothes to the charity receiving a £5 M&S voucher – a project they claim has diverted 1,400 tonnes of clothing (3 million garments) from landfill sites in its first year alone.

And true to his beliefs, Kurien, who recently took over as President of the Retail Lifestyle division of the US$35 billion turnover Reliance Industries, is making benevolent marketing work again. He has piloted schemes for jewellery recycling and with some pride recounts a major scheme he has just launched to recycle textbooks. "As students progress to their next year of study they need a new set of textbooks. Although some pass their old books to siblings many books just gather dust in a bedroom. We said, if you can bring in a full set of text books for the year you've just passed, we will give you a 20% discount on any future purchases. We then give these old textbooks to schools where the children cannot afford to buy them."

Charitable redistribution does require additional stock handling and supply chain planning, and of course the cost of refurbishment of watches in Titan's case. But Kurien claims the additional footfall generated by such promotions more *with thought, a little soul can be injected into a commercial transaction* than covers these costs. He's also seemingly learnt how to drive home the message that buying a Titan watch meant donating to charity, without suffering charges of profiteering – hardly surprising when orphanages and the truly needy of India are involved.

But retail has always talked of the need to engage with communities. And there can be few better ways than recycling product. It is plainly a 'model' whose time has come. With discussions on waste, sustainability and the planet's fragility – not to mention the gap between the haves and have-nots widening – such endeavours richly deserve the success they achieve.

The revelation and key learning from this case study is how, with thought, a discount can be *loaded* with emotion. How, with thought, a little *soul* can be injected into a commercial transaction. This not only makes the promotion better, it makes it differentiating.

And if customers *love* anything – it's an idea that surprises and delights.

45
Case History

Betsy McLaughlin
CEO, Hot Topic

Interviewed February 2010

Money can't buy

All successful retailers change with time.

Sometimes proactively, sometimes re-actively. And sometimes the metamorphosis needs to be so profound that it changes the business model completely.

"Music is a primary driver of teen fashion preferences," says Betsy McLaughlin, the Los Angeles-based CEO of Hot Topic, a free-spirited fashion chain aimed at 12 to 22 year olds. "Back in the early 90s I guess there were 10 or 12 genres of rock music that devoted fans and teenagers aligned themselves with. We built our business back then selling fashion to these discreet audiences. We not only sold products that had licensed images of artists on them but also carried whatever fashion appealed to those types of fans, usually the sort of things the artists themselves were wearing. About 50 per cent of our business was licensed, and 50 per cent pure

Cast of Vampire Diaries on Hot Topic tour

fashion. Things were going really well, we went public in '96 and experienced big growth. Most of our stores generated positive cash flow in their first year – it was an incredible time."

Hot Topic was formed in 1989. McLaughlin joined four years later from a retailing background and in 2000 became CEO of a 200-store estate. Today the company has grown to three concepts: *Hot Topic* which now has 680 stores from Hawaii to

Music is a primary driver of teen fashion preferences

Florida, focusing on teenage music and pop culture; *Torrid* which launched in 2001 and has 150 stores targeting young women who are plus size; and *ShockHound,* a music digital e-commerce concept that launched in 2008. Sales turnover for the group has grown from US$200 million to $700 million since McLaughlin has been at the helm and for 2009 she delivered over $63 million of profit.

But all businesses have their ups and downs and it was shortly into McLaughlin's reign that a potentially terminal influence loomed onto the horizon.

"I'd only been in the hot seat for a while when along comes a huge change in the music scene – the iPod!" says McLaughlin. "Music became freely available online, and all of a sudden teenagers had all types of music available to them. The whole thing was turned upside down. Their iPods suddenly started shuffling between Elvis, Madonna, Bruce Springsteen and Green Day. Before they were locked into one genre, exclusively listening to one type – metal, ska, rock or whatever. But with the arrival of this wafer thin box, they could have an unlimited amount of music. Today 95 per cent of these kids share music files."

Simply put, almost overnight the music tastes of America's 12 to 22-year-olds became more diverse, their choices more eclectic and the Hot Topic specialist business model, increasingly less relevant.

So in an open plan area surrounded by 800 free-thinking young fashion and music executives (including the odd dog), and shielded by a frighteningly huge gothic centrepiece in reception, McLaughlin set about steering the business back to relevance. She's unmistakably Californian. Smiling readily, listening deeply and seemingly very at peace with herself. She is sharp, vibrant and in a very relaxed way, in a hurry.

Hot Topic was about to reinvent itself as a cool place to *discover*, not follow, music, entertainment and fashion.

Taking the iPod phenomenon head-on, McLaughlin bought into the idea: "Hot Topic needed to step into the role of taking teenagers on a different journey, helping edit and connect with music and fashion they hadn't connected with before. A major turning point for us was the whole idea of hosting live 'gigs' in our stores, celebrating and tapping into the enthusiasm for local music talent."

"We went to all 680 store managers and said if you want to have acoustic music performances in your stores that would be great, but if you do, let's make sure we provide a *real* experience for our customers. They went absolutely nuts," says McLaughlin. "Everybody loved the idea, store teams rallied around instantaneously, they came up with all sorts of ideas and great local contacts. We had no trouble engaging the workforce. We did three months of testing in a few stores which went fabulously, and by the end of 2008 we'd done 2,000 live performances in our stores. The response was incredible – in that year sales growth of licensed merchandise went from minus 12 per cent in the first quarter, to plus 25 per cent in quarter four, so it was obvious we were converting this new footfall too."

reinvent itself as a cool place to discover, not follow, music, entertainment and fashion

In 2009, the number of performances in stores hit 10,000, often coinciding with new ranges and back to school/college fashions, as well as all the big seasonal events, including Valentines and Halloween. "Stores that do it well, that select the right bands and market them well, are really starting to see big dollars roll in. Fans are coming, seeing the new product and going for it, it's working very well."

Success breeds success. And more recently, Hot Topic has begun growing the 'idea' by hosting bigger gigs in the communal areas of their malls, with signings and promotions taking place back in the store – again converting to sales. The chain is now also focusing on the wider pop culture. Teen-targeted films and TV shows, as well as the latest bands, are now a cause for in-store and mall-side celebration, with licensed products promoted in tandem. An event with the cast of the hit USA TV series *Glee* drew a crowd of 5,000 and an impressive 10,000 fans arrived in Dallas to meet the cast of *Twilight*. "We just did *Vampire Diaries* last weekend and we had 4,000 people show up," says McLaughlin. "We had exclusively designed merchandise and fashion ranges celebrating the up-coming Johnny Depp movie, *Alice in Wonderland*, where we tied-in with its launch. It's good for us, good for the studios – it helps they're just around the corner in LA."

"We've always been about connecting fans with artists but now we have an idea that's really breaking the retail mould. We're even re-modelling our stores to feature an integral stage and we've just launched our own loyalty scheme – we've signed three million customers in two months! Benefits already include names drawn for special invites to the bigger gigs in their local areas, special screenings of

an idea that's really breaking the retail mould

movies and all-areas passes for concerts – that sort of thing. So for our customers we're all about accessibility and for us and our partners, it's about connection. Everyone's happy!"

The interesting lesson here is how McLaughlin has changed her business model, yet stayed true to her brand. Hot Topic is still about connecting fans to artists but the reason for connecting is somewhat different. She now helps her customers discover and then access popular culture and fashion, not slavishly follow it. And by doing so, has elevated the status of her brand. The physical space that was once dedicated to satisfying and retailing a specific need has metamorphosed into an experience that promises newness, inspiration and difference. What teenager wouldn't want that?

And what teenager wouldn't love a brand that stands for access, money can't buy?

Thank goodness for the iPod!

SECRET FIVE – SUMMARY

Ideas: Tips for success

- Ideas must be celebrated as the lifeblood of a business

- Ideas need a forgiving culture of 'lid-lifting', where everyone is encouraged to think outside their box without fear of failure.

- The best ideas are simple and single-minded – betraying the complex thinking involved.

- 'Well-poisoners' must be named, shamed and restrained – drowned if needs be!

- Fortune favours the brave. The more creative an idea, the more it punches above its weight

- Effective protocols for recognising great ideas must be agreed and implemented.

- Bonded teams should always champion ideas, not individuals.

- An idea is useless if it can't be remembered.

So if you only remember one thing from this section, remember:

Make sure your ideas stick.

SECRET 6

BEING DIFFERENT

BEING DIFFERENT

Last thought

The really successful retailers are all the same. They love to be different. This is my observation and the final secret of retail success.

Unforgettable

Over the years, I have shared many speaking engagements with a good friend and colleague who often starts his presentations by asking for permission to take his jacket off.

Following the inevitable approval, he carefully removes his impeccably tailored jacket and proceeds to swing it around his head. And with theatrical flourish, hurls it into the audience. As the shocked laughter dies away he quietly asks the audience if they can remember the last speaker they heard talking about marketing at a conference.

the most effective way to remembered is to be different

Leaving his jacket in the lap of a delegate, he then quietly says his name is Neil Kennedy and is there to talk about marketing. At the end of his piece he asks for his jacket back. And then politely enquires if the audience will remember him.

'Certainly' is the guaranteed response! And why? Because he was not only very good, he was different.

What's this got to do with retail?

Well you can't *be chosen* if you're not remembered. And the most effective way to remembered is to be different. Preferably for the right reasons!

Better to be different.

Barry Urquhart, an Australian colleague, reasons 'it's better to be different than it is to be better'. A slightly tortured expression, it certainly hits the mark – it is in itself different. And it certainly stood out in one of his monthly E-Zines buried in my deluge of e-mails. Barry is famed for his keynote presentations and at the heart of this particular one is 'differentiation'. A premise that has been championed many times in this book and is at the heart of all great brands.

Having spoken to so many successful retail leaders it comes as no surprise that being different is high up on their agendas. Common sense dictates it's a great starting point to attract customers and a wonderful way to keep them coming back. We all fondly remember how so many great businesses started out by being totally different, challenging the status quo – customers love it.

The pioneering Southwest Airlines in America and its equally legendary co-founder Herb Kelleher insisted on being different by making sure absolutely everything they did was geared to making them *the* low cost airline. And I mean everything! No-frills is now informing and shaping the agenda for all other airlines around the world whether they deal in frills or not. Sam Walton at Wal-Mart determined to be different by giving ordinary folk the chance to buy the same things as rich people. His business methods too have shaped retailing ever since. And just in case you're getting the idea that cheapness is the criterion for being different, spare a thought for companies like Nike, Apple or Starbucks – none of these iconic businesses could be accused of being driven by price.

Being different can be touched or felt

Being different comes in many different shapes.

Both, is best

Being different can be touched or felt by customers – either way being highly effective.

But given the choice, most of the leaders I've interviewed would prefer to be emotionally rather than rationally different. This is because emotional differentiation is more sustainable and near impossible for competitors to copy. But given the ultimate choice, they'd all love to be both. Again Apple springs to mind as a great example of this; so does the John Lewis Partnership in Secret Two. The John Lewis Partnership fundamentally promise never to be beaten on price but enjoy an enviable reputation as one of the world's most trusted retail brands.

As argued in Secret One, in order to *be chosen* the great retailers are now actively seeking to imbue their rational differences with emotional qualities, as magnificently explained by the COO of Wal-Mart China in Secret Four and the boss of Macys in Secret One.

A magical difference

The trouble is, it's getting harder to be truly original. Mark Taylor, a wonderfully strategic and creative thinker at my old agency found particular success when seeking a different perspective by looking outside the normal 'sources' for inspiration. In his work he'd encourage different thinking by working with a stimulating mix of poets, set designers, architects, novelists, broadcasters, theatre producers, psychologists, semioticians, cultural historians, product designers, screenwriters — purposely eclectic, all observers of 'life'. Each bursting with creative energy and their own unique interpretations, people like this are not easy to facilitate. But it's something Mark does to extraordinary effect.

From these sessions he'd distil fresh thinking from creative people who understood, practised and were passionate about the new and original. Individuals whose training, experience and approach to creativity are different to the traditional sources most businesses rely on for their creative thinking.

Magical thinking, geared to be different.

Stolen difference

The continuing quest for "difference" has meant that modern retail has become notorious for imitating when it can't think of ways to innovate. Somewhat paradoxically, being different can be stolen from others.

But ideally, if this dark art is to be used as a credible point of difference, the imitation must come from a different retail sector.

There is limited merit in simply copying a successful initiative from a competitor. A particularly interesting piece of shameless 'borrowing' has been used to great effect to reposition Sprint-Cass completely differently in the minds of airport shoppers. Featured in Secret Six, this retailer turned to supermarkets for inspiration.

Many of the retail bosses talked euphemistically to me about how they have sought inspiration from other retailers. But as testament to the relative purity of the customer business model of retail, I have found that more sectors borrow from retail than the other way round. Jack Shewmaker, one of the first Presidents of Wal-Mart has spent much of his time since retiring consulting around the world on the principles of 'every day low pricing' and Len Roberts of Radio Shack fame is currently heading up an American Hospital organisation sharing his retail learnings with them. Indeed in the recent UK political elections there was much talk of what retail could teach government – the problem is where to start!

There is limited merit in simply copying a successful initiative from a competitor

Default settings

The most inspiring leaders I've interviewed seemed to have an agenda to *not* make life easy.

To them, establishing, maintaining and refining their status for being different is so important that they refuse to default to simpler solutions. In Secret Six, the boss of La Rinascente seems determined to take on the whole of Italy is his pursuit of being different. In Secret Three, Harvey Nichols sees a normally mild-mannered boss tear-up recruitment protocols to deliver true brand differentiation. And the boss of Bloomingdales in Secret One insists on *not* training any of his workforce – because that's what you do with animals. As we saw in that section, all learning at this iconic department store has been elevated to a series of educational programmes. A truly laudable mindset for deeper learning and an ideal conduit for differentiation.

an agenda to not make life easy

Entrepreneurial

But I guess the most prevalent trait I've witnessed amongst the world's successful retailers in the pursuit of being different, is an almost youthful enthusiasm to achieve it. With a bold and certainly brave agenda fuelled by the oxygen of self-confidence, these executives go out of their way to recreate the good bits of entrepreneurism. Trinity, part of Li & Fung in Secret Two, are fine exponents of this and have built a global empire acknowledging its strengths within corporate life. And in Secret Six, A S Watson has taken the whole thought process of being different to unimaginable extremes by delivering a different kind of difference to the landlords of greater China and their ever evolving customers.

It's a particular skill to keep entrepreneurial spirit alive and celebrated in major corporations but for those who do, I have noticed success is as near guaranteed as is possible. It takes a special leader to achieve it and they are certainly different from those who can't.

Let me finish by *not* being different

So many people have quoted this that I find it hard to credit the originator, but I agree with whoever first said '*it's the difference that makes the difference*'.

If a business can capture the essence of the need to be different, not just better, it will be driven to own a special place in the hearts and minds of customers and equally importantly its workforce. As I argued in Secret One, if

it's the difference that makes the difference

uniqueness is all part of *being chosen,* I would now add that being different must be part of the strategy.

And here are some particularly fine examples of this thought process.

The interviews

- **La Rinascente** is on course to become Italy's first state-of-the-art national department store group. This 150-year-old brand plans to regain iconic status by creating totally different shopping experiences, turning each location into architectural celebrations, building 'places not stores'.

- **Challenger Technologies Group** is enjoying loyal success in the punishingly competitive and promiscuous world of electronics retailing in Singapore. With some highly original thinking and a ground-breaking customer reward initiative this business is looking to keep its customers happy for a life time.

- **Pak 'n Save** dominates the New Zealand grocery scene. With several of its stores individually in the country's top 100 businesses, this giant brand continues to deliver an ever-evolving and radically different shopping experience through a deeply engrained culture of doing things differently.

- **Sprint-Cass** has taken thinking differently to a different level. Shamelessly borrowing from the ruthless world of supermarketing, this Singapore-based electronics retailer is creating a whole new genre of airport retailing by persuading travellers to rethink their prejudices.

- **Jay Jays** is the largest youth fashion retailer in Australia and New Zealand. With a father's simple observations, cutting edge instincts and outstandingly different lateral thinking, a failing denim store chain, catering to the middle-aged, metamorphosised into a cult brand for the young.

- **Sports Authority** has just under 400 giant stores in the USA and Japan and is now poised to move into China. It all started with a belief that the retail sports market was ready for something radically different. With some radically different thinking it took a radically different character to deliver one of retail's big wins.

- **Lord & Taylor** is America's oldest department store group and has, with some highly relevant and compellingly different thinking, embarked on a programme to grab back market share lost to the specialty fashion retailers. A three-dimensional merchandise matrix, cut by lifestyle, is at the centre of this initiative.

- **A S Watson** is a huge retailer and has a burgeoning food division in Greater China. With some stylish and distinctly radical thinking, this highly successful retailer is attempting to future-proof itself from the demanding and all-powerful landlords of the region.

- **Somerfield Supermarkets** was the talk of UK financial institutions. First for its precarious financial position, then for its breathtaking turnaround. With some exquisitely counter-intuitive thinking and strategically defiant manoeuvring the management ruthlessly engineered the business to stock market success.

46

Case History

Vittorio Radice
CEO, La Rinascente

Interviewed May 2009

Focused on tomorrow

There are some who say, by failing to adapt to a changing world department stores, like dinosaurs, face extinction. But Vittorio Radice isn't listening to this theory.

He is passionate about department stores, passionate about change and, more importantly, passionate about being different.

Stunning La Rinascente store setting, Piazza Duomo Milano

Radice is Italian, wholly charming and totally visionary. To date he's probably best known for transforming Selfridges from a staid British department store to a cutting-edge brand – its statement stores in London, Manchester and Birmingham have become icons of style the world over.

Now, back in his homeland and CEO of the 150-year-old department store group La Rinascente, Radice is working his modernising magic and creating something different again. He's developing stunning new stores, painstakingly renovating ancient outlets and bravely closing others

– which in conservative Italy is a radically different strategy. Five years into a seven-year turnaround, he's on course to deliver Italy's first state-of-the-art national department store chain.

For the first time in over 100 years the big idea is to stir up excitement about the La Rinascente brand, its retail experience, its aesthetics and its merchandise. Celebrating the stunning, often historic locations, from Milan to Sicily, from Venice to Naples, Radice is also creating the only 200,000 sq ft department store in Rome.

But bold plans need bold actions. "Be prepared to change constantly – this is the name of the game," says Radice who argues there's no point settling for 10-year plans. He advocates stepping outside the business (both metaphorically and literally) and, with an objective eye, visualising its long-term future. "Don't look at the store from inside, look at it from outside and ask: can this store be around 50 years from now? And if the answer is no, close it today!"

Radice's admired and profitable transformation of Selfridges is testament to long-term thinking and investment – neither of which he enjoyed during his truncated spell at Marks & Spencer following his 'Lifestore' project in the north of England. But he readily admits it takes courage to be different, to be a moderniser. "You have to be ready and confident to upset everything for the sake of commercial longevity. It comes

Can this store be around 50 years from now? If the answer is no, close it today

with acute frustrations, particularly in Italy where trade unions, political activists and layers of bureaucracy seem to obstruct progress (change) at every turn. For companies like La Rinascente, that haven't changed in 100 years, when you bring in the changes – boom – you're faced with a revolution!"

Change always brings high emotions. Where store closures have been announced, employees with long service are understandably distraught – shoppers too. "Yes, but they've not been shopping enough with us, things have to be different – we're going bust," say Radice, believing sentimentality must be set aside, unlike others retailers who stumble along avoiding progress. "Of course as you go along, it's better to keep up with the times with a rolling change programme, but if you haven't, there comes a time when you need to take a drastic decision. If you don't stand outside your company and look in, you'll never be able to do it and more importantly, you'll never see what needs to be done."

In situations like this, clear direction is required. One of the purposes of a well articulated brand is to work like a signpost – helping inform business decisions, developing and protecting emotional bonds with customers. "Branding is everything," says Radice. "Everyone must know and feel, very clearly, what you *stand for* and as the manager, you need to know what must change to deliver it for tomorrow, *not* how it was done for yesterday." His vision for La Rinascente is to build on the inherited brand values dating from its 1920s heyday – when the original Milanese retailer championed and celebrated Italian design excellence – and sympathetically introduce contemporary values inspiring a new shopping generation.

In typical Radice style he explains his brand vision: "I want to be different, creating stores that become *the second church* or a *monument* in a city – effectively becoming 'must-visit' destinations for tourists and locals alike. Not merely being shops." Just as he created civic, community hot-spots within Selfridges in the *designing places* UK, hosting major art and cultural events on *instead of stores* site, he wants the stunning new flagship La Rinascente stores, planned for Milan and Rome, to be 'too good to miss'. He has similarly grand plans for the rest of his estate. But for now this means investing in the fabric of old buildings, creating new architectural experiences, making them contemporary and inspiring – in his words, "designing places instead of stores".

The locations themselves are certainly spectacular enough to draw the crowds. The refurbished Milan flagship overlooks the city's enormous cathedral, the Duomo, while in Florence La Rinascente's doors open onto the famous Piazza della Republica, and the Rome store will be a coin's throw from the impossibly beautiful Trevi Fountain.

But to keep the purity of Radice's dream, the estate, for now, is being culled to just 14 showcase stores with a critically focused merchandise selection. As well as world-renowned Italian fashion labels, Radice wants to source locally produced food and well-designed homewares – all celebrating high Italian art and skill. Increasingly, local artisans will be given the opportunity to sell their specialist products throughout the stores. Already, in Milan, the store's food hall, tucked away on the seventh floor, is such a draw that locals mingle with tourists to enjoy indigenous skills – an unlikely confection of street-market authenticity and up-market chic. In July 2009 a 'Design Supermarket' opened in the homewares departments. An excited Radice explains: "Italy is famous for design – not just fashion, beautiful design for the home, for the table, and yet there's no *one* place in Italy that brings it all together. Imagine all those designers working throughout Italy, taking three weeks to design a 'cup' or whatever. How do they show off their work? Where do they sell them? We're going to be different, giving them the chance."

But all this vision needs a workforce 'living the dream' Italy's employee protection laws are notorious and change has proved challenging for Radice, so he's pushing for innovation too. "I want to inject more energy, with sales assistants closer to understanding the brands they sell. We need more engagement and passion. If Armani himself were on the shop floor, he'd be the best salesman ever, explaining what he had in mind when he designed each piece."

But despite Armani spending eight years as a window dresser at La Rinascente, not even Radice can persuade him to run training sessions! So senior designers from all the big fashion houses, and eager artisans of every persuasion, personally educate employees. Regularly offering insight into their product and brand values.

Nine stores have been closed, yet group turnover has increased by 40 per cent in the same three-year period. Radice is certainly doing things differently. He's giving Italian design back to the Italians, and they love it! But the true learning from this *Armani spent eight years as a window dresser at La Rinascente* case study is the power of an easily understood brand vision, where being different is founded on a truth but focused on tomorrow.

An iconic brand has been re-born, and another dinosaur theory laid to rest.

47
Case History

Loo Leong Thye
CEO, Challenger Technologies Group

Interviewed, June 2008

In the club

Win-win must be a magical thought to Loo Leong Thye.

As Chief Executive of Singapore's Challenger Technologies, a flourishing chain of 22 small to mega-sized (44,000 sq ft) stores selling IT and Electrical goods, Loo Leong Thye puts much of his considerable success down to luck.

Even acknowledging the roll luck plays in oriental culture, there is a great deal more to this man and his retail empire. Leong Thye has a ready smile, a steely gaze and is quick to giggle but don't let the man distract you with his charm – he keeps his *loyalty cannot be bought* notoriously fickle customers coming back to his stores in the fiercely competitive and over-supplied Singapore market through rigour and creativity. His business is different.

Attracting customers and encouraging repeat purchases to grow *customer lifetime value* is an essential element of successful retailing – chasing this Holy Grail has seen many retailers both large and small turn to loyalty and reward programmes with mixed results. But get it right, as Loo Leong Thye has done, and this marketing tool can be an extremely valuable asset to a business.

The starting point and universal truth has to be that loyalty cannot be bought. It is also well understood that when someone pays for something, they value it more.

And it was these two profound thoughts that led Leong Thye to cleverly design a customer membership club with a difference, to reward loyalty. With no need for plastic cards, just national identity numbers, his concept was as simple to use as it was compelling (foreigners use their passport numbers). Besides all the benefits of enhanced customer service that comes with membership – for a two-year subscription of US$20 members are *guaranteed* a minimum US$33 saving on their purchases during that same period. If they don't achieve these savings they get a US$27 refund, a US$6 profit on their subscription – which according to a smiling Leong Thye, "seldom happens."

How does this price saving guarantee work?

In addition to an overall promise of the lowest prices in town, policed by a 110 per cent refund of the price difference, membership includes access to a dual-pricing structure. Unlike many other retailers around the world, Leong Thye overtly displays two prices on each product, in each store – the lower being for members only. As he admits, "membership is unashamedly price-based with store ticketing constantly reinforcing the key benefit of membership as well as stimulating new applications. The ticketing also serves as a reminder to our workforce to talk about all the other benefits and extra freebies."

And it works, as Leong Thye explains. "We launched the scheme in 1999 and in the first year signed up nearly 3,000 customers a month on average. Today, we have over 160,000 members and when membership expires they renew – it's different and they love it!"

It isn't lost on Leong Thye that his initiative has created a new way to generate income. "The membership gives us a pure revenue stream when we collect each US$20. It might be a small amount, but tens of thousands of customers become members so that's a lot of money. At the same time it's producing loyal customers who come back to us again and again."

But loyalty can be generated in many ways. Service and convenience speaks to shoppers at an emotional level with a disproportionate effect. Challenger offers car park refunds to members – SG$2 back when spending at least SG$50, which on the minimum purchase, Leong Thye says, is equal to a 4 per cent discount. "In Singapore's oppressive heat many people drive to purchase things from us, it's a small token that shows we are interested in all their purchases not just the big stuff. It means a lot."

The guiding principle is that members are made to feel truly special.

There are privileges on a host of services including reduced delivery and installation charges, a 50 per cent reduction off all repairs and much more. "We are always looking for exciting ways to add value for our membership and from 2006, a points-based rewards programme was introduced. For every dollar spent members earn one point. If we need to stimulate a particular product line we may offer two points for each dollar. It's a great tool and very flexible, and just another way for us to say thank you to our members."

Although Leong Thye acknowledges plenty of programmes around the world offer financial benefits, rewards, service discounts and price guarantees, he believes the Challenger scheme *a bespoke service* is different being among the very few to offer *in real time* all these plus an additional customer engagement tool. "A key aspect of our programme is we allow members to check their purchases from the previous three years, accessing this data online or on in-store terminals. Soon my teams on the shop floor will have handheld devices so they can immediately look up members' purchase histories. Very useful for advising on equipment compatibility or the appropriate 'best value' ink cartridges for the printer they bought from us a couple of years ago, or what sort of connection is needed for a new piece of add-on equipment. It's a bespoke service in *real time*. We value our members highly and I think that shows. They love the personalised help we give them on the shop floor."

By profiling the purchase history of individual members, Challenger is developing plans to proactively offer equipment upgrades, trade-ins and replacements to its membership. Besides the obvious benefit of driving sales, if sensitively executed, this development presents great opportunities for deeper relationships between Challenger and its membership – consolidating a true sense of belonging to a club.

With mutually compelling benefits for both the company and its customers it is not surprising that membership of the programme continues to grow by around 15 per cent each year and now accounts for an impressive 60 per cent of total group sales. Leong Thye wants that figure to be 100 per cent but will settle for 80.

What are the learnings here?

Leong Thye intuitively understood reward is better than bribery as a platform for emotionally engaging customers. And by making his proposition sufficiently compelling he has found his customers valued it enough to pay for it. He has also avoided the short-sighted trap of launching a scheme to reward loyalty that doesn't actually do so in any meaningful way. And in the process of using hi-tech methods to attract and retain his target market, he has nurtured some *good old-fashioned* customer relationships. Normally the envied domain of small, owner-operated stores.

reward is better than bribery as a platform for emotionally engaging customers

In an unforgiving marketplace defined by its promiscuous shoppers, Leong Thye is understandably proud of this different initiative. He has created and developed a well rounded, almost holistic membership club capable of delivering ever-increasing customer lifetime value.

With some strategically and tactically different thinking Leong Thye's customers are winning and so is his business – he may think its luck, but don't bet on it.

Case History

Hugh Perrett
Founder, Pak 'n Save

Interviewed June 2008

Fabric of the business

Attracting customers with low prices is nothing new. Neither is the knowledge that this sort of retailing attracts promiscuous shoppers.

What then did Hugh Perrett, one of the founders of the iconic New Zealand grocery chain, Pak 'n Save do to defy the odds? How did he create the fabulously successful, low price brand famed for its loyal customers?

First we must understand the man. Hugh Perrett, who has now stood down from running this 44-store group, is rather like his country's national rugby football side – a confection of charm, politeness, intelligence and rugged ruthlessness. You wouldn't want to have to take anything from him in order to win.

It was while Perrett was at the co-operative supermarket chain, Foodstuffs Auckland, that he and a colleague Richard Reilly came up with an idea that would add a totally different and highly successful new business to the group based on *extremely* low grocery pricing.

Unsurprisingly, their early research confirmed that customers wanted, and would travel for, really low prices but only if it came with a 'proper' choice. And better still if it came *Price had to be* with top quality fresh food. Nothing ground-*our dominant* breaking here! But having scoured the world *attribute* for inspiration they soon realised the only way to deliver their vision efficiently was through scale, owner-operators and malleable suppliers. Here lay the genesis of Pak 'n Save.

As Perrett coyly reflects, "Price had to be our dominant attribute. Most price-based operators rely on a *very* limited assortment to try to generate their buying leverage. We wanted to be different. Pak 'n Save gets its buying leverage firstly through a controlled range, but secondly, and very importantly, through an incredible domination of the catchments in which our enormous stores operate. No supplier wants to miss out on so much business – we knew that and so did they! A number of our individual stores today would be in the top 100 businesses in New Zealand in turnover terms; some account for as much as 1.5 per cent of our national supermarket turnover."

Whether retailers in other parts of the world would be able to succeed in this manner is open for debate, New Zealand is unique in its size, geography and population dynamics but as Perrett proudly points out, "we now stock almost 75 per cent of the SKUs a fully ranged major supermarket stocks – including quality fresh foods. So there might be a couple of things our customers can't get but they don't seem to worry about it. I would say, the standard format competitor supermarkets are still 12 to 13 per cent more expensive than Pak 'n Save. Initially people were getting together and jointly hiring buses to travel 20 miles to use our stores. We had never seen that before in New Zealand – no-one else has either, before or since."

Operationally speaking, strategic ranging and massive stores (up to 100,000 sq feet) leading to catchment domination, all offered huge leverage with suppliers. But to deliver true success Perrett looked for an emotional connection with customers and staff. For this, semiotics (the use of signs and symbols) always played a big part in supporting the Pak 'n Save brand – how the look and feel of the stores made people feel. Enormous warehouse-like cubes, with warehouse-style racking and a distinctly no-frills flavour hammering home the message to shoppers of bulk buying and *semiotics has always played a big part* low, low prices throughout the shopping experience. "From the outside they looked very different and dominant. The first time you saw one of these stores you stood at the door and your mouth dropped open. They were designed to be overpowering, a huge perception of buying power and deal prices. You just *felt* Pak 'n Save were going to give you a great deal."

But for Perrett and the team, the real beauty of this store presentation was reduced operating costs.

In store, the 16-feet-high warehouse-style racks, cathedral-like in their homage to low prices, are replenished directly with fork lift trucks. Most of the goods are either put up in carton lots (often access panels neatly cut out for self service at customer level) or tipped into dump baskets, with everything designed to keep handling costs to a minimum. This high-level warehouse racking enabled the business to buy very deeply into deals and keep really strong prices running for a long periods of time, with the desired effect of putting pressure on the competition – it also meant promotions seldom become 'temporarily' out of stock.

Pak 'n Save are masters at stripping out infrastructure costs and streamlining the logistics operation into stores. "We cut out the central distribution element of normal supermarket supply chains and negotiated for suppliers' trucks to *we cut out the central* deliver pallets directly into our stores." *distribution element of* Sophisticated, centrally controlled *normal supermarket* ranging together with the huge shop floor racking meant that Perrett could *supply chains* warehouse the goods in-store – "paring down our administrative and storage costs to the absolute minimum; currently over 80 per cent of stock arrives direct to our stores."

Returning to the 'softer issues', and as expected from a business founded out of a co-operative holding company, each Pak 'n Save is franchisee-owned. Consequently, the individuals running them are emotionally engaged and this in turn means that their workforces can't help but be emotionally involved too. After all, they're rubbing shoulders with the owner and not just working for a corporate entity. Perrett is clear on the type of franchisee needed. "They must be great retailers, great business people, achievement driven and hard-nosed traders. Typically with 300-400 staff they must be people people too."

It soon becomes clear just how trusted and important these franchisee owners were in delivering Perrett's very different vision.

With gentle guidance, Pak 'n Save cleverly let each franchisee negotiate and tailor their promotions to specifically suit their catchment dynamics – but with only one aim: to outmanoeuvre everyone else. Just imagine the headaches each 'different' promotion causes their national competitors!

Inspired by the best of the best grocery retailing methods from around the world, Pak 'n Save's transparent beauty is that through low operating costs the business delivers low low prices, and without erosion of margin. As Perrett says, "Full price operators often reduce their prices by margin cutting. We're different. We don't. A discount offer from a supplier has the same percentage margin applied to it as we have on our every day prices. We're not cutting margin."

In 1985 Perrett and his colleagues had the vision to create something different. They created Pak 'n Save. It now dominates the New Zealand grocery scene by executing a finely tuned business model. At its heart was difference. They understood that to successfully trade on price, it couldn't just be an add-on feature; it

the business delivers low low prices, and without erosion of margin

has be embedded into the very fabric of the business – a simple thought, but one not always appreciated by others.

Whether all this success could be achieved outside New Zealand is academic to Pak 'n Save's loyal customers. But have the audacity to ask about promiscuous shoppers and Perrett gets the last word and he's not wrong: "Those retailers are not usually very good at price!"

Case History 49

Casey Lim
COO, Sprint-Cass

Interviewed June 2008

Innovate by imitating

One of the many golden rules of retailing is if you can't innovate, imitate! Copy the best of the best and why wouldn't you succeed?

Casey Lim is the quietly spoken, rather intellectual chief operating officer of the Singapore-based Sprint-Cass. This IT distributor and now blossoming Photographic, Electronics & Computer products retailer is brilliantly led by Lim with sound common sense and interesting tricks of the retail trade.

Lim is growing a highly profitable retail business. He is thinking differently by copying!

First a bit of lateral thinking and good old common sense. Why battle it out in the shopping centres and high streets, side by side with the competition, when there is a place that has virtually three times the footfall and where you are almost on your own?

"In Singapore there are hundreds of shops like us out there selling to a total population of around four million people plus a small percentage of tourists," says Lim. "Whereas *thinking differently by copying* in Singapore's Changi international airport the orientation is totally different. 10-12 million people pass through each of its three terminals, most being tourists, business travellers or connecting with flights. It's a different landscape altogether and we decided to aggressively pursue this opportunity. We now have five retail outlets there and only one in a normal shopping centre. The rents and operating costs are higher at the airport but so is the pay-back."

Retailing at a major international airport is not for everyone. Each airport seems to work in different ways taking pride in aggressively leveraging their greatest asset, huge captive audiences. The retail rents and their associated financial conditions are notorious but the skill, as Lim soon learned, is to think differently. Accepting that costs are costs, he looked for different ways to overcome the other primary downside – the customers' mindset.

Unsurprisingly, being at an airport, most of Sprint-Cass's sales were categorised as *needs-based*. Traditionally involving low-value goods with few proactive initiatives that could be introduced to encourage or boost additional sales. "Undeniably there were lots of people but they were not in 'buying' mode," explains Lim. "Not apparently for major electrical & computer purchases, anyhow."

So having exhausted 'best practice' customer flow and speed-of-service initiatives, Lim turned to retailers from a very different sector for inspiration.

"Mass stacking is not new – but it is at airports, especially ours. I would say most of the time if you look at retailers in airports they are very neat, prim and proper and the displays are very pristine. There's no 'mass' or 'mess', so we thought, let's be different, let's create some!"

This involved putting a platform on the floor the size of a big pallet. It was then loaded with products such as DVD players with Philips, Shinco and Panasonic devices piled high. "This created a kind of hype and made it look as if the products were on special offer whereas the retail price was the same as before. It was an illusion; it made people think of supermarket style offers. It created a perception that it was price-driven. We create a hype where people say 'wow there is so much of this, it must be on offer.' They were attracted and came in to take a closer look. We were then able to induce *impulse* purchases. Business increased by 15-20 per cent on this initiative alone."

There's no 'mass' or 'mess', so we thought, let's be different, let's create some

Inspired by supermarkets, this particular initiative helped Lim attract and adjust the mindset of the passing footfall in his favour. Supermarkets and their like are experts and have engineered phenomenal business success by developing a keen sense of how to create *impulse* purchases.

But flush from the success of his mind-meddling initiative, Lim pondered how he might capitalise on his new-found retailing skills. For this he looked at the fundamentals of his situation and how his competitors outside the rarefied surroundings of the airport operated.

He didn't have to look far.

The great attraction of shopping at Changi airport is its duty-free status – a saving of 7 per cent. Not much of a pull when all you need to replace is a forgotten memory stick or battery but as Lim dared to dream, certainly irresistible if it could be applied to the very latest high-value products as sold in the normal retail outlets. Or even better, to models never seen before. Acknowledging the sort of appeal this would have, Lim called it *demand* shopping and set about refining this different approach.

Demand shopping became Lim's biggest retail challenge and forms the latest part of his airport business development programme. It involved delicate negotiations, many presentations and the picking off of one manufacturer at a time. Until, using peer pressure and the fear of missing out, he gradually persuaded the big brands to fall into line and supply him the same merchandise and enjoy the same promotions as other retailers throughout Singapore. "This was a little bit tricky because when suppliers have a marketing campaign they tend to do it on a local basis and in the past travel retail has been excluded."

suppliers soon realised the quality and quantity of our customers

But increasingly now, the manufacturers have extended their localised campaigns to include Lim's stores at the airport. "Because airport retailing is free of tax at 7 per cent, this has become an advantage for our company. And it's worked for the suppliers too. With a lot of prompting from us, the suppliers soon realised the quality and quantity of our customers. They appreciated our new-found ability to engage them and saw just how big travel retail could be for selected products. They started to oblige us in terms of extending their local programmes to the airport. We are now even launching new models through our outlets at the airport – this is very different for them and very exciting for us."

Sprint-Cass have set their own successful and different agenda. They looked to their immediate competition and also to retailers from different sectors for inspiration and direction. And in doing so have metamorphosed into a retailer of beautiful proportions. Enjoying continuous 15 per cent year on year profit growth and a business split of 30 per cent *demand*, 30 per cent *impulse* and 40 per cent from the original *needs-based* purchases.

The learning here is obvious. Customers like to have their heads turned. Make the time to get out there to imitate the best of the best and your customers will like you too.

Interestingly however, by shamelessly copying something from a different sector, it effectively becomes innovation.

And we all know how much customers love something different.

Case History

Howard McDonald
Former Managing Director, Just Group

Interviewed June 2008

It's not normal

Keeping it in the family may be nepotistic but retailers' kids can help in all sorts of different ways. It's well known that observing everyday life informs a retailer's business but it's by interpreting life that great retailers gain the insight to make their boldest moves.

Howard McDonald is a human dynamo who seems genetically unable to switch off.

He is a fashion retailer through and through and counts re-inventing Jay Jays into the largest youth fashion retailer in Australia and New Zealand as his most audacious achievement. "Being observant is the first characteristic of a great retailer," he says. "Watch the good ones in a room, particularly those in fashion, and in seconds the whole room is summed up. What you're wearing, how you're wearing it and assessing it too." It's plain to see McDonald is talking about himself as well.

Jay Jays was a fledgling denim business with 50 stores in the suburbs of Sydney and Melbourne. It was just one of a stable of fashion retail brands in the Australian-based Just Group when McDonald took over as group managing director in the late 1990s. "Jay Jays was designed to appeal to the lower demographics with a price focus, but it was undifferentiated and underperforming," says McDonald. "I had watched the successful emergence of fast fashion visiting the likes of Zara and H&M in Europe and Old Navy had even surprised America with the boldness of its $4 and $9 items. Back in 2000 I realised there was a great opportunity in Australia to get a brand like these out there. I was looking for a spark to inspire me, something really different!"

Living with his daughter struggling to 'express' herself during the tense, teenage years gave McDonald the inspiration he was looking for. A fashion destination where she could put a statement wardrobe together herself – and do it on a budget and do it fast. "You know that triumphant moment where mum says I'd like you to wear that and she says *no* – that's the girl I wanted, that was the customer!"

Under fiscal pressure, McDonald chose not to open new stores but to develop the ailing Jay Jays format for his new venture – not an obvious choice. As he says, "it involved a 360-degree repositioning of the brand, but it had an infrastructure of sorts. I utilised buying and personnel expertise from the 600 stores in the rest of the group which kept the start-up costs down." Incredibly and in a totally unorthodox manner, his strategy was to shift the centre of gravity of the Jay Jays business from 40-year-olds to 18-year-olds and from cheap denim to fast fashion, while trading to both! As McDonald confesses, "It was certainly different. I was getting in younger product for the kids and attracting them on Thursday afternoon, Friday and Saturday ready for their socialising schedule centred on the weekend. The mums and dads I had previously been attracting through the older-style product were coming in Monday, Tuesday and Wednesday."

that triumphant moment where mum says I'd like you to wear that and she says no

Whilst the prudent approach might have been to wait until more funds were released, McDonald understood perfectly what this short-term obstacle represented.

Here was a chance to engage emotionally with the youngsters in an almost co-conspiratorial way. "How cool was that, the kids could *discover* just what they were looking for in a boring old-people's denim store – what a great start for a youth brand. They loved this different approach." He was confident that with their highly developed social networking skills and modern communications his audience would find and share their secret with like-minded friends. But McDonald also knew the Jay Jays ambience needed to change. Music was brought in and turned up, window displays became anarchic, younger more expressive sales assistants were hired on a part-time basis towards the end of the week and lots of 'rummaging' displays were introduced.

McDonald's team were not subtle. "We put in shower recesses with curtains and fake shower heads as changing rooms, which, as planned, caused some consternation among the older customers. Everything we did *spoke* to our young customers on their terms."

Although he was intentionally making it uncomfortable for the older audience there was still reluctance by the company's board to abandon them altogether. "There was a lot of pressure internally to hold onto the older market. If we let it go there was a fear the kids weren't going to be there in the first half of the week. The critical period for us was when the new offering

Everything we did spoke to our young customers on their terms

started to take off and the old market began to suffer badly. But we held our nerve and as soon as the younger crowd began generating 50 per cent of the profits we catered solely to them."

The *coup de grace* for Jay Jays' old business model was the level of stock turn delivered by McDonald's visionary business. "We enjoy seven to eight turns per year compared with Zara at 5.5 and the industry average now half of ours. It helps recover margin, little is marked down and we have very few Sales periods. Turnover is now three to four times more per square metre than before," claims McDonald. To overcome low gross margin on low price products, store fit-outs and rentals were kept to a minimum. "The kids weren't looking for glamour and didn't mind being off Broadway," as McDonald appropriately puts it!

In five years Jay Jays grew to 220 stores with much of its continued success being the fanatical observation undertaken of its young customers. "I encouraged the buyers to be 'out there' on public transport, in bars, being part of the demographic. When a new idea or trend emerges it emerges fast and it's certainly not coming from formal research," says McDonald. "We got this thing started in the most unusual and different way and that has to be our guiding principle and approach to everything we do to keep it successful."

Incredibly the very thing that cemented Jay Jays' renaissance could have been its death. McDonald, who has since retired from Just Group, had to operate in a corporate environment where other members of his board failed to see what he had seen. McDonald understood the deeper meaning of what he had witnessed in his daughter and embraced it in a way that turned short-term obstacles into a long-term vision. *It's not a normal place to shop*

Most teenagers are easily embarrassed by their parents' choice of clothes. But by interpreting this perfectly normal dynamic a dad created a shop like no other. It didn't start in the normal way and doesn't sell normal fashions. It's not a normal place to shop.

It's different – so where's the attraction in that to a teenager?

51
Case History

Jack Smith
Founder, Sports Authority

Interviewed March 2010

One swing

"In 1987 I opened my first store. 18 months and eight stores later, I sold the business for US$75 million cash. It had cost my investors just $9 million."

So recounts Jack Smith, the pioneering retailer who founded

Jack Smith, setting the scene

Sports Authority, the market-leading chain of big box sports stores in North America.

Having sold his business Smith stayed on as CEO and over the next five years grew it to over 150 stores, eventually floating it on the New York stock exchange.

Now in 2010 the business turns over $3.5 billion and has 330 stores in the USA. "There's an additional 50 stores in Japan doing around $ 1 billion and getting ready to push into China," says Smith who stepped down in 2000 "to enjoy my time sitting on other boards".

Smith is a born retailer and was inducted into Nova University's Entrepreneurs' Hall of Fame. He is fast-thinking, fast-talking and fast-acting. He's charismatic and incredibly sure of his instincts. He learned his craft with some of the biggest names in American retailing, ending up at Hermans, a chain of 7,000 sq ft stores selling sporting goods. "I soon realised that for certain markets successful retailing was evolving into something different. Big box formats were big news: Home Depot, Office Depot, Toys R Us. I just knew sports retailing could be next, thriving in a 40,000-square-feet environment. I'd seen first-hand how lack of space had stifled opportunity. To me 'sports' was ripe for big box formats. I reached out and found some very good venture capital players. Mitt Rommelly who recently ran for American President, was one of my first investors."

All great retailers crave some kind of authority. From day one, Smith's different concept was about having an unrivalled range, competitively priced and always in stock. "We were all about breadth and depth – assortment. Our small store competitors would have, maybe, three facings *for certain markets successful retailing was evolving into something different* of golf equipment. We'd have *eight times* that. I feel bad saying it but we'd go out of our way to have category-killing ranges and prices. So in the northern States, we'd go aggressive on ski equipment or surf gear in California. And for the hot lines, I'd shoot anybody rather than let them break stock."

Smith is adamant that big box didn't mean warehouse. "We were different. My apparel departments had carpets. We had fashion fixtures. When the customer walked into our big stores, they could've been walking into Saks Fifth Avenue – the ambience was perfect."

No-one had ever *seen* anything like Sports Authority before and that's just the way Smith wanted it.

"But we had *Authority* in our name and that meant service was essential. We were an 'every day low price retailer', we didn't have Sales, we had the same price every day of the week. So the only way we were able to get any loyalty from the customers was through service. Not unreasonably, everyone I employed had to be keen on sport, not built like athletes but certainly keen on sport. We made sure vendors did fantastic educational programmes with our teams and we had awesome fixtures and photographs of sports celebrities, complete with personal appearances – customers were blown away. And unlike other big box operators at the time, we had greeters. It was a nice little touch that made a big difference. With nearly 50,000 SKUs you needed someone to take you right to what you were looking for."

And true to his retailing and leadership instincts Smith always made it clear how much he valued the people on the shop floor. "In meetings I'd ask, is it managers or buyers *big box didn't* who are critical to our success? No I'd say, its *mean warehouse* people on the shop floor, they're who customers relate to – especially the cashiers, they're the last people our customers see. That has to be perfect, or they won't come back."

In the early years Smith would ask anyone who'd listen a simple, yet compelling question: "Why would a customer go to a small store with a limited range and no service when they can come to me and get better assortment, better prices, better service, in a fabulous one-stop shopping experience?" But it was Smith's customers that gave the positive response he was looking for and he, in turn, ruthlessly delivered on his big promises.

"When we opened up the first store in Fort Lauderdale, we did a million dollars in the first month. I knew I had a tiger by the tail and I made a promise to myself that we may be a big box operator but we would never lack for service. I knew we had to be different; we'd only expand successfully if we had the right staff. What I call *disciplined* staff. People who understood what was needed and who were prepared to deliver it. So even when we were madly opening new stores, I always made sure all new store management completed a 13-week course at an established store before moving to their new store. And you know what, we drug-tested our people too. I've seen too many problems when people get involved with that stuff. And yes, I was the first to be tested. My company was recognised and celebrated by the White House for our stance against drug abuse."

Smith made sure he always led from the front. He frequently visited every store, making sure everyone knew what was expected. "We made a point of promoting from within. They'd proved they could be trusted, it was good for moral, and we saved millions on recruitment fees. Everyone always knew how important service and sales were to success – even the specialists in the gun department weren't allowed to use the bathrooms until another accredited member of staff covered for them. The law states you can't sell guns unless you're accredited. I respected that, but we weren't going to lose a sale because someone needed the bathroom."

Smith grew his business, *"with people who believed in what I believed in,"* creating a phenomenally successful and visionary brand by being different. Not just different in size or price points but different on almost every dimension. He was certainly dictatorial and his workforce loved him for it. He was loyal to them and they loved him for that too. And when the business was floated he rewarded their love with share options. "It's one of the great things about being public," explains Smith.

Not just different in size or price points but different on almost every dimension

What Smith did 25 years ago has now been largely copied – certainly the big-format retailing and cheap prices. But he is equally sure that had he chosen to stay on, things would be very different at Sports Authority now.

Employment lawyers may have an opinion on that, but it's doubtful Smith would have listened very hard. "We warned our people one time. They only had one swing at the ball and after that they weren't going to be working for me."

Case History

Jane Elfers
President and CEO, Lord & Taylor

Interviewed, June 2008

Making life easy

Being different in retail can take many forms. But Jane Elfers, President & CEO of Lord & Taylor, America's oldest department store chain, is determined to be as relevantly different as possible.

Elfers herself is different. She's a force of nature and proud of it. A born leader, assured, charismatic and unbelievably comfortable with change. As she puts it: "Our challenge was to make Lord & Taylor relevant again, *grabbing back* share from the specialty fashion stores who had effectively stolen it!"

"Successful specialty fashion stores have made an art of honing their merchandise mix and store layout to meet the precise needs of distinct customer types. Whereas traditional department stores, like us, have been at a disadvantage.

grabbing back share from the specialty fashion stores

us, have been at a disadvantage. Historically we've strived to appeal to a vast number of customer types in a great many product areas."

The colossal challenge for Elfers was to re-engineer the business's merchandising strategy to win back a profitable spectrum of key but diverse customer groups.

Editing was Elfer's answer.

But with her this familiar and seemingly innocuous solution was so different, executed with such rigour and guile, that it was considered by some as an industry first.

Elfers advocated editing fashion and accessories according to a three-dimensional matrix cut by lifestyle. "This resulted in up to a 40 per cent sales uplift for stores that had been 'lifestyled'. It was very different and in my view a strategy to secure Lord & Taylor's future as a speciality department store across our 47 sites in north east America."

In 2003 Elfers, who was CEO for eight years until she stepped down in late 2008, audaciously re-orientated and segmented her entire target market into just three distinct groups: *contemporary*, *modern*, and *updated classic*. "Age was not central to all this," says Elfers. "But broadly speaking, the *contemporary* lifestyle refers to the young, slim and trendy set; *modern* is for those who want on-trend but slightly more wearable styles, and *updated classic* is for shoppers who are mature but still style-conscious." Although primarily geared for women, Lord & Taylor also applied these fundamentals to menswear and to a certain extent children's merchandise too.

> *re-orientated and segmented her entire target market into just three distinct groups*

Elfers and her 'all-women' merchandising team intuitively felt they knew where their potential customers would be 'coming from' and precisely how they wanted to shop. And they set their stores out accordingly. It was different and they were convinced.

"When you're a woman you don't wake up in the morning and think, I need a dress... hummm, should I get a long gown or a sun dress.. you wake up and think, I need a sun dress! You don't decide between special occasion and casual, you already know in your head what you need. You simply say, hey its hot outside, I need some sleeveless dresses because I've got some summer parties. Whoosh... you know if you are *contemporary* or an *updated classic* kinda gal... so if you're an *updated classic*, boom.... over there is just the sort of dresses I like, all my dress choices and brands in one area of the store. You know you're not going to wear these flimsy little low-cut *contemporary* things, because that's simply not you. But if you are a *contemporary* person you're not going to wear these things with sleeves that are mid-arm, you've got the shape and you'll want to be sexy, bang.... all sexy dresses are over there... your sorts of dresses are right here if you're a *modern* woman... well here's some dresses that have gorgeous styling and you know they'll fit you... boom... it's obvious, *that's how* customers want to shop. We then marry up the right 'must-have' accessories in each section. They're not fighting and fighting racks of clothes to find what they want. We do the editing so they don't have to. It takes huge merchandising skill, ruthless control and selection – and untold *gut-feel*." Elfers adds a word of caution to would would-be imitators: "It's not easy; please don't attempt this at home folks!"

Elfers is different and enjoys thinking in this animated way.

According to her, "it's a bit like a whole bunch of speciality shops in one place so there's no walking." Elfers and her team delivered all this by dramatically reducing inventory in stores, cutting SKUs by 45 per cent and logistics costs too. There was also a purge of suppliers who did not fall into the three lifestyle camps with a particular move away from the more staid womenswear brands. "Almost 85 per cent of the vendor base was changed. And as you would expect from such a focused culling the stores are different and now incredibly coherent."

The strict segmentation was introduced through all dimensions of the business, with each segmentation given a colour code as shorthand for internal alignment purposes, red, orange and yellow. "Buying and merchandising personnel were required to become completely *obsessed* with achieving delivery for their particular lifestyle segment – living and breathing their *colour*. We also took every vendor and allocated them by segment, and during 2003

people taking ownership of their 'colour'

and 2004 all stores were painstakingly set up according to these lifestyle groups. Within each segmentation we further refined by *tailored* and *casual*. I can't tell you the debates about whether something was orange or yellow or whether such and such had the depth of range to be a yellow vendor or if that handbag was red enough – but that's the skill, people taking ownership of their 'colour' and making sure they're getting it right!"

By 2005 Lord & Taylor had won over many of the customer groups it had single-mindedly targeted. But what has been particularly rewarding was the high incidence of multi-generational shopping. Mothers, daughters and even grandmothers, arriving together and enjoying their separate lifestyle sections before meeting up again in the shoe department (the shoe department is not segmented as yet because of huge 'back-of-house' operational challenges).

The company was sold by Federated Department Stores in October 2006 to NRDC Equity Partners, and a timely injection of US$60 million funded further store improvements and brand marketing. A high-profile campaign was launched in Autumn 2007. Created by marketing guru David Lipman it used genuine customer testimonials to champion Lord & Taylor as 'my favourite store', neatly underlining Elfers' relentless pursuit of merchandising perfection.

When the banking crisis struck in 2008/9 a number of fashion stores found themselves facing a fragile future. Thanks to Elfers' vision and innate customer understanding, Lord & Taylor were better placed than most to deal with the challenges.

Customers love going somewhere where someone has done all the hard work for them

And here must be the learning for retail in general. Customers want an easy life. Customers love going somewhere where someone has done all the hard work for them. That's not to say they don't want to be surprised or inspired, but for most, it should be within limits.

Elfers' vision is different, yet paradoxically it's cross-generational. She has understood it's about emotional and lifestyle influences, not choice per se. She knows her customers want what they want, and love knowing exactly where to find it – ideally sharing the experience with someone else.

The choice she's skilfully masterminded is certainly different.

Case History

Philippe Giard
Managing Director for Greater China, Food
Retail, A S Watson Group

Interviewed, November 2009

All things

Everyone in retail knows you can't be all things to all people.
Everyone except A S Watson.

As one of the largest retailers in the world, this Hong Kong based
conglomerate, owned by Hutchison Whampoa, has a relatively small
yet burgeoning grocery business in Asia. Boasting a complex network
of seven retail brands/formats, this retail division operates across
Hong Kong, Macau and ever increasing parts of China.

With a US$2.5 billion turnover and 280 stores in 2009, over the
next five years this fast moving division aims to double in China and
increase fifty per cent overall. "We're
now successfully appealing to the
individual needs of a particularly
diverse audience," says Philippe
Giard. "With our portfolio of retail
brands we can adapt to the nuances
of any location in Greater China and
react immediately to changes in circumstance. We're effectively future-
proofing as we grow, giving customers and landlords a reason to
prefer us!" But critically, Giard is achieving all this profitably by
operating a centralised management system.

*future-proofing as we
grow, giving customers
and landlords a reason
to prefer us*

What he is doing is certainly different.

As the whole region flourishes and shopping centres & malls
mature, its all-powerful landlords ensure their mix of tenants is

ruthlessly flexed to satisfy the rapidly changing requirements of an increasingly sophisticated shopper. And food retailers are not immune from this imperative. But as Giard explains, pressure like this suits his company's mindset. "Park 'n Shop was founded in the early 1970s in a small town on Hong Kong Island – specifically catering to the mercurial food needs of an ex-pat community. As the business grew it became very comfortable with segmenting its 'offer' by location, instinctively catering to the rich diversity of the region and its customers. So I guess adapting is in our DNA."

And this chameleon-like capability is the genesis of Giard's business success today.

"Effectively, the present-day multi-format model was forced on the business in the mid-nineties. Back then, our only format was the Park 'n Shop brand – we had around 200 supermarkets and superstores. One particularly successful 33,000 sq ft food anchor superstore was in the Kowloon Tong shopping mall. But without warning, the landlords decided our brand didn't match the growing aspirations of the new affluent middle classes in the area. We were given just two months to re-present plans for a new shopping experience or our soon-to-expire lease would not be renewed!" Remarkably, in this limited time frame, the business successfully created a new format, called 'Taste'. Whether or not the landlord would approve, it was decided that this entirely new brand would be managed by the same Park 'n Shop team.

In 2004, Giard was brought in to grow and refine this multi-format model. "Back then things were on track but barely profitable," explains Giard, a classically French and obviously driven executive – sporting MBAs from French and American universities, and enjoying impeccable brand credentials including Haagen Dazs and Carrefour. He is supremely confident in his abilities to build something different – a single retail portfolio that profitably meets the exacting demands of the notoriously challenging landlords of Greater China.

In truth, most retailers concede that it's difficult enough to develop *one* truly successful retail brand, but Giard only talks of the need, not the difficulties, of multi-brand/format retailing. "One-size-fits-all is not the future. It doesn't cater to the rapidly changing needs of modern customers, particularly the complexity of needs in Asia.

We are different, we have learned to move fast here and I think the world will have to learn too – that's the future. Basically we have embarked on a journey where we try to satisfy the needs of *local* customers, one store at a time. Rolling-out for us is not an option. Cookie cutter templates won't work. Hey, we've got two stores, 20 seconds walking distance apart, doing very different food retailing jobs and I'm not talking about one being a convenience version of the other."

It will come as no surprise that Giard has monumental ambitions.

His business already has store sizes ranging between the 1,000 sq ft and 120,000 sq ft. There are 'Express' convenience stores, specialist supermarkets in commercial and residential districts, supermarkets with a comprehensive fresh offer, superstores, megastores and a prestigious new Food Hall format. "But we always concentrate on four customer segments: Budget, Lifestyle, International Asian and International Western," says Giard who has his own *peculiar* definitions for these segments. "Our stores are selling product from 120 countries. From everyday essentials to huge varieties of produce, including fresh and cooked food, live fish, market-style fruit and vegetables, Chinese sui mei, freshly prepared sushi, and in-store bakeries. Every store has product and pricing carefully reflecting the local tastes, needs and spending power."

we have learned to move fast here and I think the world will have to learn too

But, Giard explains, his secret weapon is the impressive intelligence his loyalty card scheme delivers. "In little over 12 months it has grown to capture and analyse over 70 per cent of total sales, representing 65 per cent of households in Hong Kong and Macau. We now know what they buy, where they're from, if they are more western, Asian or Japanese and on which shopping occasions related purchases occur – few retailers in the world capture and analyse this level."

"Keeping the back-office functions lean enough to work across the entire network is key to profitability – certain functions may have to be split as our presence in China grows, but we've managed with only one team so far," says Giard.

There are many who would question the wisdom of non-specialist buyers and multi-brand marketers but at his current size, Giard is proving detractors wrong. He claims the only things holding back explosive expansion are a studied capital expenditure regime (rents are over five times the European levels) and finding the right people to join up and share his dream!

Is this different business model working?

Giard highlights a continuous like-for-like growth averaging 25 per cent per annum over five years. He also believes that after Tesco he runs one of the world's most profitable food retailers per square foot – always easier for smaller businesses in densely populated regions but nevertheless impressive. But the true lesson here is in the power of being different. Imagine Giard and his team presenting or re-presenting to the tough landlords of greater China, claiming *allows the landlord to finely tune and indeed re-tune, a 'food offer'* that for any shopping destination and any target market, they can offer a successful stable of retail brands that allows the landlord to finely tune – and indeed re-tune – a 'food offer'. A tenant partnership that is capable of moving up or down the socio demographic scale and one that's effortlessly geared to the psychographic needs of their customers. A business that has a proven track record of re-inventing a brand/format within a few of weeks when necessary.

Let's not forget the customers either. They have a constantly evolving food-shopping opportunity specifically designed for their food aspirations – even the indigenous population of the region are made to feel special in Giard's new format, budget stores.

But Giard's biggest challenge will be to continue to grow the model profitably.

If he can do this, he will secure a place in food retailing history by *being all things, to all people.*

Case History

David Simons
Former CEO, Somerfield Supermarkets

Interviewed December 2009

Different accolade

It takes a confident executive to yin, when everyone else is distinctly yanging!

And in retail, if you do something different you can look forward to instantaneous verdicts from customers and peers alike.

When David Simons took the helm of the UK's Somerfield supermarkets in the early 90s, the company was in dire straits. Following a leveraged buy-out five years earlier, and the acquisition of a plethora of small supermarket groups, Somerfield was a sprawling giant of disparate brands. Haemorrhaging sales and owing international banks an eye-watering US$2 billion. What's more, while all other supermarket groups were opening out-of-town superstores to satisfy consumers' new-found love of big, bountiful grocery temples, Somerfield had sold its bigger units in a desperate bid to raise money.

Newspaper picture of David Simons leading from the front

Its remaining 800 small stores were firmly, and very unfashionably, *in-town*.

Despite these seemingly terminal problems, Simons gleefully grasped the opportunity to take on his first Chief Executive role. From a financial and retail background, he's profoundly bright and a master of strategy. But more importantly, he's supremely confident in his own judgment. While peers and business press wondered openly what kind of 'madman' would accept such a daunting job, Simons approached it with a typically philosophical optimism. "If I failed, everybody would've said it couldn't have been turned around anyway. And if I succeeded, I'd be hailed a hero. I thought it was a no-lose situation."

On his arrival, the banks set Simons the challenge of devising a new strategy within *one week*. "And I was naive enough to say, I can't do it in a week. Give me a month."

Incredibly, Simons went on to achieve a remarkable turnaround for Somerfield. His strategy was to come to terms with exactly what he could *and* couldn't achieve – financially and operationally. And then find an attractive customer proposition that would fit. It soon became apparent that his portfolio of 800 town-centre small supermarkets should not be written-off as the rump of a depleted business but rather, the key to a strategy of being different, a possible key to success.

its 800 small stores were firmly, and very unfashionably, in-town

Despite the competition moving to large, out-of-town destination shopping, Simons put his money on re-inventing 'local'.

"Not huge food and grocery replenishment expeditions that required *four-door fork-lift trucks* to take the shopping home," explains Simons. "But a different proposition. Unbelievably convenient shopping. Well stocked stores, with the majority boasting edited ranges reflecting local needs, all offering fresh meat, fruit and veg. Prices occasionally were a bit higher than out-of-town, but unbeatable deals and a friendlier community spirit was always present. Today it's normal to have quality 'top-up' supermarkets in towns and villages but before we arrived on the scene, the local independents and specialist chains were, quite frankly, doing a very poor job."

There was a gap in the market but was there a market in the gap?

Quantifying his instincts, Simons found research revealed a large customer base, a third of the shopping public, preferred the convenience of staying local rather than going to soulless out-of-town sheds. "Our ad agency had a wonderful verbatim quote about a wife asking her husband what he wanted for supper on Thursday during a shopping trip out of town. He said he couldn't possibly know because today was Saturday!"

"I wanted Somerfield to boldly own what I called the *neighbourhood* market. A monumental programme went into understanding what 'local convenience' meant to customers and we painstakingly engaged our workforce – they couldn't deliver it if they didn't understand it! At the beginning I remember surprising stores with Sunday visits. The stores were a mess. Directors never visited on Sundays, so neither did regional managers. And usually the store manager or deputies didn't work either. No wonder things didn't operate as they should on this most *important* day for convenience. Standards and sales rocketed as soon as this was addressed. Everybody was growing to appreciate what it took to deliver the *neighbourhood* concept."

> *Everybody was growing to appreciate what it took to deliver the neighbourhood concept*

But Simons needed breathing space and cash to roll out his transformational vision. He needed time to be different. As an interim measure, he introduced another trail-blazing idea that has since become part of the arsenal of modern retailing – deep cuts. Called 'Price Check', Simons claims it ruffled feathers. "Instead of moderate general discounting, we were the first to deep-cut key quality products at key times. We had half-price grade 'A' turkeys at Christmas or, 'buy a bottle of Famous Grouse whiskey and get another for a penny'. This caused near riots in our Scottish stores at New Year and consternation about brand devaluation from producers."

But Price Check was a phenomenal stop-gap success. It raised awareness, generated cash and bought Simons valuable time to continue aggressively converting the estate to his visionary *neighbourhood* format. Research now proved that Somerfield was increasingly standing for quality products and unbeatable bargains, with its convenience dimension starting to be appreciated too. An extra million customers a week came into the stores, staff morale lifted and sales declines were reversed. "Somerfield had been in despair but a new focused vision and Price Check changed everything. It gave heart to the business. We also now had the cash to invest in better systems and improve efficiency. All this convinced the bankers that there might be some life in the business after all, and with increasing enthusiasm they supported my transformation programme!"

So from a business without a 'rudder' losing a quarter of a billion dollars a year when he arrived, Simons turned Somerfield around with some well executed, counter-intuitive thinking. Within seven years he delivered annual profits of close to US$375 million, re-floated on the London Stock Exchange at 145p and peaked at 485p. He delivered near US$10 billion in sales at its height and was handed the ultimate compliment of being copied by competitors like Tesco *Express*, Sainsbury's *Local* and M&S *Simply Food*.

Counter-intuitive thinking is an amazingly effective tool. And a pre-requisite for being different. It's certainly a useful skill for any retail executive. It's a thought process brought about through creativity or necessity. And in one impossibly difficult business venture, Simons demonstrated his skills in both – an audacious leap into deep discounting with 'Price Check' and a visionary return to localness with 'neighbourhood' retailing. Both were very different and his customers loved him for it. Both were meticulously explained to the workforce and they rewarded him for it. And both were uncompromisingly executed and his banks supported him for it.

And as Simons confides the lesson is simple: "In retail, counter-intuitive thinking is no different to ordinary thinking – the same rules apply but only more so. Make sure you know your customer, engage your workforce and compromise on nothing. Absolutely nothing. Candidly, any disappointments in my retail career have always involved a failure to follow these guidelines."

But throughout a 40 year retail career Simons has taken his own advice more often than not and it's been recognised at the highest levels.

He has now been honoured by the Queen for services to retail – Commander of the Order of the British Empire is a highly prestigious accolade for a man who enjoys success by being different.

SECRET SIX – SUMMARY

Being different: Tips for success

- Understand and appreciate all great businesses started by being different

- Successful businesses continue to be chosen because they strive to be different, not just better.

- In a world crammed with options, being different delivers an immediate emotional connection with customers and builds brand equity in a business.

- The actual difference, however, can be emotionally or rationally based. Each being highly effective.

- But given the choice it's better to be emotionally different; it's harder for others to copy. Given the ultimate choice, be both!

- Ironically, being different can be copied. But it's only really effective if the business you're copying is not in your market.

- Businesses that are different make a point of not defaulting to simpler solutions.

So if you only remember one thing from this section, remember:

When uniqueness is the objective,
being different must be part of the strategy.

CONCLUSION

Success

Let me conclude by testing my theories of success.

Let's take two companies that couldn't be more different if they tried.

Two global brands who have built phenomenal success and enjoy iconic status.

One, a retailer & manufacturer, the other a manufacturer & retailer. One, a brand customers love to hate. The other, a brand customers love to love. One, where everything is predicated on price. The other where everything has nothing to do with price.

So what do they have in common?

Well firstly I haven't been able to interview the bosses. So I too am going to be different this time and view them as a customer – to see what my mum, your mum and anyone else's mum, daughter, son, dad or friend might see and think.

Secondly both have a flair for design.

And thirdly these two companies both dominate their own particular worlds.

Depending on currency rates and who does the research, Ingvar Kamprad, the founder of Ikea, is either the wealthiest man on the planet or eleventh, it really doesn't matter. What does matter is how this remarkably reclusive genius has grown a chain of mega-sized stores into an empire of some 300 outlets in 35 countries, making it the world's largest and most successful furniture retailer.

On the other side of the coin, Steve Jobs relishes publicity. The co-founder and genius who in recent years has led Apple to become the agenda-setting computer and electronics manufacturer and now, retailer. By early 2010, Apple products were universally available in stores around the world and also through what I believe to be one of the most intuitive websites on the planet. Products, information and advice are now also readily available in 284 of Apple's own stores in ten countries. At the same time the business startled many with a market capitalisation exceeding Microsoft!

One can safely assume from these figures, each business shares the common position of being securely perched at the top of its game.

What's in a name?

Ingvar Kamprad named Ikea in a totally functional way. Being the acronym of the founder's name, the farm where he grew up (Elmtaryd), and his home parish (Agunnaryd). On the other hand, Apple's name and logo is completely different – it's different and emotionally stimulating. It comes from Isaac Newton's fabled apple tree where the offending fruit helped him understand much. Interestingly the Apple logo was created with a bite mark to prevent it being mistaken for a cherry.

Ikea celebrates the founder's name and somewhat appropriately his home details as inspiration for the brand name. Apple skilfully borrowed from an inspiring genius.

For Ikea the guiding purpose has always been to democratise design, a lofty and creative ambition. Rather paradoxically it chose a totally logical path to achieve this. By ruthlessly keeping the cost of manufacturing its beautifully designed products to a bare minimum and by ensuring operational costs were kept famously low, Ikea's adoring fans have been able to enjoy exquisite levels of design and creativity normally reserved for the rich. With a mantra of not paying to transport or store 'air', most of Ikea's products can be de-constructed and come in flat boxes. Apparently, in the name of cost efficiencies, the company even defends what many believe to be one of the worst customer service experiences in modern retailing.

the guiding purpose has always been to democratise design, a lofty and creative ambition

So with Ikea we have a highly functional, 'no frills' retailer, operating in the rarefied reaches of top design. Offering only the occasional and legendary Swedish meatball in their restaurants to soften the harsh in-store experience.

Contrast this with Apple who seemingly never worry about money – obviously they do but it doesn't appear to shape their thinking. And certainly never at the expense of their customer experience. They are the antithesis of Ikea, sharing nothing with them except success and a love of design. Apple touch their customers with a thought process so refined and so emotionally deep that without fail, recession or not, people pay whatever it costs to own a piece of real-time computer and electronics history. Exponentially deepening their customer relationships by offering a piece of tomorrow, today. These pieces of tomorrow's history are beautifully designed and branded and have competitors dancing to Steve Jobs' tune. Like Ikea, customers really love Apple products but unlike Ikea they really love the experience of buying them too.

> *Exponentially deepening their customer relationships by offering a piece of tomorrow, today*

Apple stores are cathedrals to experiential shopping. Indeed so authoritative are they, one feels the need to book an appointment to browse. I don't truly know what's going on in these shops or in indeed in the majority of their products but my ten-year-old daughter does. But she's the living future not me. Enough said.

Silently speaking

And let's finally acknowledge how these brands have developed their public profile, how they groom the minds of new and existing customers.

Ikea appears corporately secretive. Seemingly only communicating through channels-to-market, product and wonderfully quirky marketing. Skilfully centred around observations of life and home, its advertising uses peculiar stories beautifully told, beautifully presented and beautifully crafted. Please take a look on Youtube, tap in *Ikea dog commercial*, it's the one where the dog goes through a flap in the door. It's one of my all time favourite pieces of communication. It's brilliant. You can almost feel the personality of the company: functionality of thought, wrapped in creativity.

And now consider Apple. The name and logo is the work of a creative genius. The apple, with a byte (*sic*) taken out, originally in a stripy colourful version to add warmth to technology as well as demonstrating on-screen colour functionality is now only used in chic monochromatic tones. So much thought loaded into a simple icon, impeccably articulating what the company stands for – an innovative brand for creative minds. The corporate and public face of Apple is now Steve Jobs famously striding a stage, microphone kissing his lips, personally responsible for launching technological epochs to global adulation. Ably supported by rich communication from Ridley Scott's '1984' commercial in the beginning, to the highly awarded advertising launches of the iPod, iPhone and iPad. Everything this company does is a study of creativity and thought. Again brilliant.

So what's my point?

The point I am trying to make is that these two brands couldn't be more different but they are unified by knowing exactly what business they are in. They achieve continuous success by staying ruthlessly focused in that business.

Steve Jobs never sells the functional elements of his products; he sells what functionality will *deliver*. He sells the dream of how peoples' lives will be changed for the better, forever, simply by using them.

lives will be changed for the better

Even if Ikea doesn't always talk about the cost of individual items in its marketing, everyone knows everything they sell is miraculously low-priced. They are committed to bringing breathtaking design excellence to the masses, not the few. Ikea won't do anything that distracts from this vision. Everyone shopping at Ikea knows things hardly ever seem expensive. Everyone can afford to dream, everyone knows how their personal space will be changed forever with very little money. And most who visit will even accept the less than enjoyable customer experience, logically and creatively filing it under the heading: a small price to pay for small prices.

As a retail observer and customer both touch me. I love the products they sell. And emotionally both speak loudly to me. I can't think of a credible reason not to buy from them.

a small price to pay for small prices

Six secrets

At the beginning of this book I talked about an objective to get customers to turn left into your store, not right into your competitor's store. Millions of customers have turned to Ikea and Apple – what are their secrets?

- Both companies know the business they're in and constantly strive to emotionally engage their customers – even if it's in totally different ways.

- Both build exponentially on their roles as trusted agents for their customers and stakeholders. They fiercely protect their reputations by doing what's right.

- Both deeply acknowledge their brand is their workforce.

- Both reflect, lead and dictate their markets through visionary thinking.

- Both brim with ideas to bring considered and intuitive thinking alive. They do things differently but their ideas stick.

- Both companies are strangely similar. They are totally different from anyone else in their markets, hugely successful by making sure things stay that way.

Secret or not

With Ikea and Apple we see two global companies with very different ideologies. They share credentials in design excellence, and some may argue this is what joins them. But I beg to differ. I think it's because their expertise is in design, that they are comfortable with the power of emotions in the decision-making processes of their businesses. And to me it is through this that they both come together in their understanding of the business they are in. And like Steve Mavuso, a world apart in a Township in deepest South Africa, they too totally embrace the fact that they're in the emotional business of *being chosen.*

comfortable with the power of emotions in the decision-making processes

Certainly I believe this to be the case with all those I have had the honour to interview and interrogate for this book. I have found the truly successful retailers run emotionally aware and emotionally intelligent businesses – this is what defines retailing today.

To me there is no future in simply buying and selling – traders went out, as the internet came in.

The future is exemplified by Ingvar Kamprad, Steve Jobs and Steve Mavuso as well as everyone one else in this book. If ever a secret, it certainly isn't now.

Success is all about the *art of being chosen.*

P.S. When asked what they would do differently, 94 per cent of the leaders interviewed simply wished they'd done it sooner – so what are you waiting for?

INDEX